THE COLLECTED ESSAYS OF SIR LEWIS NAMIER
Volume II

CROSSROADS OF POWER

By the same Author

THE STRUCTURE OF POLITICS AT THE ACCESSION OF GEORGE III

ENGLAND IN THE AGE OF THE AMERICAN REVOLUTION VOL. I

SKYSCRAPERS

ADDITIONS AND CORRECTIONS TO SIR JOHN FORTESCUE'S EDITION
OF THE CORRESPONDENCE OF KING GEORGE III

IN THE MARGIN OF HISTORY

CONFLICTS

1848: THE REVOLUTION OF THE INTELLECTUALS

FACING EAST

DIPLOMATIC PRELUDE, 1938–9

EUROPE IN DECAY, 1936–1940

AVENUES OF HISTORY

IN THE NAZI ERA

PERSONALITIES AND POWERS

VANISHED SUPREMACIES

SIR LEWIS Bernstein NAMIER

Crossroads
of Power

ESSAYS ON
EIGHTEENTH-CENTURY ENGLAND

THE MACMILLAN COMPANY
NEW YORK

PRINTED IN GREAT BRITAIN

ACKNOWLEDGMENTS

Acknowledgments are due to the Cambridge University Press for permission to reprint the Leslie Stephen Lecture, 1959, to Messrs. Macmillan & Co. for permission to reprint Essays 1 and 3 from *Skyscrapers* and Essays 4, 8, 10, 11, 12, 13, 17 and 18 from *In the Margins of History*; also to the Director of the Institute of Historical Research, London University, and to the Editors of the *English Historical Review* and the *Observer* for permission to reprint Essays 2, 6 and 14 respectively. Essays 5, 9, 15 and 20 are from *Personalities and Powers* and 16 is from *Avenues of History*. Essay 7 has not been printed before.

CONTENTS

THE BIOGRAPHY OF
ORDINARY MEN

STUDY-CIRCLES of working men, when asked what subject they would like to take, almost invariably answer with a request for 'economic history'. Political history, they reason, is about kings and statesmen and wars, while they want to learn about 'the likes' of themselves—as all the other classes and professions did before them. But how much of that desire is satisfied by stories about the enclosures, the spinning-jenny, the Poor Law, the Factory Acts or the Free Trade controversy? Students are landed once more in the sphere of legislative enactments and of Government measures; for these are 'documented' and can be easily dished up, whereas the tale of those ordinary men and women about whom they want to know is buried in casual remarks, in crevices of unknown texts—pins in haystacks. In the correspondence of the upper classes remarks occasionally occur which throw a flood of light on the life and condition of 'the lower orders', but will anyone ever collect and blend them into a picture? Why, even a history of the rank and file of what may best be described as 'the political nation' is seldom attempted; biographies of famous men still hold the field, though hero-worship is no longer the creed of the writers. But, then, a biography has well-defined limits, a natural sequence and an established practice, and can be compiled by an individual writer in a reasonably short time; nor is it attempted unless materials are ready to hand. Lastly, the public is accustomed to read biographies, and so they continue to be produced.

In biographies, as in plays, the central figures act and speak, the others being mere dummies in the background, 'citizens', 'soldiers', etc. In most cases the biographer does not profess an exclusive interest in the psychology of his 'hero' and would not deny the importance of the men who surround him; and yet they remain a dark, dumb, nameless crowd. We have written about Parliamentary leaders and great administrators, and more or less ignored those whom they led and with or through whom they had to do their work, the individual Members of Parliament, the Civil Servants, etc. We have written about changes in methods of production, the rise of modern finance, trade statistics, but very seldom about the men behind these developments, the merchants who turned manufacturers or bankers, the landowners who became mining adventurers, etc. Now the heroes of biography are often approached in a sceptical, would-be humorous, depreciatory manner, and this is the main tangible expression of the doubt which besets the writers as to whether these men truly deserve the prominence they receive. The outstanding figures are reduced to ordinary dimensions, but continue to fill the picture, mainly because information about them can be easily obtained. Still, what can one expect from the lonely student, not given even the most elementary help (e.g., of a secretary or an assistant to do for him some of the more mechanical work) or the necessary leisure for his researches, as usually he is compelled to earn his living by teaching? Is he to attempt to cross an ocean in a boat of the most primitive construction? Our interests and requirements have changed and broadened, we want to know about the life of crowds, to hear symphonies and not arias, and then a single virtuoso is invited to perform them. Occasionally we take refuge in collective works, and fondly expect 'fifty men to make a centipede'; more often than not, these attempts at joint and yet individual work end in failure. Historical research to this day remains unorganized, and the historian is expected to make his own instruments or do without them; and so with wooden ploughs we continue to draw lonely furrows, most successfully when we strike sand.

The biography of the ordinary man cannot be profitably attempted unless one writes the history of a crowd. It would not pay to go through hundreds of volumes of manuscripts and many thousands of books merely to fish out some twenty documents or passages about one man. Proper returns cannot be obtained from the work except by following up many threads, by establishing the average and selecting the typical. The student has to get acquainted with the lives of thousands of individuals, with an entire ant-heap, see its files stretch out in various directions, understand how they are connected and correlated, watch the individual ants, and yet never forget the ant-heap. An interesting piece of research into economic history could be done by studying the lives of the members of any great trading company in the seventeenth and eighteenth centuries, or, say, of the directing personnel of the East India House. But most of all there is that marvellous microcosmos of English social and political life, that extraordinary club, the House of Commons. For centuries it has been the goal of English manhood, and besides those who found seats in it on the strength of a tradition or of a quasi-hereditary right, there were in every House many scores of men, for whom its membership set the crown (and often the coronet) on achievements and success in other walks of life. Generals, admirals, and pro-consuls entered it, business men who had made their fortunes and now aspired to social advancement, Civil Servants, lawyers and political wire-pullers who tried to raise their professional status, etc. The rise of 'interests' and classes can be traced through the personnel of the House of Commons, the forms of English gregarious existence can be studied, the social structure of England is reflected in it, the presence or decay of independent political life in boroughs and counties can be watched in their representation. When the sons of peers or leading country gentlemen begin to invade the representation of boroughs, it is clear that Parliament is becoming the governing body; when the brewers, clothiers and iron-masters start acquiring seats in the House, it is obvious that fortunes are being made in these branches of trade, and that the early capitalists have made their appearance; by the number of West Indians in the House one can measure the prosperity of the 'sugar islands'; when many families of country gentlemen, who for generations had sat in it, withdraw from the House of Commons, one can guess that agricultural rents are falling—on a careful inquiry it will be found that the coming in of American wheat has wrought a greater change in the composition of the British House of Commons than the first two Reform Acts. From the 'circular letter', the whip which in the eighteenth century was sent to Government Members at the opening of the session, one can learn a good deal about political groupings; about 1750, independent country gentlemen sitting 'in their own right' received it usually from the leader of the House, relatives or retainers of politically prominent peers through them, members of professional groups through their chiefs (naval officers through the First Lord of the Admiralty, lawyers through the Lord Chancellor, Government contractors and financiers through the Secretary to the Treasury, etc.), and lastly, in one or two cases, territorial managers made their appearance.

We have discussed kings and statesmen and wars, and when desirous to show our appreciation of 'progress'—institutions, inventions and 'reforms'. But how much do we know about the real political life of the country, even about that body which before the eyes of the nation has for centuries shaped its joint existence? How much do we know about the Members of the Long Parliament, or about the changes which came over the House between the accession of George III and the voting of the First Reform Act? When did local citizens disappear from the representation of most small provincial boroughs? When did rich City merchants begin to plant themselves out on them? When did provincial business men of the new type start entering the House in considerable numbers? When did national politics become the dominant issue in elections? When and how have parties got the upper hand over individual candidates? When was the loyalty of the average elector transferred from organic constituencies to party organizations? In the eighteenth century as many excuses had to be made for 'disturbing the peace' of a county or borough as in our time for starting a war, and every candidate in an election contest naturally tried to prove that it was not he who was the aggressor, but that his opponent, by an inexcusable disregard of his 'just pretensions', had forced a contest on him, in which he himself confidently relied on the fairness of his neighbours to secure his victory. The idea that constituencies should be contested for the political education of the electorate was as alien to the eighteenth century as would be to us a proposal that the summer manœuvres of our army should take the form of a three-days' battle with that of some other nation. Even about the middle of the nineteenth century, in a good many constituencies the local issues still predominated, and, e.g., the Radicals could form an almost separate body in the House without producing any considerable number of triangular contests, for the battle was not fought on a national scale. Without underrating the value of work on what is called the political history of the British nation, one might wish that at least a start should be made with a history of the British 'political nation'. And a biographical history of the House of Commons, covering the seven centuries of its existence, could well supply the spade-work for such a new venture along lines consonant with the general change in our outlook and interests.

Parliamentary histories based on the biographies of Members have been attempted for various counties, and much of this work has been done by real scholars. Useful as these books undoubtedly are, they suffer from the following of 'vertical' lines—what has Adam Fitz-Richard, returned for Liverpool in 1295, in common with some big merchant of the eighteenth century, or with George Canning who represented Liverpool 1812-23? By taking counties or single constituencies, one can study, e.g., the degree of heredity in their representation, but one touches merely the outskirts of political life, and cannot properly follow up the personal connections even of the Members in question, for these extended in most cases far beyond the borders of their constituency or county. Much better results could be reached by doing the work 'horizontally'—an attempt of that kind seems to have been planned by Mr. Pink, one of the greatest antiquaries of our time, who collected biographical material about the Members of the Long Parliament, but died without having published anything on the subject. The student of Parliamentary biography whose work is limited to one period, but extends over the entire country, can do what is impossible for those working on vertical lines—he can plunge into the mass of manuscript and printed material extant for his period and obtain from it a living picture of the men. Still, no such study of one single period can fully realize its aim unless similar studies, on the same plan, are available for other periods; only by comparison can we gauge movement and correctly define its nature.

In short, the task cannot be undertaken by individual researchers, working independently of each other. It has to be organized on a national scale, given national standing, and financed from national resources. A central organization is required, an editorial board composed of experts and working under the auspices of a Parliamentary Committee, co-operating with various county organizations, with bodies such as the editors of *The Complete Peerage*, with scholars working on the biographies of members of universities, colleges or schools, with other experts specializing in cognate subjects. *A Dictionary of Parliamentary Biography* should be compiled, but based on periods, and not on the alphabet. The entity and individuality of consecutive Houses have to be clearly preserved, for the pageant of history must not be arranged under capital letters, like the luggage on the pier at Liverpool. The value of such work executed on a sufficiently large scale and according to the highest standards of scholarship could hardly be exaggerated. It would be a *Who's Who* of politics and social life throughout the ages, the most indispensable reference book for everyone engaged on English political history and for every editor of historical manuscripts—and it would save us from having to do the same work over and over again, often without sufficient means or knowledge. But of equal or perhaps even greater importance would be the attempt inherent in that work to organize historical research, and last, but not least, the training which the work would give to younger collaborators. It is difficult to imagine a better preparation for history work on any given period than a study of the lives of the men of that time, in the course of which a proper knowledge of the available materials would naturally be acquired.

2

DANIEL PULTENEY, M.P., AN ORDINARY MAN

EIGHT men of the name of Pulteney sat in the eighteenth-century House of Commons: William Pulteney Earl of Bath, the most famous of them all; his son William Lord Pulteney, who predeceased him by a year; his uncle John; his brother Harry, in 1764 heir to his 'mountain of riches'; his cousin Daniel (son of John) whose daughter Frances was next heir to his wealth; her husband William Johnstone, who assumed the name of Pulteney; and the husband of their only child, Henrietta Laura, Sir James Murray, Bart., who did likewise. The story of the family seems to turn round the million pounds of the miser's fortune, who, when his son died, renounced probate to avoid paying his debts. Only the eighth Pulteney, another Daniel, the subject of this essay, stands alone: he does not appear in the Pulteney pedigree, although he bore their one less common christian name and came from Somerset (a county from which William Pulteney took his titles—Viscount Pulteney of Wrington, Somerset, and Earl of Bath).[1] In his case it was not wealth which formed the basis of his parliamentary career, but debts which admittedly supplied the incentive: the seat in the House was to secure for him immunity from arrest by creditors, and next some lucrative appointment to retrieve his financial position. Fellow of King's College, Cambridge, for nearly forty years, dean and vice-provost, he flits across the parliamentary stage; and there is singularly little known about him except through his letters to Charles Manners, 4th Duke of Rutland, preserved at Belvoir Castle.

Daniel Pulteney was the eldest son of the Rev. Charles Pulteney, rector of Curry Mallet, Somerset, by Betty Speke: the fullest information about the family is contained in a letter from W. J. Gadsden in

[1] The reason for this choice is not clear; his main family connection was with Leicestershire.

The Genealogical Magazine for October 1901[1] (who Gadsden was, what caused him to take an interest in Daniel Pulteney, and whence he derived his information, is not known to me). The trustee of Betty's marriage settlement was George Speke whose daughter married in 1754 Lord North, the Prime Minister. There were four children of Charles Pulteney's marriage, three sons and a daughter who died an infant. Daniel, by his will dated 8 October 1810, left a legacy to his next brother, Charles Speke Pulteney, of or from whom he had 'never heard any account . . . since the year 1780 or thereabouts . . .' Charles was a doctor at Sherborne, Dorset, and married at Yeovil in 1772; but, adds Gadsden, 'I can find nothing at the College of Surgeons in Lincoln's Inn Fields respecting him'. The third son, George Ann, is a bare name in Gadsden's letter; but a memorial tablet to him in the parish church at Curry Mallet, Somerset,[2] states that

> after twelve years distinguished services, [he] was promoted by Sir George Rodney to the command of his Majesty's ship the Prince Edward of 64 guns, and died on board her off the coast of Ireland, May 20th, 1781, aetat 27.

Daniel Pulteney was baptized 19 September 1749; entered Eton as King's Scholar in 1762; was admitted scholar at King's College, Cambridge, 1769; B.A. 1773; Fellow of King's 1772–1811; vice-provost 1798–1801; dean 1801–3; and again vice-provost 1803–10; admitted student of the Middle Temple, 1772; called to the bar, 1788. This is as much as we know about the formal side of his education and of his academic career. There is no indication in the accounts or records of King's that Daniel Pulteney was ever a teaching Fellow, not even during the years when he held office in college; but a glimpse of the life he led at Cambridge before his incursion into politics can be obtained from the memoirs of Henry Gunning, an undergraduate at Christ's 1784–8:[3]

> There were a few men amongst the Masters of Arts of pretty high standing, who cultivated the acquaintance of the young nobility, and contrived to keep a handsome establishment, and live in a very expensive style, without any other apparent resources than their fellowships. Two of the most celebrated (I was very near using the word notorious) were Akehurst and Pulteney, both Fellows of

---

[1] Vol. V, pp. 273–4.
[2] See Collinson, *History of Somerset*, vol. i, p. 34.
[3] *Reminiscences of Cambridge* (1854), vol. i, pp. 22–3. I am indebted to Mr. John Saltmarsh, Fellow of King's College, Cambridge, for the information concerning Pulteney gleaned from the College records, and for the reference to Gunning's memoirs.

King's. At a dinner given by the Bishop of Llandaff[1] to the Duke of Rutland and some other young men of high rank, the Bishop was pressed by Akehurst to take a seat at a table where there was a vacancy, and at which they had been playing for very high stakes. This was the very significant answer of the Bishop,—'I have no estate to lose, Sir; I am not desirous of winning one'.

Daniel Pulteney, though nearly five years older than Charles Lord Roos (who on his father's death in October 1770 became Lord Granby, and in May 1779 succeeded his grandfather as 4th Duke of Rutland), was his contemporary at Eton and Cambridge. Pulteney, highly intelligent, versatile, and flexible, burdened with no strong views of his own or moral principles, a good observer and talker, but probably also a good listener, formed a contrast and a complement to the serious, tense, and rather solitary Rutland; and he knew how to render himself both agreeable and useful. A close friendship grew up between them—in a letter undated except by the title, Pulteney addresses him as 'Dearest Granby'.[2] Then follow a few unimportant letters, till one, again undated but probably written towards the end of 1782, opens on a sudden note of reproach and despair.

As I cannot think but with extreme horror of any breach with your Grace, I shall not state ... without it is required from me what I conceive is my present situation in respect to a connection formed so long ago.—I shall at present only say ... that I really beleive no person living is so entangled in all sorts of difficulties, and sunk into such certain ruin as myself without being immediately brought into Parliament; ... this has arose without any kind of doubt from my expectation of being now in the House of Commons. That this step may be attended with difficulties and inconvenience to your Grace I have no kind of scruple to beleive. ... But if your Grace will fairly consider that £1,500 or 2,000 is what you would stake at play or give for a picture, and that to me it makes the difference of rank in life or immediate ruin ...; I can only judge from myself, that there is no person I had so lived with, even without my having raised his expectations, that should not claim from me a sacrifice of that inconvenience to his preservation.

... ten years ago I could not have beleived it possible such a letter as this could have passed between us. Indiscretions of several sorts

---

[1] Dr. Richard Watson, Fellow of Trinity, Cambridge, who had been tutor to the Duke of Rutland, and partly through his influence was made Bishop of Llandaff in 1782.

[2] This, as all the other letters from Daniel Pulteney preserved at Belvoir Castle, is noted in the Hist. MSS. Comm., *14th Report*, pt. I, Rutland MSS. vol. iii. From the originals I have been able to check and complete the texts there given, and my best thanks are due to the Duke of Rutland for allowing me access to his papers.

aggravated into God knows what magnitude from a jealousy of the intimacy I was then honored with by your Grace have done me injury in your opinion; but except in the Cambridge election where I was pre-engaged,[1] I have never acted contrary to your wishes. I am now at extremity and the only solution to all this undoubted despair and ruin to me . . . is—that your Grace should apply to Lord Shelburne or Orde[2] for a seat from any one who has offered such to them without doubt at a price, that your Grace should give that price by a draft at 6 months or by any manner your Grace pleases . . . I solemnly beleive if such a sum was now advanced at 6 months by means of my liberty I could raise it, if not I am left to this sort of fate that delay of a fortnight will be certain ruin.

If it was necessary to mention my dependence on your Grace and the numberless consequences, I could mention one probably known to G. North[3] but certainly to Lord North of an offer he sent me by Mr. Coombes[4] and which I thought would clash with the connection your Grace had honored me with.

From the next letter (again undated) it is possible to gauge the duke's reply: Pulteney assures the duke that he had meant no disrespect by the expressions used, but had written under pressure of a desperate situation.

Your Grace's message . . . that you intend to bring me into Parliament the first opportunity that occurs will tend very much to releive me from a most embarrassed situation, which would have been more effectually avoided . . . if it had happened that I had been now in Parliament.

Thus alone will he be enabled to live in this country—'half the House of Commons perhaps are in a worse situation'. He estimates that he owes the duke about £3,000; but the way in which he puts it suggests conscious understatement.

In April 1783 there are two letters from Newmarket (hopelessly bankrupt the spendthrift went in for racing).[5] But the next, of

---

[1] Presumably the election for the university, 9 September 1780, in which Pulteney voted for John Townshend and James Mansfield, and not for William Pitt.

[2] This reference to Shelburne as First Lord of the Treasury and Orde as its Secretary, approximately dates the letter.

[3] Probably George North, son of Lord North. He was at Eton 1766–74, and therefore three years together with Pulteney.

[4] Probably Richard Combe, M.P. (died 1780), one of North's agents.

[5] In the Protocollum Book of King's College, 1760–96, p. 246, under date of 29 November 1771, there is an entry of Pulteney having been admonished for 'having been engaged in a horse race lately at Newmarkett', 'confined to his room for a fortnight except at the hours of chapel, lectures, and commons', and assigned some appropriate exercise (probably copying Latin verses) by the vice-provost. In the Racing Calendars for 1784, 1785, and 1786, three horses are mentioned which belonged to 'Mr. Pulteney', probably Daniel; but it may also be William Pulteney.

7 November 1783, was written, significantly, from Southampton: in readiness to slip across the Channel.

> . . . a week or two ago I received intelligence from a friend that some of Bingley Fox's[1] creditors to a considerable amount indeed, had determined to execute writs against me . . .
>
> On the idea that Lord Shelburne intended from your Grace's recommendation to put me out of their reach I kept myself almost without a guinea last year by paying the demands that came in and this has encouraged others who preferred persecuting me to a settlement offered by Fox of 5 per cent on Sir John Goodricke's death.—As nothing was done by Lord Shelburne . . . I must leave England immediately; and as I cannot without danger appear in Town nor can I raise money without appearing there I beg the favour of your Grace to lend me £200. . . .
>
> . . . A bare existence in England out of a jail by means of Parliament is, I assure your Grace, no object with me in my present circumstances. I should endeavor to make myself as usefull as I could there to Pitt for half a year or a year, and in the meantime settle as well as I could all my affairs, and I then think the being thus patronized by your Grace, together with Lord Chatham's and perhaps Pitt's own good wishes, might get me some appointment to the East Indies. I should by this means leave your Grace's borough open for any of your Grace's friends, and perhaps stand some chance of repaying your Grace a sum which I am sensible is a considerable object with the greatest estate. . . .

He received from the duke 'effectual assistance', and on 29 December was setting out for France, with wishes and hopes for an early dissolution of parliament. But if there is 'no prospect of a dissolution, and Pitt will bring me in for some Looe or Newton, I will engage to speak as much nonsense for him as his opponents for the most part do against him'.

In February 1784, the Duke of Rutland went to Ireland, as Lord-Lieutenant, and on 23 March Pitt wrote to him[2] that parliament would be dissolved the next day. And he added when discussing candidates and elections:

> Forgive my telling you how anxious all your friends are that Pulteney should, if possible, be disposed of some other way than by a seat in Parliament; and yet I hardly know how it can be done.

---

[1] 'Bingley Fox' was undoubtedly James Fox Lane, nephew and heir of Lord Bingley of the second creation who had married the daughter and heiress of Robert Lord Bingley of the first creation. But Sir John Goodricke, M.P., who had married that lord's illegitimate daughter, had a life interest in the estate.

[2] See John Duke of Rutland, *Correspondence between William Pitt and Charles, Duke of Rutland* (1890), p. 10.

Nor did the duke; and on 31 March he had Pulteney returned
for his pocket borough of Bramber in Sussex. A month later
Pulteney was back in England, busily 'engaged in searching for a
qualification'[1]—'Mr. Hill [the duke's agent] says he knows how
to do it if you order him in a particular way.' Rutland, who did
not relish such transactions, had already once refused, and did so
again; still Pulteney persisted: he was trying others, but if they all
fail him he will have to renew his application to the duke. 'In
point of law' any scruple on the subject is 'absurd'; and as for
his creditors, these, to lay hold of the land named in the grant,
would have to know the terms of the grant, the situation of the
land, and have 'sufficient time to sue out a proper process against
it'; whereas he would receive it in the morning, deliver it in and
swear to it, and reconvey it to the duke at night.[2]

> I have seen half-a-dozen executions against Fitzpatrick's and Fox's[3]
> horses; the latter's books have been sold in the streets; Lord E.
> Bentinck's horses have been sold by advertisement; Will Hanger,
> Stanhope, and 50 others have at this time all sorts of demands
> upon them and judgements against them, but nobody ever thought
> or heard of any claim on a qualification, which with one third at
> least of the House is known to be fictitious.

Pulteney's parliamentary statistics, intended to show that he was
not out of place in the House, must not be taken too seriously; and
it will be noticed that all those he names were friends of Charles
James Fox, a set he resembled but which he could not join: as a
dependant of Rutland he had to adhere to Pitt.

Pulteney entered the House with the hope of leaving soon for
distant lands in quest of rich prizes, as he might well have done
under North or Fox or the combination of the two; and he remained to observe and to fret, eyewitness to a change of scene
and methods detrimental to his plans and purpose. Yet frustrated
as he was, he could not help paying at times high tribute to Pitt,
and that not only from a wish to please Rutland. The reports of
parliamentary debates and political transactions which during
the next three and a half years he regularly sent over to the duke
in Dublin, contain remarkable thumb-nail sketches of men in
action during that short interval when British politics and Pitt's
steersmanship were unaffected by external events; and owing to

---

[1] By 9 Anne c. 5, borough members had to possess landed property worth £300 p.a.
[2] In the end Rutland sent orders to Hill, 'but as it could not have been done in time
for the first division', Pulteney had obtained a qualification from another friend; see
Hist. MSS. Comm., *Rutland MSS.*, vol. iii, p. 98.   [3] Charles James Fox.

these reports a more than merely personal interest attaches to the amusing, but politically insignificant, figure of Daniel Pulteney.

The parliament which emerged from the electoral defeat of the coalition met on 19 May 1784, and Pulteney's very first report,[1] of 27 May, shows Pitt's growing strength and the crumbling of 'the poor forlorn minority' which, barring the leaders, 'seemed at last to join in the laugh at their ridiculous situation'. 'Mr. Pitt's ministry is fixed beyond any possibility of danger from without, with a greater strength at the opening of the session than ever was before possessed by . . . any . . . modern Minister.' Independents returned on their own interest were coming over to him. Thus Lord Delaval 'astonished a great many by a very warm explicit declaration' that while in the previous parliament he had opposed Pitt 'as a supposed Minister of secret influence', he would now give him as the people's Minister 'all the support he deserved'. Similarly, Osbaldeston, previously a follower of Fox, now openly opposed him, and 'was in every division against him'. But Pulteney criticizes the government's management of the House. On an election question of doubtful merits Fox

> could only muster 60 against 210, though so little pains had Steel[2] taken about members that I suppose 100 of his friends were absent and did not know of any debate. Sutton[3] and I were just in time to be locked out, as nobody had an idea there was any business so soon, and Pitt did not think it worth while to prolong the debate in order to encrease his numbers.

Here was a minister who appealed to the House and neglected marshalling his own cohorts—would he look after needy followers? Pulteney does not as yet ask the question; but he was exceptionally good at sensing trends and forecasting the course.

Then followed weeks of wrangling over the technicalities of the Westminster election—dull stuff and very long hours, 'low bustle and absurdities' laboured in order 'to tire out the independent Members, who were literally sleeping at full length by dozens this morning'. On 8 June, Pulteney spoke for the first time, another member having promised on that condition to stay and vote.

[1] In Hist. MSS. Comm., *Rutland MSS.*, vol. iii, p. 97, two reports dated by the editor 25 and 26 May 1784, are made to precede that of the 27th—supposed interim accounts of the same debates. Even on a superficial reading of the three, serious discrepancies appear, while a more careful examination of the two allegedly earlier reports and a comparison with Debrett's *Parliamentary Register* date them definitely as of 25 January and 1 February 1785.

[2] Thomas Steele, M.P., Secretary to the Treasury.

[3] George Manners-Sutton, M.P.

I rose and spoke ten minutes, . . . not knowing what was the question
before the House. I took care, however, to get into no scrape . . . but
I certainly felt no more embarrassment than in a private room, and
will venture to assure your Grace that you cannot employ any of
your Members who will more readily speak on the Turnpike Bills
of Leicestershire, Cambridgeshire, Grantham, Newark, Scarborough,
or Bramber,[1] whenever such business is before the House. . . . Fox
who followed me . . . has declared at Brooks's, he wondered only
at my want of embarrassment and want of information. . . . I am
perfectly ready to execute all the minor business your Grace will
direct me to do. . . .

—'in the higher departments' he will avoid 'diminishing the
effects of Pitt's speeches'.

On 17 June Sawbridge, supported by Fox, raised the question
of parliamentary reform favoured by Pitt himself. Pulteney, with
most of Rutland's members, had 'the mortification to vote against
Mr. Pitt, who was in the minority with Fox, Sir F. Bassett, etc.,
etc., almost all the House dividing against their friends and with
their enemies'; and reform was put off, 'for this session at least,
by 199 to 125, on the previous question'. Everything else he now
expected to pass smoothly. As for himself he saw no prospect 'but
your making me a Nabob'.

For after all the world is not such a dupe at present as to think there
is any sort of difference in the object for which all people go to India.
Everyone I know expects I should get there . . .

He returned to the subject about a week later—such an appointment would vacate the seat at Bramber for another friend of the
duke.

On 6 July Pitt outlined the India Bill which he was about to
bring in. The speech was highly applauded from every side of the
House, Fox alone rising to answer him. A grand debate on it was
expected: 'I really feel great difficulty from want of your Grace's
directions and presence in England.' With Pitt his connexion was
very slight—

We have no sort of plan, or system, or discipline. We conquer at
present by numbers, and shall run no sort of risque this year at least;
but I foresee what *may* happen if Pitt's ministry is to be conducted
on such a narrow system as public virtue, for the House of Commons
must and will be what they have been this last century.

[1] All of them constituencies in which Rutland had a considerable influence or of
which he was the patron.

Further reports of debates follow, and appeals to the duke to send him 'to India or Africa, or somewhere else' where he could fill his purse. Meantime the House was growing thin as the summer advanced—'it is almost impossible', wrote Pulteney on 15 July,

> to bring down above sixty or seventy members; and I really think your Grace's members are the most usefull in the House, for I don't believe Pochin,[1] Sutton, or myself have ever missed a single day, and Lord Tyrconnel[2] is seldom or never absent at any expected business.

Occasionally he sends Rutland his own worldly-wise criticisms of Pitt's measures—for instance of the India Bill; but he cuts them short—'as it is Sutton's business and mine to approve the Bill throughout, I fear it is mutinous to make any observations on this voluminous code'. Still, he let himself go over Pitt's additional tax on racehorses, which made the 'jockies' in the Lords declare that they would give up racing unless it was amended; which it was, but Pitt caused disgust 'by a great want of politeness' to a delegation which waited on him. Grafton was reported to have said that 'they could expect nothing otherwise from such a young man', and Lord Chatham that 'his brother's ideas on the racehorses were only fit to humbug an old woman'.

> I foresee [wrote Pulteney on 31 July] things will not go so smoothly next year as at present, for in a division yesterday not forty of those who voted came in consequence of Treasury letters. Except Rose[3] and Stevens,[4] there is hardly one man of any service either in the Treasury or the Admiralty.

Shelburne's friends are 'very slack'; there are 'murmurs about the inordinate power and patronage of the Duke of Richmond'; some of Pitt's country supporters think him 'too full of *concession* to his East Indian friends'; there is jealousy of Dundas and the Scotch 'for whom everything is claimed and granted'. Still, no great address will be required to prevent such discontents from having fatal effects: the House, Pulteney shrewdly remarked, 'will always have the *real* Minister a Commoner, or be dissolved every year in attempting to keep such a *valuable* companion

---

[1] William Pochin, M.P. for Leicestershire, elected with the support of the Rutland family.
[2] The Earl of Tyrconnel, married to Frances Manners, daughter of Lord Granby, and returned on the Rutland interest at Scarborough.
[3] George Rose, M.P., Secretary to the Treasury.
[4] Philip Stephens, M.P., Secretary to the Admiralty.

amongst them'. He concludes the letter of 13 August with a new appeal:

> Some place might perhaps be obtained for Sutton in which I could act as his deputy, and not subject your Grace to the expense of a re-election.

The House rose on 31 August, and on 17 October, in the middle of the recess, there is yet another appeal:

> I really think if, on returning to town, I can't get any prospect of going to Calcutta, or some sort of employment at home, G. Sutton and myself shall be starved before the end of this winter, or sell ourselves to Fox for the sweepings of his faro table.

Did Rutland act on these urgent appeals? There is nothing to show it in his extant correspondence before August 1785. But in a letter to Pitt, of 13 September 1786, he stated that he had repeatedly applied in favour of Pulteney during more than two years;[1] and in the meantime was paying Pulteney £400 a year from his own pocket.

At the opening of the new session, on 25 January 1785, Pitt, writes Pulteney,

> spoke warmly for his Reform, but there is no sort of chance that it can be carried, let him exert, even in earnest, every power of Government.

And in a postscript:

> Sutton says he hears your Grace is pledged to support the Reform here. It is therefore necessary for us to know how to vote, for God knows we are not pledged, and should hardly think of dividing in any manner opposite to the views of your Grace. . . .

In reply Pulteney received, as he told Pitt, 'instructions from my *constituent* to support his Reform'; and he would do so, 'even if it goes to destroy the rotten boroughs', the branch on which he sat. But he did not think there was any great probability of its being carried; many on the Treasury bench 'and two-thirds at least of the independent part of the House' were against it.

On 9 February 1785 Pitt found himself in a minority when trying on technical grounds to delay a return being made of the Westminster election.

> . . . contrary to the wish of all his real friends, and only supported by Dundas, Lord Mulgrave, and Bearcroft, Pitt persevered in this

---

[1] See John Duke of Rutland, op. cit. p. 168.

cursed business, to the disgust of his most independent supporters, and the numbers against us were 135 to 174, a very different division from what we have hitherto experienced. . . .

The consequence of this will be trifling if Pitt will now recede, and agree to order the return; but . . . many will form a very different idea of the Administration if such an odious business is forced down by a small majority. . . .

. . . Pitt . . . should not pretend to offer such resolutions to the present *virtuous* house as Dundas and Mulgrave were used to propose to Lord North's majorities of Whitworth, &c.[1]

In one division over the Westminster election Pulteney went the length of voting 'in opposition to G. Sutton and the Ministry'; and on 4 March supplied the duke with a laboured explanation: by the time he voted it was clear that there was a majority against the government; 'the difference of one vote was nothing'; it lessened the triumph of the Opposition if they required the support of so 'notoriously a steady attender on Government divisions'; the vote will help him to bring back 'some of our friends' on the succeeding question. And he tried to make light of adverse votes on that election:

The explanation to all this is . . . that the House of Commons, being at present perhaps *too independent*, that *incorrupt* body has many whims and caprices, and will decide against any Minister, sometimes without ill-will to him in the main.

He himself seemed to be harking back to the system on which he had banked when he entered parliament: 'for every purpose except entertaining the galleries,' he wrote on 14 February 1785, 'Jenkinson, Atkinson the contractor, and Dundas possess almost all the good sense in the House'. Yet a certain measure of admiration he feels for its new complexion: this is 'the most independent House that has sat since the Revolution' (19 March); 'there never was a Parliament where election justice was so impartially dispensed'. And on 21 March: 'Pitt will gain credit with the public, at the risk of making some personal enemies, by his reforms in the offices.' Introducing the report on the Commission on Public Accounts Pitt treated the auditors of the exchequer and imprest with great asperity,

[1] This letter, dated 10 February, starts: 'In continuation of the letter I had the honour to send your Grace last night . . .' That previous letter seems to be missing. For the early career of Charles Whitworth, whose name is here used as a by-word, see my *The Structure of Politics at the Accession of George III*, chapter on 'Parliamentary Beggars'.

for he said almost in as many words, that their 'laziness was even superior to their avarice'; and these auditors are the Duke of New-castle, Lord Mountstuart, and Lord Sondes. Though nobody doubted the truth of his assertions, there was at least one in this number whom we did not expect to hear mentioned in such terms.[1]

Next the question came up of parliamentary reform. Rutland instructed his members to vote for it—on what grounds does not appear from his correspondence. But Pulteney, while willing to obey, was outspoken in his criticisms. 'I regret Pitt's attachment to this Reform . . .',[2] he wrote on 6 April. 'Fox will take advantage of it to injure Pitt with the King and the most respectable part of the country. . . .' The reform was expected to be thrown out by a considerable majority—'I think the greater the better'. During the debate of 18 April, a very long speech by Pitt was listened to

> with that sort of civil attention which people give to a person who has a good claim to be heard but with whom the hearers are deter-mined to disagree . . . the generality of Pitt's friends only lamented that he would not keep clear of this absurd business. . . .

On the bill being thrown out by 248 votes to 174, Pitt looked 'as grave as if he had really suffered a Ministerial defeat', while Pulteney clearly agreed with those who felt happy 'at our good riddance from such a troublesome affair'. He did not report to Rutland how his members had voted. In the extant list of the minority appear John Macnamara,[3] John Sutton, and Tyrconnel, with Pulteney paired on that side; but as there is no list of the majority, it is uncertain whether Pochin and George Sutton were absent or voted against Pitt.

After about a year's observation, Pulteney describes Pitt, in his letter of 23 April, as very much 'fettered in his conduct on great affairs'.

> From a very partial and confined knowledge of the world, he is too full of caution and suspicions where there does not exist the shadow of a pretext for them; and, from having no immediate intercourse with the generality of the House of Commons here, he is as ignorant of their opinions on particular questions as if he was minister of another country. His whole conduct proves he can only be minister

---

[1] Presumably the Duke of Newcastle, an influential supporter of the administration.
[2] On another occasion Pulteney speaks of Pitt as 'encumbered or enamoured with —I am not certain which—this Yorkshire system of Reform'.
[3] Member for Leicester.

with an independent House; and the very proofs they give of indepency, *i.e.* dissenting from him on points where, according to plain common sense, I think they have been in the right, startles him so much that he is too much frightened for some time to bring questions before them where he is equally sure of decisive majorities in his favor. His living and conversing with a very small circle and acting only on abstract general principles will, I foresee, involve him at some time or other in difficulties, from which no minister of this country can be free without more extensive information. But the aversion to the Coalition is still so strong in the House that he may continue many years, if he pleases, a very usefull Minister to the country, though not so absolute in majorities as some of his predecessors, and, whenever he was to quit, I think no ministry, not founded on corruption, could stand against him.

Naturally the new system had a discouraging effect on men with a preference for 'the old plan of Lord North, and afterwards of the Coalition, to divide the profits of a Ministry in their several proportions down to the lowest of their adherents. . . .'

But if Mr. Pitt can long persuade a House of Commons that they are to spend their time and fortunes *independently* to support an *independent* Minister in great power and an income of 8,000*l* a year, it will certainly be better for the country and more honorable to themselves. . . .

Still, even some of 'our most virtuous friends' complain that they never before supported a minister a fortnight without at least one dinner in the time, 'and it seems in this great duty of a good minister Pitt has almost deserved an impeachment'.

In letter after letter Pulteney complained at being left unprovided for, and begged Rutland to intervene on his behalf.

All sorts of people are getting all sorts of places here . . . but according to the vulgar proverb of the nearer the church the further from God, Sutton and myself, who are the most constant adherents Pitt has, are to be kept as pure and independent as Lord Chatham, Banks, Wilberforce, &c.

Hard pressed by Pulteney, Rutland wrote to Pitt on 31 August 1785:

I very much wish to obtain an office of about 400*l*. *per annum*, not preclusive of a seat in Parliament, for Pulteney. He has nothing to live upon. I must either support him out of my own pocket, or he will be forced into the arms of Opposition upon future expectations. He has in truth been very useful to me during the progress of the

adjustment, by transmitting to me clear, distinct, and regular accounts of all that was passing. He would have no objection to considerable duty and attendance. I think you might employ him to
effect. If no office of that description should offer itself, might I point
out some situation in the East Indies. It would vacate a seat *for me*,
and *he* would be provided for.

But again nothing happened; and another year passed without
Pulteney realizing the aim with which he had entered the House.
In July 1786 Rutland wrote from Dublin to his secretary, Thomas
Orde:

> Pulteney is here, stating his constant attendance, and the use he
> could be of to Pitt if he were employed. I believe it to be true. Pray
> press Pitt to give him something to relieve me from importunity and
> from expence. He has talents and industry, and he might, I think,
> be turned to advantage.

Orde replied on 14 July:

> I have again urged Mr. Pitt to remember Pulteney, and I trust, that
> he will do so. I am indeed most anxiously impatient to relieve your
> Grace from importunity and expence, which you ought not to be
> burthen'd with to any degree.

But again nothing happened, and on 13 September 1786 Rutland
wrote to Pitt complaining that 'after repeated applications' from
Orde and himself, Pulteney was still an 'expectant'—his finances
'oblige me to make up the income of such an office as I have
troubled you for to enable him to attend to his duty in Parliament. . . .' And still always nothing happened, and complaints
and requests continued; and so did the parliamentary service and
reports of debates of a Pulteney despairing 'of your Grace's system
of attachment and attendance ever doing me the least service'.
Consequently, on 7 May 1787, he approached Rutland with a new
request: for a loan of £1,000 to enable him to establish a faro
bank, in partnership with Lord Foley, Lady Duncannon, Lady
Harrington, and others.[1] The bank was to begin with £6,000. 'I

---

[1] On such a bank run in 1781–2 by C. J. Fox, Richard Fitzpatrick, and James Hare,
and on its profits, see Hist. MSS. Comm., *Carlisle MSS.*, pp. 476 et seq. *passim.* Thus G.
Selwyn to Lord Carlisle, 24 April 1781, on 'Charles's and Richard's damned Pharo
bank, which swallows up everybody's cash that comes to Brooks's. . . .' Same to same, 16
May: 'I saw Charles today in a new hat, frock, waistcoat, shirt, and stockings; he was
as clean and smug as a gentleman, and upon perceiving my surprise, he told me that
it was from the Pharo Bank.' Same to same, 29 May: 'Charles, Richard, and Hare
are alternatively holding a bank . . . by which they must have got among them
near 2,000*l*', etc.

mean to subscribe £1,500, and shall have the additional advantage of occasional pay for dealing.' And on 3 July:

> The faro project, though so essentially advanced by your Grace's means, is from the absence of some of the gang from town, in no condition to commence this summer; though some of our allies at Bath (the Duchess of Devonshire and Lady Duncannon) are in a rage at our having suffered Sir Watts Horton to set up a mushroom bank of 500*l.* in their absence. Little as I can pretend to any great knowledge of fine ladies, I cannot foresee what obstacles the very proposers may suggest in future. All I know is that it is as much their interest as mine, and . . . as much their inclination.

The Duke of Rutland died suddenly on 24 October 1787, at the age of 33; and henceforth only the bare facts can be ascertained of Pulteney's career. On 6 June 1788 he was called to the Bar, sixteen years after having been admitted—was he preparing to take up legal work? On 9 May he spoke in the House at some length in defence of Sir Elijah Impey, chief justice of Bengal, and in the ensuing division voted on the government side. But this was his last recorded vote for early in December 1788 he was appointed collector of customs at Roseau in the island of Dominica —did Pitt honour the request of a dead friend? or did he perhaps fear lest Pulteney, now at a critical juncture, sold himself to Fox? It seems doubtful if he ever went out to Dominica[1]—more probably his duties were performed through a deputy. Had he gone to the West Indies he would have had to resign his Fellowship at King's; whereas he continued to hold it, and in 1794, at the age of 45, seems to have retired 'to a comfortable bachelor life in College, with easy duties as a College officer'.[2] During the years 1772–5 and 1782–93, Pulteney did not attend a single Congregation or college meeting; during 1776–81, eight out of thirty-nine; but during the last eighteen years of his life, 1794– 1811, 204 out of a total of 251. He was clearly in residence, undoubtedly in daily contact with Charles Simeon, of the Clapham sect, who from 1782 till 1836 was of the small band of resident Fellows of King's, vice-provost 1790–2, one of the deans 1792–8, and of the bursars 1798–1805. But even during Pulteney's regular

[1] His work in Dominica was probably as fictitious as that which, according to the Protocollum Book of King's College, p. 135, was solemnly assigned to him in accordance with the Founder's Statutes for the Fellows of the College: on 2 June 1788, the Provost, in presence and with the assent of the Dean of Divinity, 'diverted . . . Daniel Pulteney, M.A. . . . to the study of Astronomy'.

[2] *Ex inf.* Mr. John Saltmarsh to whom I am indebted also for the further details of Daniel Pulteney's college activities.

residence in Cambridge, and while he held office in college, there is no evidence of his ever having been a tutor; and the stipend of £3 a year which he drew *pro lectura philosophica* during his two years as second dean of arts (1801–3), seems to have been just another sinecure. On 24 July 1811, Daniel Pulteney died of apoplexy at the Rainbow coffee-house, in King's Street, London; and was buried in King's Chapel at Cambridge.

A parasite throughout, he had sensed and recorded during his short parliamentary career the change that was coming over British politics.

3

LORD FIFE AND HIS FACTOR

WILLIAM ROSE was factor and confidential friend to Lord Fife, and their correspondence,[1] which lasted from 1763 till about 1800, together with accounts, bills, etc., all carefully preserved, filled 'seven immense cases'. Lord Fife knew its value and, in 1788, wrote to Rose:

> I wish some time, at leisure hours, you could arrange all my letters and libel [*sic*] them by the year, only just to separate them on business from general correspondence. I am certain I could make a pretty good history of many events, if ever I took time to review them, with the additional recollection of my mind—but this only speculation, for I never shall think of such a thing.

Nothing was done, and it was left to the present editors to 'disentangle the valuable from the useless', read and sort some 20,000 letters, and choose from them for publication. Their workmanship points to the selection having been made in a competent manner. Amateurs in history-writing are primarily people who take themselves more seriously than their subject, which certainly cannot be said about the authors of this book. They have done their work with care and devotion, and in an interesting series of well-annotated letters have given a vivid picture of one of those who formed the political set in Great Britain; this, as presented by them, makes a story, to some of us, at any rate, more interesting than any novel.

Lord Fife sat in the House of Commons from 1754 to 1790; till 1784 for Banffshire, which, between the Union and the first Reform Act, the Duffs represented for fifty years, and after 1832 without break from 1837 till 1893. He was no place-hunter: 'I am in such a way in the world', he wrote to the Duke of Newcastle in 1754, 'as to have little or no occasion to trouble your

[1] *Lord Fife and his Factor. Being the Correspondence of James, second Lord Fife, 1729–1809*, Ed. by Alistair and Henrietta Tayler.

Grace with demands.' But, though independent, he usually supported the King's Government, considering this the proper rule of Parliamentary conduct. Whig orators and historians have managed to confuse Tory gentlemen biased in favour of authority with parasites intent on places and pensions, while the Tory accounts of the 'Whig oligarchy' give an equally incomplete picture of the other side. A series of monographs about minor Members of Parliament, whose names and ideas are hardly ever considered and whose influence is usually underrated, would yield a different picture of one of the most gifted, active, inventive generations in British history, which, by its wit and love of humorous stories, has created an unduly derogatory legend about itself. The authors of this book have done the redeeming work for their own ancestor, simply by letting him speak for himself.

Lord Fife's political thinking at the time of the American Revolution is typical of a vast volume of British opinion. Though from the first anxious to avoid war (of which, as a true Scot, he disliked the expense), in January 1775 he could not join Chatham in 'praising the *Loyal* Americans for all they had done, and desiring to move the King for the immediate recall of the troops from Boston'. In 1776 he saw that 'we gain no credit by our operations in America', and by 1777 wished for 'a period to this American war. Our most sanguine and victorious expectations will not make all up, we are exhausting ourselves.' In February 1778 he welcomed Lord North's Conciliatory Proposals as 'the only means of getting out of the horrid scrape we are in', adding:

> I pray God that punishment may fall on the heads of those who have made so bad a use of the great exerted force of this Country and misspent so much blood and treasure. . . .

He voted (against the Ministers) for a special war tax on Government salaries and pensions, and was becoming sarcastic about the King himself:

> The King is amusing himself with going about to visit ships, etc. . . . It looks like playing with rattles and whistles when so tremendous a power is armed to attack us. The Toulon fleet is certainly sailed . . . ours is waiting till great Personages be amus'd with the sight of it.

Still, he continued to support the Government, as is shown by the circular letter from Lord North in November 1779, inviting his attendance. But by 1783 Lord Fife had travelled the full length from North to Shelburne, whose Government he supported on the peace treaty in February 1783:

> I have no connection with them, but I love Peace and wish to give my vote of disapprobation of this, and abuse came but ill from a set of men who has brought the bad peace on us, for I think whatever is humiliating in it is owing to war-makers, and not to peace-makers.

In 1789, during the King's illness, Lord Fife's warm monarchist feelings once more became apparent; he did not, like many others, turn towards the expectant, jeering heir—his heart 'unfeignedly' prayed for the King. After his recovery Lord Fife went to Kew, but when he saw the King mount his horse, 'went to the other side of the road to see and not to be seen'; the King, however, hailed him, and addressed him in the most friendly manner:

> All this I bore and returned my grateful thanks. He then called out: 'Lord Fife, you are no gambler, you are no rat.' I then forgot all distance between King and subject, took him by the thigh, prayed the Almighty to bless him, and added: 'Yes, Sir, I am at present a gambler; my greatest stake is on that horse; for God sake take care of it, don't ride too hard.'

Lord Fife's correspondence, of which politics form but a small part, admirably displays the cares, business and interests of a big Scottish laird in the latter part of the eighteenth century; also his mentality, unlike that of English lords or country squires, and completely different from that of the man about town which is most familiar to us from contemporary literature. Even his humour is different, composed of terse common sense and good temper, dry and unpolished, sometimes personal and even coarse. His mind was free of cant; on the death of a friend he writes to Rose:

> I think your wife expected a legacy, but I suppose he has forgot that, otherwise I should have heard more regret for him. Nothing on the death of a friend calls forth more affliction than a legacy.

Where other people might grow angry, Lord Fife remains humorous; thus after having suffered a loss of about £200 through a cousin of Rose's, he remarks:

> When you have done with such cousins as that, of your own, I can furnish you with some of mine, in the same stile.

But his humour does not spare people; on one occasion, describing things which he sends home from London, he mentions 'one

hen fully as large as your wife. I hope she shall be as breedy'
(Mrs. Rose had twelve children). And Rose's own person invariably was in for it; thus in the letter of 29 March 1777: 'I
receiv'd your letter from Edinr., it was all over snuff nose-drops,
so I condole with you on that accomplishment'—annotated on
the back by William Rose: 'Lord Fife anent snuff-taking. *Nota*.
Gave it up on this reproach, 25th March.'

But directly on this banter in Lord Fife's letter follows a sentence which makes one's imagination wander to things unre-
corded:

> There din'd here last Sunday *Genl. Grant*, Genl. Fraser, Col.
> Morris, Lord William Gordon, and Troup, so you see I am washing
> away offences in a moderate way.

As the editors add, 'these were some of Lord Fife's political
opponents'; but yet another interest attaches to their persons.
'Genl. Grant' was probably Francis Grant of Dunphaile, M.P.
for Elginshire from 1768 till 1774, when he was ousted by Lord
Fife's brother, Arthur Duff; he had served in North America in
the Seven Years' War, commanding the Royal Highland or 42nd
Regiment.[1] 'Genl. Fraser' was Simon Fraser, M.P. for Inverness-
shire, the son of the Lord Lovat executed in 1747, himself attainted
but pardoned; barred by Hardwicke from standing for Parliament in 1754, he proved his loyalty in the Seven Years War by
raising the Fraser Highlanders and serving with them under
Wolfe; and in 1776 he again raised two Highland battalions for
service in America. 'Col. Morris' was undoubtedly Staats Long
Morris, M.P. for Elgin Burghs, a New-Yorker by birth, brother
of the American revolutionary and ambassador, Gouverneur
Morris; he married the widow of the third Duke of Gordon and
died a general in the British Army. A dinner with these men in
the year of Saratoga, at the height of the American crisis! But
perhaps they did not talk about America at all; foremost in their
minds was probably the old feud between the Duffs and the
Gordons.

---

[1] To begin with I thought that 'Genl. Grant' was James Grant of Ballindalloch,
M.P. for Wick Burghs, home on leave from America, where he had served in the
Seven Years War, been Governor of East Florida 1763–73, and was now serving once
more; and where his over-bearing manners had done more harm than his service had
done good. But on further consideration I am inclined to think that the 'Genl. Grant'
here mentioned was Francis Grant of Dunphaile.

4

SO COME AND JOIN THE DANCE

AN EIGHTEENTH-CENTURY POLITICAL TRANSACTION

Dramatis Personae

JOHN CALCRAFT was a well-known regimental agent; for a long time he was the right-hand man of Henry Fox, but deserted him in 1763. In 1757 he bought the estate of Rempston in the Isle of Purbeck, in Dorset, within walking distance of three Parliamentary boroughs, Corfe Castle, Poole, and Wareham, and set to work to capture them. He succeeded in having his brother, Thomas Calcraft, elected for Poole in 1761; in 1767 he purchased the Manor of Wareham from Thomas Erle Drax, 'and also all the lands of George Pitt, John Pitt, and John Bankes, esqres, and almost all the freeholds in the borough soon after'.[1] He failed in his attempts at Corfe Castle, and gave up whatever footing he had gained in it to Mr. Bankes in exchange for his 'interest' at Wareham; Corfe Castle had for a century been owned and represented by the two families of Bond and Bankes, and remained with them until disfranchised by the Reform Act of 1832.

The Fursmans, a West Country family, are mentioned by Hutchins at Wareham early in the eighteenth century. A Rev. John Fursman of Lamerton, Devonshire, appears in Joseph Foster's *Alumni Oxonienses*, and died as Canon of Exeter Cathedral in 1757. William Fursman, to whom Calcraft's letters are directed, was a 'waiter and searcher' at the Custom House at Deal, as can be seen from a letter of his to the Duke of Newcastle dated 12 June 1744.[2]

The letters which follow are from one of Calcraft's letter-books at the British Museum.[3] Fursman's replies are not extant.

John Calcraft to W. Fursman at Deal, 3 October 1757:

Your very obliging letter of 28 September found me in Wilts on Fryday, or should sooner have been answered. You are very wise to

---

[1] Hutchins, *Dorset*, vol. 1, p. 82.   [2] 32703, f. 113.   [3] 17493, f. 96.

provide for your son who, Captain Pool tells me, is a proper person for the Army, and if you will accept a pair of colours for him, I will immediately procure them. Should he dislike the Army, the Custom-house place may in that case be applied for, which if it could be ever got might not be soon and 'tis pity the young gentleman should not at his time of life take to some profession. If the Army proves agreeable you may depend on my continued attention to him. I do not mean or wish to prejudice Mr. Bond but on the contrary hope to cultivate his friendship, and I hope you will allow me to purchase your burgages at Corfe. I shall be obliged to you for an immediate answer because I forsee a speedy opportunity of getting an ensigncy, if your son chooses it, and am, with great regard, etc.

J.C.

William Fursman's son obviously chose the Army, and on 19 November 1757,[1] John Calcraft wrote to Lord Home, Governor of Gibraltar, for whom he was agent:

Ensign Fursman of Jefferey's [Regiment] will have the honour to deliver you this letter; he is son to a gentleman who is kind enough to give me his interest in a borough where I hope your Lordship will see either my brother or some other friend of mine chose next election, and is a very promising young gentleman. Wherefore I will earnestly recommend him to your Lordship's protection. . . .

But young Fursman does not seem immediately to have started for Gibraltar, for on 26 February 1758, John Calcraft is found writing another letter to Lord Home for him with a new recommendation:[2]

Fursman is a friend's son at Corfe Castle where I have an estate that I hope will in time give me some influence, so I will recommend him to your Lordship to shew him any little civility that lyes in your way.

This time Ensign Fursman started out on the *Prince George*, Admiral Broderick's flagship, the squadron acting as a convoy to a numerous fleet of merchant ships bound for the Straits.

On 15 May 1758, John Calcraft wrote again to Lord Home:[3]

What a terrible misfortune is happen'd to Broderick's ship on board of which was my poor friend Fursman who I doubt is lost as I hear nothing from him. He had a long private letter for you and when I shall have an opportunity to send you another I don't know.

Two days later, Calcraft, seeing his last chance of making capital of poor Fursman's 'ensigncy', wrote to his father:

---

[1] Ibid., f. 111. [2] Ibid., f. 149. [3] Ibid., f. 166.

I wish I could ease the anxiety your mind must be under but I am sorry to say I cannot get any certain tidings about your son, the minute I have you shall know. Duplicates of all my letters recommending him shall be forwarded, I have already received answers to some in which I mentioned him, so doubt not but if it has pleased God to spare him he will be well received. If you will desire your friend at Corfe to support me in my undertakings there, you will oblige me. Make yourself, dear Sir, as easy as you can 'till you hear more of this melancholy affair and believe me always, etc.

Young Fursman was dead, for in a letter to Colonel Jeffreys dated 4 June[1] Calcraft mentions that Mr. Bruen is 'to succeed poor Fursman'.

A full account of the disaster of the *Prince George* will be found in the *Gentleman's Magazine*, vol. xxviii (1758), pp. 228–30. The ship caught fire at sea in broad daylight and of a 'complement' of 715 and 30 passengers to Gibraltar, 745 in all, only 260 were saved. The other ships seem to have feared to approach it, for 'not knowing we had taken care to float our powder, were under sad apprehensions we might blow up' (letter from Mr. Parry, an officer on board the *Prince George*). The Rev. Mr. Sharp, the chaplain, gives an even more sinister account of what happened during that catastrophe on 13 April 1758:

> ... More might have been saved had the merchantmen behaved like human creatures; but they kept a long way to windward the whole time; and if possible, to their greater shame be it spoken, instead of saving men that swam to their boats, they were employed in taking up geese, fowls, tables, chairs, and whatever else of the kind came near them.

[1] Ibid., f. 172.

5

COUNTRY GENTLEMEN IN
PARLIAMENT, 1750–84

In common parlance 'country gentlemen' can be equated with commoners possessed of armorial bearings and landed estates, but the term denotes also a way of life: Colonel John Selwyn was a country gentleman, but no one would describe his son George Augustus Selwyn, the wit, as such—a rustic touch is implied in the term. And there are outer rings to the indisputable core of any social group. At what point do men in the line of succession to a peerage merge back into the country gentry? And what about Irish peers, especially those with nothing Irish to them except their titles? In the mid-eighteenth-century House of Commons, excluding sons of British and Scottish peers on the one flank (an average of about 80) and those with 'no claim to arms' on the other (less than 30) we are left with about 80 per cent of the total. Yet in Parliament the term 'country gentleman' is never made to cover anything like four-fifths of the House; its character is residual: certain categories are subtracted, and not the same by everybody, and what is left is called country gentlemen.

There are elaborate lists in the Newcastle Papers[1] analysing the House of Commons as it emerged from the general election of 1754; and the results appeared of sufficient importance to Lord Hardwicke to copy them out for his own use.[2] A peculiar feature of these lists is that, having abstracted several professional groups —officers in the Army or Navy, placemen, merchants and planters, and practising lawyers—they describe the rest as 'country gentlemen', including among them even courtesy lords. Roughly the category is meant to denote men without professional interests and in less obvious dependence on Administration. And in fact while in the professional groups only 25 are classed as against the Administration, 6 as 'doubtful', and 170 as 'for' (yielding an

[1] 33034, ff. 169–181.　　　　　　　　　　　　　　[2] 35876, f. 1.

over-all majority of 139) among the country gentlemen the corresponding figures are 124, 28 and 162, leaving a narrow margin of 10.

Still, these 'country gentlemen' on both sides formed groups of a mixed character. Among the 162 friends of the Administration a great many, while they held no places or pensions, depended on Government support for their seats, and drew heavily on official patronage for their relatives, friends, and most of all their constituents; others were connected with peers or leading politicians in office; and it was a small and shrinking group of truly independent Whigs of the country gentleman type which differed basically from holders of places, commissions, or contracts. Similarly on the Opposition side a distinction should be drawn between mere 'outs' panting to get in, and the real independents; but of the 152 country gentlemen classed in 1754 as 'against' or 'doubtful', at least two-thirds were such independents.

The distinguishing mark of the country gentleman was disinterested independence: he should not be bound either to Administration or to any faction in the House, nor to a magnate in his constituency; if a knight of the shire, he should owe his election to the free choice of the gentlemen of the county, and if a borough Member, he should sit on his own interest: so as to be free to follow in the House the dictates of his own judgment and conscience. The monumental inscription in the church of St. Mary, Astbury, for Richard Wilbraham Bootle, M.P. for Chester 1761–90, reads: 'in Parliament his conduct was uniform in the support of his King and his country, in the respectable character of an independent country gentleman'. And a newspaper about 1780[1] described him as

one of the most independent Members in the House. He attaches himself to no party but is governed in the vote he gives, by the unbiased suggestions of his judgment, and the fair operation of that influence only which originates in the several arguments he hears. . . .

A similar attitude was taken by Lord Belasyse, son of the Earl Fauconberg, but in character and outlook a Yorkshire

[1] Some 25 years ago I picked up, I do not remember where, a book of newspaper cuttings headed 'Parliamentary Characters. From the *Public Ledger*, 1779; and *The English Chronicle*, 1780 and 1781'. The cuttings are not dated nor marked with the name of the newspaper. At the end there are some cuttings and papers referring to William Strahan, M.P., the printer, and his wife, which suggests that the book may have been started by him, and completed by someone connected with him.

country gentleman, when he wrote to his father on 20 April 1769:[1]

> Last Saturday I sat twelve hours in the House of Commons without moving, with which I was well satisfied, as it gave me the power from the various arguments on both sides of determining clearly by my vote my opinion. . . .

And about William Drake, Member for his own pocket borough of Agmondesham during half a century, 1746–96, a newspaper wrote in the early 1780s:[2]

> . . . the late Earl Temple took great pains to enlist this gentleman under the banners of the Chatham party; but tho' Mr. Drake uniformly supported the measures of that great statesman, he could never be prevailed upon to form a partial connection which might deprive him of the constitutional freedom of sentiment which *ought* to be the characteristic of a British senator. . . .

Here was a conception of Parliamentary duties radically different from our own: such Members did not deem it a function of Parliament to provide a Government—the Government to them was the King's. Their duty was to support it as long as they honestly could, while judging of questions which came before them with the impartiality and disinterestedness of a jury. As late as 1793, R. B. Jenkinson (subsequently 2nd Earl of Liverpool and Prime Minister) in a debate on Parliamentary Reform,[3] described 'the landed interest, or country gentlemen', as seldom ambitious of exercising Government functions.

> Indeed, it may, perhaps, be more proper that such persons should be employed in watching over the conduct of those who exercise the functions of executive Government, than that they should be employed in exercising those functions themselves.

In short, not partisans but judges; and therefore without party label.

Things were as yet somewhat different about 1750 when 'independent country gentlemen' was wellnigh a synonym for Tory. Between 1688 and 1714, Whigs and Tories alike had a Court and a country wing, and neither side being permanently in office, the balance of that double division was maintained. But during

---

[1] Fauconberg MSS. in the possession of Captain Malcolm Wombwell, at Newburgh Priory, Yorks.

[2] G. Eland on 'The Shardeloes Muniments' in *Records of Buckinghamshire*, p. 294. The cutting can be dated approximately from internal evidence.

[3] *Parliamentary Register* (1793), vol. xxxv, p. 389.

the Walpole-Pelham era, the Tories' forty years in the desert, the Court-minded among them, that is most of the nobility and the 'flesh-potters', drifted over to the 'Whigs', while among these the country gentlemen were being gradually absorbed by the Administration group. Thus the Tories were losing their Court, and the Whigs their country wing.

It would indeed have been wholly unnatural, and even priggish for a supporter of Administration by a self-denying ordinance to preclude himself from ever asking a service or favour of his friends in office. It was merely a question of how frequent and urgent such requests were, whether the favours were for the Member himself or for others, and what conclusions were drawn from their being granted or refused; most of all, how far the Member would go against his own convictions in his support of Administration. There were country Whigs of an older stamp: such as John Garth (born in 1701), M.P. for Devizes 1740–64, who in 1755 could speak of 'fifteen years' of 'constant and steady concurrence in support of the measures of Government in Parliament without any assistance or return';[1] Robert More (born in 1703), M.P. for Shrewsbury, who claimed to have been chosen 'without solicitation, without influence of Minister of State or Lord', in 'contempt for the influence of the greatest';[2] John White (born 1699), M.P. for East Retford, and John Page (born 1697), M.P. for Chichester, two strong independent characters. There were also some younger men, such as Brooke Forester (born 1717), M.P. for Much Wenlock, against whose name it was noted in a list of the House prepared for Lord Bute: 'Old Whig', 'by Whiggism attached to Lord Powis as the head of that party in Shropshire, but soliciting very few favours of Government'.[3] And in 1785 his son George, pointing to his own record, during 30 years' service as Member for the borough, declared:[4]

> To preserve independence, to support the consequence of Parliament is I conceive the only means of protecting and preserving the rights and liberties of the people, and in order to do that, I will be independent myself whilst in your service.

Most of all, there was the group of Yorkshire Whigs, which hardly finds its counterpart in any other county. There was Cholmley Turner whose 'distinctive characteristic was a dislike of aristocratic domination in the county', and who with the support both

---

[1] See 'Charles Garth and his Connexions', by L. B. Namier, in *The English Historical Review* (1939).   [2] See *The Structure of Politics*, p. 258.   [3] 38333, f. 93.
[4] Forester MSS. in the possession of Lord Forester at Willey Park, Salop.

C

of Whig and Tory gentlemen was 'able to show a certain coolness towards some of the greater magnates'. In 1734, and again in 1741, he would not accept nomination from the Whig peers but would await what he called 'the command of the gentlemen' in a county meeting; and 'in 1747, he could not be persuaded to stand again, giving as his reason that there were "so many noblemen" who were "thought to have the interest and direction of the county"'.[1] A similar attitude was adopted by his nephew: in 1768 when Rockingham wanted to recommend him as Parliamentary candidate for York, Charles Turner was reluctant to join the Rockingham Club (the society of York Whigs) since he did not wish to seem to owe his seat in Parliament to aristocratic patronage.[2] Further, there were the two Armytages, the three Lascelles, old William Aislabie, and young Belasyse. And foremost among these Yorkshire Whigs was George Savile, a close friend of Rockingham's, who declined nomination by him either at Higham Ferrers or York, but would only stand for the county, with the support of its gentlemen;[3] who neither in 1765 nor in 1782 accepted office from his friends, and during his many years in Parliament probably never gave a factious vote: and in the list of the Commons drawn up for Shelburne in August 1782, after Rockingham's death, is placed in the residual column of 'country gentlemen and persons unconnected'.[4]

Still, these independent country gentlemen were a mere trimming to the Whigs in Administration or in Opposition, just as a few peers were to the Tory country gentlemen. It is the gradual identification of Tories with the independent country gentlemen which empties the party name of specific contents. There were men whom political managers hardly knew how to label. Thomas Hill, M.P. for Shrewsbury, was nephew and heir of Sir Richard Hill, a Tory of the reign of William III; Thomas, who never held any office, entered Parliament under the wing of Lord Powis, head of the Shropshire Whigs, and with the support of Sir John Astley,[5]

---

[1] See Cedric Collyer, 'The Rockinghams and Yorkshire Politics 1742–61', *Thoresb* *Society Proceedings*, vol. xli, part 4 (1954), No. 99.
[2] Rockingham MSS. of Earl Fitzwilliam in the Sheffield Public Library.
[3] Collyer, loc. cit.
[4] Dundas Papers in the National Library of Scotland.
[5] Sir John Astley to his agent, 28 February 1748/9: 'Jones, Mr. Hill of tarn who i mett here i find intends to offer himself a candidate for Shresbury att the next ellection in cace a vacancy happens you must imeadetly aply to my tennants that are burgeses or any body i have any interest in and desire the faviour of them to oblige me with their vote and interest for Mr. Hill att the next ellection, I am your friend Sir John Astley.' Attingham MSS. at the Salop R.O.

M.P. for Shropshire, an arch-Tory; and he still appears as a Tory in Newcastle's list of 1767[1] although he used to receive Newcastle's 'circular letter', the eighteenth-century Parliamentary whip. There were knights of the shire such as Robert Shafto in Durham or Lord Downe in Yorkshire, members of Tory families returned 'on Whig principles' with the support of Administration, without losing that of the Tory gentry. In spite of such uncertainties, it is still possible about 1750 or 1760 to compile a list of so-called Tories; but hardly in 1770; and by the 1780s the designation of Tory is completely replaced in Parliament by that of country gentlemen, 'independent and unconnected'—men not owing suit to any political leader.

There is peculiar difficulty even about 1750 in the study of a nationwide group without a leader or program or deeper coherence; especially as its members were seldom literary men addicted to writing, and very few collections even of their personal papers have survived. Bolingbroke belongs to the age of the 'pre-exile from office' Tories. Even William Wyndham is still a politician of the Queen Anne period (and his papers seem to have been destroyed). Nor have those of Sir Watkin Williams Wynn so far come to light; they are said to have perished in the fire at Wynnstay in 1858. After his death in 1749, the country gentlemen threw up no leader approximating him in stature. Influential among them, and sometimes acting as their spokesmen, were two men of curiously disparate mentality: Sir John Phillips, the Pembrokeshire squire, long suspected of Jacobitism, and Alderman William Beckford, the richest and most prominent of the West Indian planters, and in the 1760s leader of the Chathamite City radicals. Some papers of John Phillips are at the Welsh National Library at Aberystwyth but nothing of political importance; while those of William Beckford seem lost—the papers of his son, the much biographized author of *Vathek*, survive, but not of the father. In fact, I have so far found only one very rich collection of manuscripts of a Tory country gentleman: that of Sir Roger Newdigate of Arbury, Warwickshire, and Harefield, Middlesex.[2] His experience and the range of his activities were wider than that of most of his fellow country gentlemen. In 1742, he was returned for Middlesex in place of William Pulteney, created Earl of Bath; ousted in 1747, he was returned in 1750 for Oxford University,

---

[1] 33001, ff. 357–63.
[2] The Newdigate MSS., in the possession of Mr. Humphrey Fitzroy Newdegate, are now deposited at the County Record Office, Warwick.

which he continued to represent till 1784. He had thus a triple connexion within the group: with the metropolitan Tories, with the country gentlemen of his own region, such as the Mordaunts of Warwickshire or the Bagots of Staffordshire, and with the Tories of Oxford University.

The man from whom Newdigate first heard that he was being considered as candidate for Middlesex, and who in fact proposed him 'as a very proper person', was George Cooke, Member for the county from 1750 till his death in 1768, and in the sixties a well-known Chathamite. In April 1747, when Newdigate's colleague, Sir Hugh Smithson, subsequently 1st Duke of Northumberland, proposed to him to stand as joint candidates at the forthcoming election, Newdigate declined, considering it 'want of due deference to propose ourselves without the authority of a general meeting'.[1] It was etiquette among country gentlemen to await an expression of the sense of the county as declared in such a meeting; and even canvassing would be given a tentative form pending such approval. I adduce one example only, remarkable in that it refers to much less than a county: the borough of Cricklade, converted in 1782 (as punishment for 'most notorious bribery and corruption') into a quasi-rural constituency through the inclusion of five adjoining hundreds. In May 1782, Ambrose Goddard, successful candidate of the country gentlemen against a Herbert of Wilton in the Wiltshire election of 1772, wrote to Lord Shelburne:[2]

> The nature of my situation in the county lays me under the necessity of declining to take any active part in the Cricklade election at least 'till the sense of the gentlemen and freeholders is taken at a publick meeting which is appointed for that purpose the 27th inst. at Wooton Bassett, my conduct must depend upon the result of that meeting.

Information about Newdigate's life, both in the country and in London, can be gathered from his pocket diaries. In a minute handwriting he entered each day's activities, visits, and interviews, and sometimes even lengthy reports. His social intercourse seems to have been mainly with other Tory country gentlemen; besides calling on each other, they used to meet at certain taverns, the Cocoa Tree, the Horn, the St. Albans, etc.; and in 1755 there are accounts of several meetings convened at the Horn

---

[1] Newdigate's canvass book of 1747, A. 260.
[2] Shelburne MSS. in the possession of the Marquis of Lansdowne at Bowood.

Tavern to settle the line the 'minority', as he calls them, should take over a bitterly contested election petition. These meetings are also recorded, in a derogatory manner, by Walpole in his *Memoirs of the Reign of King George II*.[1]

The Mitchell election, in which Robert Clive and John Stephenson, supported by Thomas Scawen and Lord Sandwich, had been returned against Richard Hussey and Simon Luttrell, backed by the Edgcumbes and Boscawens, turned into a major affair—and for once Lord Hardwicke and the Duke of Newcastle were taking opposite sides. 'The Court members being pretty near equally divided made this election to be of more than ordinary consequence; great sollicitations were us'd to the minority', noted Newdigate on 24 February 1755. Lord Lichfield and George Cooke supported Stephenson,[2] while another Tory, William Northey, favoured Luttrell, and both Stephenson and Luttrell, writes Newdigate, professed themselves 'inclin'd towards them [the minority], but were answer'd in general that they would attend if desir'd but would vote according to the merits'. On the 28th, some 20 Tories, led by John Phillips, voted with Fox, Sandwich's friend and his manager in that affair, who thus carried his point against Newcastle. After this Horace Walpole has a story to tell, unconfirmed by anything either in the Newdigate or in the Newcastle papers: Northey is alleged to have offered Newcastle that, if he would give up the Oxfordshire election[3] and dismiss both Fox and Pitt, the Tories 'would support him without asking a single reward'. Northey, on the same side as Newcastle, may have made approaches to him, but not on behalf of the whole group; nor do the terms seem likely. But Newcastle, writes Walpole, would not pay that price for 'nothing but about a hundred of the silentest and most impotent votes' (as if anyone could have controlled the votes of a hundred independent country gentlemen).

This notable project being evaporated [continues Horace Walpole] the Tories were summoned on the 5th [should be the 4th] of March to the Horn Tavern. Fazakerley informed them that they were to take measures for acting in a body on the Mitchel election: he understood that it was . . . a contest for power between Newcastle and Fox: . . . that he for every reason should be for the former. Beckford told him, he did not understand there was any

---

[1] Vol. ii, pp. 12–14.   [2] 35592, f. 162.
[3] Petition against Sir James Dashwood and Lord Wenman, returned for Oxfordshire on the 'Old [the Tory] Interest'.

such contest: . . . were he obliged to name, he would prefer Mr. Fox.
The meeting, equally unready at speeches and expedients, broke
up in confusion.

And here is Newdigate's account:

> A meeting 63 of the minority at the Horn Tavern to consider
> what measures to follow in regard to the two contending parties
> for power. About 40 members agreed as Michael[1] election not
> advanced far enough to judge of the merits to meet again on Friday.

On that day, 7 March, according to Walpole,

> 62 Tories met again at the Horn, where they agreed to secrecy,
> though they observed it not; and determined to vote, according
> to their several engagements, on previous questions, but not on the
> conclusive question in the Committee.

Similarly in Newdigate's account the meeting resolved

> not to vote in the decisive question in the committee of Michael
> election but to stay for the report.

On the 12th, the last day in Committee, Sandwich won by 158
votes to 141; the Tories, in accordance with their resolution,
having almost all left before the division. But eight remained and
were equally divided; their names are given in Admiral Bos-
cawen's report to Newcastle[2] — on the Sandwich-Fox side: Curzon,
Barrow, Hanger, and Cooke; against: Sir William Meredith,
Sir Armine Wodehouse, Grosvenor, and Sturt. Some twelve years
later, Meredith and Barrow were Rockinghams, and Cooke a
Chathamite; and in 1773 it was Meredith who moved to abolish
in the Universities the subscription to the 39 Articles, a motion
of which Newdigate as member for Oxford University was one
of the strongest opponents.

Next, on 24 March, Walpole writes:

> The morning of the report, the Tories met again at the Horn,
> and here took the shameless resolution of cancelling all their engage-
> ments, in order to defeat Fox. . . .

And he goes on to inveigh against 'the wretched remnant of the
Tories' crowning 'their profligacy with breach of promises'.

---

[1] According to Tonkin's MS. Parochial History, compiled between 1700 and 1730
and now at the Royal Institution of Cornwall, the original name of the borough was
'Myshell, Mitchell or Modishole, . . . and nowhere St. Michael till of late, to which
denomination it has no pretence but vulgar error.'   [2] 32853, f. 260.

Only twelve of them stood to their engagements; the Duke of Newcastle, assisted by the deserters, ejected Lord Sandwich's members, by 207 to 183; the House, by a most unusual proceeding, and indeed by an absurd power, as the merits are only discussed in the Committee, setting aside what in a Committee they had decided.

But here is Newdigate's account:

At eleven to the Horn Tavern. 68 met. Sir J. Philips propos'd to disappoint both parties by voting against both and making it a void election. Sir Charles Mordaunt, Mr. Northey, Mr. Crowle, R[oger] N[ewdigate], Mr. Bertie, against it. Nothing in the evidence to warrant it. Mr. Beckford for it. Came away without any joint resolution.

In the House, Phillips

moved to make it a void election by rejecting the petition too. Oppos'd by Northey, R[oger] N[ewdigate], and Sir Robert Long. Question Ays 201. Nos. 178. These questions were carried by the bulk of the minority who were clear from engagements to either side and determin'd only upon the merits which were very strong with the petitioners.

What, then, emerges from these reports? Some Tories were engaged on either side; a few political leaders such as Phillips, Beckford, and Fazakerley, thought of political manœuvres; but the great body of independent country gentlemen deemed it proper to judge the case on its merits. Their behaviour was highly respectable but politically ineffective.

The next meetings of the country gentlemen recounted by Newdigate deal with the projected inquiries into the loss of Minorca and the reverses in America at the beginning of the Seven Years War. Here is the entry of 14 January 1757:

Mr. [George] Townsend's met his brother Charles, Lord Pulteney, Mr. Vaughan, Sir J. Phillips, Cornwall, Sir Ch. Mordaunt, Sir A. Wodehouse, Mr. Bagot, Mr. Fazakerley, Mr. Hanger, Moreton, W. Harvey, Mr. Ward, Ad[miral] Vernon, Affleck, Vyner, Beckford, Northey, Sir R. N.[1]

G. Townsend said he had in the H[ouse] declared he would move an enquiry which made him desire the meeting, that Mr. Pitt and the Administration would support and assist with papers, etc., but desired to be excused appearing at this meeting for fear of offence somewhere but heartily desired an enquiry—consulted what method proper, by secret, select or committee of the whole House? Sir J.

---

[1] Barring the Townshends, Pulteney, and Vaughan, all were Tories.

Phillips was for the last. Ch. Townsend the only placeman there. P. the questions must be divided—that for America to go as far as the Peace of Aix-la-Chapelle and in a select committee because facts must be reported and printed as in that for the Army. But that Minorca would be best in a Committee of the whole House because it lay in smaller compass. Resolved to leave it to the gentlemen in administration to consider what expedient.

And on 1 February:

Walked to Mr. Townsend's, met many of the same gentlemen as before. Mr. Townsend said he had a commission from Mr. Pitt to say that he would support the enquiry in the House. Desired questions might be settled by the gentlemen. A good deal of conversation and that matter but not the questions were settled.

Thus Pitt is seen sending messages to the Tory country gentlemen though excusing himself from appearing personally 'for fear of offence somewhere'—presumably to George II. The country gentlemen desired to leave the decision 'to the gentlemen in Administration', and Pitt to them. And nothing was settled.

About the transactions concerning the Qualification Bill,[1] January–March 1760, we learn from the Newcastle papers only —Newdigate at that time was serving with the militia. The Duke wrote to Hardwicke on 26 January 1760:[2]

I saw Mr. Pitt . . . who told me Sir John Phillips and Alderman Beckford had been with him from the *country gentlemen*; and tell him they intended to bring in the Bill to oblige every Member to swear to his qualification at the table of the House of Commons . . . they wish'd the Administration would not oppose it in consideration of the assistance, which *they* had given to the King's measures. Mr. Pitt said he was for it *in opinion*; and should declare for it.

Thus Phillips and Beckford are seen acting for the country gentlemen; and the measure demanded was in line with the perennial motions against placemen—it might have excluded some hardworking civil servants and humbler politicians, and a few bankrupt parasites, but rich contractors, equally loathed by the country gentlemen, could undoubtedly have produced and maintained their qualification. Attempts further to tighten up the provisions of the Bill were made, arousing opposition. Lord Egmont in the debate on 5 March called it a 'wicked and weak bill' whose principle was wrong and 'leading to an aristocracy'. It certainly

[1] By 9 Anne c. 5, county members had to possess landed property worth £600 p.a., and borough members £300 p.a.   [2] 32901, f. 479.

had a class character. All that finally reached the Statute Book (33 George II c. 20) was that each Member had to take an oath at the Bar of the House that he possessed the qualification, and to deliver a schedule of his property.

On 2 November 1762, Newcastle, preparing for the battle with Bute and Fox over the Preliminaries of Peace, wrote about a conversation with the Duke of Cumberland at Windsor Lodge:[1]

> The Duke gave me some comfortable accounts of Parliament; that my Lord Grosvenor and his brother had declared for us;. . . that Sir Walter Blackett and Mr. Noel had declared for us . . . that His Royal Highness had heard that Sir Charles Mordaunt and several of the Tories would not support this Administration. . . .

Legge had similar news about his Tory friends, 'honest sensible men and by much the best of the corps'. But the Duke of Devonshire remarked on 30 November[2] that he did not think 'it will come to anything'—wherein he was right.

About the same time, Roger Newdigate wrote:[3]

> I can't answer your Qu. what my party is? I am only sure it is neither C[um]b[erlan]d nor Pelham, landed men must love peace, men proscribed and abus'd for 50 years together be presented with fools caps if they make ladders for tyrant Whigs to mount by, I like the King and shall be with his Ministers as long as I think an honest man ought and believe it best not to lose the country gentleman in the courtier.

Note: 'landed men must love peace'—presumably because of the land tax. Next, expressions of dislike of the Whigs who had proscribed them so long. But did he desire office? He thought 'it best not to lose the country gentleman in the courtier'.

Another Tory meeting, on 24 February 1763, is reported both in Newdigate's diary and in the Newcastle MSS.[4] Newdigate writes in his pocket diary:

> Mr. Blackstone and Mr. Ward came to breakfast. Walk'd to the Cocoa Tree—a meeting—walk'd to Sir Francis Dashwood's Chancellor of the Exchequer to hear the estimates read—Sir Charles

---

[1] 32944, ff. 212–13.   [2] 32945, f. 149.
[3] On a scrap of paper which I found slipped into a document of 25 November 1762, Newdigate MS. B.2311.
[4] 32947, ff. 92–3. About that meeting see also *Bedford Correspondence*, vol. iii, pp. 210–11, and *Letters from George III to Lord Bute*, ed. by Romney Sedgwick, p. 191, No. 270. Mr. Sedgwick's edition is a masterpiece of scholarship. To mention but one aspect: from internal evidence he has succeeded in dating some 330 undated letters.

> Mordaunt, Sir J. Phillips and self objected to the mode of 50 instead of 40s[1]—to the House . . .

The paper in the Newcastle MSS. reports that the meeting consisted 'of 60 or 70 persons, Tories and others', and quotes Sir Charles Mordaunt as saying that he

> loved the King; had no suspicion relating to him; but the increase of corps was an increase of expence.

Similarly Newdigate, John Phillips, Eliab Harvey, and Dr. Blackstone opposed the larger army establishment.

In my book *England in the Age of the American Revolution* I compiled a list of 'Tories returned to Parliament at the general election of 1761', 105 for English,[2] and nine for Welsh constituencies. Only four were sons of peers: Thomas Harley, Robert Lee, Thomas Howard, and John Ward. The remaining 110 were country gentlemen. During the new few years disintegration set in among them: a few turned courtiers under Bute, some joined the Rockinghams, another batch joined Chatham in 1766. Of the Tories returned in 1761, 31 died before the end of that Parliament, and only half of the original 114 re-entered Parliament in 1768. Many of their successors were no less independent; but the grievance of their exile-from-office period, imaginary in men who did not desire office, was gone. Henceforth their independence was even more obvious, and even more colourless. There was no longer a group—neither meetings nor spokesmen. For Parliamentary divisions after 1766, I therefore take as test of the vote of the country gentlemen the English knights of the shire, subtracting sons of peers, as mostly connected with Court.

For the crucial division on General Warrants, on 18 February 1764, we have the names of 220 Members who voted in the minority, and of 81 absent; and the number, though not the names, of the majority: 234. As there were two vacancies, the names of 20 Members, presumably absent, are still lacking to complete the count. Of the original 114 Tories, 104 were still in Parliament. Of these 41 voted with the Opposition, and 14 are known to have been absent. Of the 20 unplaced Members, at least four have to be added to the absent Tories,[3] which leaves 45 voting

---

[1] The figures 50 and 40 refer to the strength of infantry companies.

[2] pp. 419–21. From that list I would now delete Simeon Stuart, M.P., for Hampshire, and add to it Thomas Noel, M.P. for Rutland: the total remains the same.

[3] Three or four on a *pro rata* basis, but men who were politically independent are more likely to have been absent without being mentioned as such in the lists of absents on either side.

with the Administration, a mere majority of four on its side. But three days later, on 21 February, Newdigate notes in his diary: 'Mr. Grenville's levy [levée] where I met most of the country gentlemen by agreement.' There is nothing more about it in the Newdigate papers, nor in those of Grenville, printed or unpublished. Country gentlemen, as a rule, did not attend Ministers' levées. Did perhaps Newdigate merely mean a majority of those he consorted with? So much is certain: that most of these who voted against General Warrant were not in formed opposition to the Grenville Administration, which, bent on peace and economies, gave the country gentlemen reasonably cheap government.

At the next important division, over the Repeal of the Stamp Act, on 21 February 1766, 93 of the original 114 Tories were still in Parliament: 39 voted with the Opposition. We have no lists either of those absent or of the majority; but the total number of absents was 116 which, on a *pro rata* basis, would yield 20 for the Tories. If so, 34 voted for the Repeal.

For the division of 27 February 1767, on the question of reducing the land tax from four to three shillings, I use the English knights of the shire for my test. The vast majority of the county members voted for the reduction: 52 against 9, while 19 were absent. Of the 9 who voted with the Administration, 5 were sons of peers sitting on an aristocratic interest and not as the choice of the country gentlemen.

Over the expulsion of Wilkes on 3 February 1769, there is an almost equal division among the knights of the shire: 24 voted with the Court, 23 against, while 33 did not vote. But if we abstract the sons of peers, we get 14 voting with the Court and 21 with the Opposition—a 3:2 majority against Administration.

Over the American Revolution, as over the Stamp Act, the feeling of a majority of country gentlemen was probably against the Colonies. Some Members previously inclined to side with the Opposition—for instance Thomas Grosvenor, or even Rockinghams, such as Lord Belasyse and Edwin Lascelles—henceforth tended to vote with the Government.

From the book of cuttings about Members, 1779–81, I pick out six original Tories who voted with the Administration:

Sir William Codrington (Tewkesbury): 'Has much the appearance of being an independent man. He always gives his vote with the Ministry.'[1]

---

[1] This statement is not borne out by extant division lists.

Assheton Curzon (Clitheroe): '. . . a man of Tory principles, votes with Ministry, but sometimes affects to be conscientious, by quitting the House when the Minister's question is not agreeable to him.'

William Drake, snr. (Agmondesham): 'A respectable independent gentleman, a Tory in principle, and a great admirer of Lord North, votes with the Ministry in general, but sometimes in the Minority.'[1]

Thomas Grosvenor (Chester): '. . . a staunch Tory, and votes constantly with Government, and procures places for his constituents.'

Sir Roger Newdigate (Oxford University): 'A rank Tory, with an affectation of honesty and independence.'

Clement Tudway (Wells): 'Appears an independent man, although he votes constantly with the Ministry.'

The writer's sympathies are clearly with the Opposition; yet he does not question the honesty of any one of these Tory Members as he does in many other cases.

And here are five other original Tories:

Richard Wilbraham Bootle (Chester): 'A very honest man, and votes on both sides, according to his opinion, but oftener with Opposition than with the Ministry.'

Richard Milles (Canterbury): 'A man of fair, respectable character. He generally votes with Opposition.'

Thomas Noel (Rutlandshire): 'A very old Member of Parliament and attends but very seldom. He is an independent man, and inclined to the Minority.'

John Parker (Devonshire): 'Usually known by the name of Devonshire Parker, a very honest, sensible, independent, man, and votes in Opposition.'

Humphrey Sturt (Dorsetshire): 'With many peculiarities, is a man of inviolable integrity and a good heart. He supports his character as one of the country members, with great independency and respect, and votes with Opposition.'

In the two most significant divisions of the next two years, the vote of the country gentlemen went heavily against the Government. Dunning's motion of 6 April 1780, 'that the influence of the Crown has increased, is increasing, and ought to be diminished', could not fail to secure their support: although giving old grievances a new turn, it summed up in one striking sentence the country party's inveterate dislike of Government interference in the constituencies, and its objection to placemen and contractors in the House. Of the 80 knights of the shire, 70 voted: 9 with the Court and 61 against. But if we eliminate the sons of peers, the

---

[1] Another newspaper describes him as uniformly supporting the measures of Chatham; see above, p. 32.

division becomes even more striking: five against fifty-five, that is an eleven to one majority against the Court. Similarly when the vote of no confidence in North's government was moved on 15 March 1782, of the country gentlemen representing shires 7 voted with the Government and 51 against: a seven to one majority for the Opposition.

What, then, broadly speaking, was the influence and part of the country gentlemen in Parliament? Their votes being determined by individual convictions, and not by pursuits or manœuvres of party, on ordinary problems they were, as a rule, so much divided as roughly to cancel out each other. But whenever a strong movement of public opinion produced some degree of unity among them, their weight would make itself felt. Faced by the American crisis, they inclined to assert authority and were averse to giving in to rebellion, and their feeling of fairness to themselves told them that the Americans should be made to shoulder part of the burden of taxation. On the other hand, the more far-sighted among them saw that the struggle would be long and expensive and lead nowhere, and these, besides a small group of pro-Americans, were opposed to the war. Saratoga did not convince the anti-Americans; if anything it stiffened their attitude. But Yorktown produced a complete swing over among them, as in public opinion at large, against the American war and the North Administration. The leader of that tiny group of country gentlemen who on 15 March 1782 still voted against the no-confidence motion, Thomas Grosvenor, after the division told North that they could not support him any longer. And this was the end.

During the confusion over the dismissal of the Coalition, at the end of 1783, a body of country gentlemen reconstituted itself in the so-called St. Albans Tavern group. Their dislike of factious politics combined with the wish to avoid a dissolution and general election. They tried to reconcile Pitt and Fox, and make them unite in a King's Government on a national basis. Lord Sydney, Pitt's Home Secretary, referred to them, in a letter of 17 February 1784, as 'the foolish Committee at the St. Albans';[1] and Pitt himself wrote that day to the Duke of Rutland: 'The *independents* are indefatigable for coalition, but as ineffectual as ever.'[2] Any experienced political observer could have told them beforehand: 'I do not think that it will come to anything.'

---

[1] See Hist. MSS. Comm., *14th Report*, Appdx. pt. I, Rutland MSS., vol. iii, p. 75.
[2] See John Duke of Rutland, *Correspondence between Mr. Pitt and Charles Duke of Rutland* (1890), p. 7.

6

THE CIRCULAR LETTERS

An 18th-century whip to Members of Parliament

THERE were no party organizations in the house of commons about 1750, and there was no proper party discipline. Followers of the government, and even members of it, would on particular occasions speak and vote against it, and a government which normally could count on a very considerable majority would at times find itself in danger of defeat. Every means was then used to bring up 'votes' on the government side, and to make others stay away, and the help of group leaders and borough patrons was invoked; the whole matter being transacted in an *ad hoc* fashion.

Here is an example of such a crisis, and of the way in which the house was managed. Although the general election of 1754 had given the duke of Newcastle a majority of over 200, the second reading of the highly unpopular Plate Bill was carried, on 17 March 1756, by only 129 to 120 votes. The same day James West, secretary to the treasury, reported to Newcastle:

> Mr. Campbell of Calder voted with us. Mr. Whichcote against us, as were Hitch Young, Lock, Olmius, Sir James Creed, Mr. Leveson Gower etc. Our friends are of opinion it will be very tight work to go through with it. I speak to every one, but I submit that there should be some large meeting upon the necessary steps to be taken.
> Alderman Baker went away.[1]

Almost every one of the members here mentioned had received government support in his election, and to that of Hitch Young the treasury had contributed £1,000 from secret service money.[2]

On 20 March Henry Fox, then secretary of state, reported to Newcastle:[3]

> I spoke to *The* Duke [of Cumberland] this morning, who most cordially assur'd me that he would have ev'ry officer apply'd to that

[1] 32863, fos. 332–3. [2] See my book *The Structure of Politics*, p. 200. [3] 32863, fo. 398.

46

he could. I understood Rigby, that the D. of Bedford had sent to ev'ry body on whom he had any influence, consequently to Dickenson, Sir William Morton and Bob Lewson. I will, however, particularize them. . . . I am by no means a proper ambassador to the Cavendishes. . . . Morgan, who was against us, will be with us, Lord Shelburne will stay away, I have wrote to Capel Hanbury, and to Mr. Edwards etc., etc.

Thus the duke of Cumberland, as Fox's patron, on this occasion supported Newcastle, and so did the duke of Bedford who in 1754 had counted as opposition.

To quote one more application and reply; Lord Northumberland wrote to Newcastle on 21 March:[1]

Both our county Members will certainly be there, and I sent to Sir William Beauchamp and the two Delavals and had a great deal of conversation with them last night, and they have all promised me to attend and to vote for it.

The case is typical: divisions on specific questions were not strict party musters. There was a sufficient measure of independence in the eighteenth-century parliament—real independence, or dependence on individual patrons rather than on the government—to establish occasionally a connexion between a division and the question on which it was taken. Only 'general support' was expected from 'friends to Administration', while a certain latitude of judgement on particular issues was conceded to them, at least so long as the government was not in serious danger. It was the line taken on the king's speech and the address which served as a primary test of political alinement, and the importance which to this day attaches to these theoretical party exercises is, possibly, an unconscious reminiscence from an age when not every single issue in the house was a 'party question'. It was at the opening of the session that forces were mustered; and the 'circular letters', whereby the attendance of 'friends' was requested, are a rudimentary form of the party-whip. Under Sir Robert Walpole the custom grew up of summoning the friends of administration to meet the leader of the house of commons at the Cockpit on the night before the opening of the session, and these meetings were continued under his successors. The following entries appear in the 'Historical Chronicle' of *The Gentleman's Magazine* for November 1742:

Monday, 15th. Met at the Cock-Pit 178 Members of the House of Commons, to whom His Majesty's Speech was read, and received with approbation.

[1] 32863, fo. 420.

Tuesday, 16th. His Majesty went to the House of Peers, and open'd the session with a Speech from the Throne.

In anticipation of the preliminary meeting, an article adversely commenting upon this custom had been published by *Common Sense* on 6 November 1742 (it was subsequently republished in *The Gentleman's Magazine*):

> The practice of summoning the Members to the Cock-pit, by a Ministerial writ, and haranguing them there before His Majesty opens the session with a Speech from the Throne, is but of modern date, and may be justly ranked among those improvements which have been lately made on our Constitution.
>
> There is something very ridiculous as well as very unparliamentary in these Ministerial Conventions. . . . The Minister produces a copy of the Speech; which being read and received with great applause, it is resolved, *nemine contradicente*, to promote a loyal and dutiful Address to His Majesty upon it. . . . Then the persons agreed upon before to move and second the Address, are proposed . . ., and unanimously approved. . . . That there have been such practices in former times cannot be deny'd; but as they are certainly unparliamentary and unconstitutional, they ought to be prevented for the future.

These preliminary meetings at the Cockpit were continued by Henry Pelham throughout his term of office at the treasury; the following letter to William Mure, dated 23 October 1753,[1] may serve as an example of the 'Ministerial writ' asking members to attend at the opening of the session:

> Sir,
> The meeting of the Parliament being fixed for the 15th day of next month, when it is expected to enter upon the publick business, I take the liberty to acquaint you, that your early attendance there will be very agreable to your friends, and particularly, Sir, to your
> most obedient, humble servant,
> H. Pelham.

Pelham died on 6 March 1754, on the eve of the general election, which his brother, the duke of Newcastle, managed to carry through to his entire satisfaction.

> The Parliament is good, beyond my expectations [he wrote on 14 May 1754], and I believe there are more Whigs in it, and generally well dispos'd Whigs, than in any Parliament since the Revolution. . . . The great point will be to keep our friends together, and that they

---

[1] Published in *Selections from the Family Papers preserved at Caldwell* (1854), II. i. 108.

should do right, when they are chose. For from the enemy, we have nothing to fear.[1]

The new parliament was summoned for 14 November, and on 2 October 1754 the duke of Newcastle wrote to Lord Hardwicke:

> It is always usual to write circular letters to our friends in the House of Commons to attend. I beg you would let me know, in whose name those letters should be now wrote. I was thinking that Mr. West might write them and say, *that he was directed*.[2]

Hardwicke replied:

> I am quite a stranger to the method of writing to friends in the House of Commons to attend. I had a notion that those letters us'd to be writ in Mr. Pelham's name, but West or Roberts[3] can inform your Grace correctly. If they us'd to be in Mr. Pelham's name, it may possibly be thought a slight to do it in the name of one of the Secretaries of the Treasury. But, if this last way has been practis'd before, that will warrant what you propose. As your Grace is a Peer, I apprehend that such letters cannot properly be in your name; but had better be in that of Sir Thomas Robinson, or of Mr. Legge, if it has not usually be [*sic*] done by the Secretaries.[4]

William Murray (subsequently Lord Mansfield), another of the duke's intimate advisers to whom he habitually appealed when in difficulties, having reviewed the situation in the house of commons, concluded: 'as to the circular letters, they shou'd be wrote by Sir T. R—n [Robinson]'.[5] On 12 October Newcastle once more asked Hardwicke's opinion as to 'who should write the circular letters', adding: 'I own, I now think, it must be Mr. Legge.'[6] Hardwicke replied the next day: 'I entirely agree with your Grace that Mr. Legge is, by his station, the most proper person to write the circular letters.'[7]

The point at issue was not without significance. Henry Pelham had been first lord of the treasury, chancellor of the exchequer, and 'the Minister' in the house of commons. These three functions were now separated; the duke of Newcastle was at the head of the treasury, H. B. Legge was chancellor of the exchequer (at that time a minor office, as the first lord of the treasury himself still presided at its board), and Sir Thomas Robinson, the secretary of state in the house of commons, was the chief representative of the government in it, though hardly its real leader. The treasury

---

[1] 32735, fo. 268.   [2] 32737, fo. 26.
[3] John Roberts, late private secretary to Henry Pelham.
[4] 32737, fo. 28.   [5] Bath, 6 October 1754; 32737, fo. 48.
[6] 35414, fo. 201 (the original letter), and 32737, fo. 109 (copy).   [7] 32737, fo. 148.

managed elections and the house of commons; and as Newcastle
did not want any particle of parliamentary control to pass out of
his own hands, he preferred the letters to come from the treasury,
even though Legge had to sign them.[1]

A year later Fox was on the point of assuming the secretaryship
of state, which he had refused in March 1754, because real leadership in the House of Commons and the handling of government
patronage had been withheld from him. The question of patronage
was now passed over in silence; Fox would have as much as he
could wring from Newcastle. The issuing of the circular letters
was one of the first marks of authority to which he turned his
attention. On 2 October 1755 he wrote to Legge who, though still
in office, was by then practically in opposition to Newcastle:[2]

> You know that His Majesty has declar'd his intention to make me
> Secretary of State and to give me the conduct of his affairs in the
> House of Commons.
> You have hitherto call'd the majority of that assembly together as
> usual at the Cockpitt to hear H.M.'s Speech and the words prepar'd
> for the Address in answer to it. If you have a mind to do so now I shall
> be indeed extreamly glad, but I am afraid you will not; and it may
> not perhaps be proper or pleasant that another should. I see some
> difficulty (I imagine so at least) that you will meet with in deciding
> either way, which when you have consider'd, I will wait on you, if
> you will give me leave, to know as much of your opinion in this
> regard, as you shall think fitt to impart to etc.[3]

Of this letter Fox sent a copy to Newcastle,[4] who remarked to
Hardwicke that he did not disapprove of it, though he thought 'the
expression *to have the conduct of the House of Commons* perhaps might
have been better turn'd'.[5] Hardwicke, who loathed Fox, replied
on 6 October:

[1] That it was he who signed them is confirmed by Newcastle's letter to Charles
Townshend, 2 November 1754; 32737, fo. 249.

[2] Newcastle wrote to Hardwicke on 12 October 1755: 'Mr. Legge cannot stay. He
told Nugent . . . the other day, *that he could not be for the subsidies*'; 32860, fo. 20.

[3] 32859, fo. 323; marked in the docket 'Copy of Mr. Fox's Lre, of 2d Oct. to Mr.
Legge'.

[4] See covering letter, ibid., fos. 345–6.

[5] 4 October; ibid., fo. 358 (copy), and 35415, fo. 91 (original letter). There is a
curious discrepancy between the text of Fox's letter to Legge as given above, and the
way in which Newcastle quotes it: Fox's letter mentions the conduct of the affairs in
the house of commons, and not of the house of commons itself. But this was what Fox
was actually going to say at least in some copies of his ill-judged circular. The idea
naturally occurs that it was that circular which Newcastle discussed in his letter of
4 October; but both the contents of this letter, and the way in which he and Hardwicke
write about the circular a week later, seem to indicate that it was only the letter to
Legge with which, so far, he was acquainted.

I think the letter to Mr. Legge one of the oddest I ever read. Can it proceed from anything but great confidence in, or great contempt of, that gentleman?[1]

In the letter to Legge, Fox apparently referred only to the formal circular inviting the attendance of members at the opening of the session. Meantime, independently of Legge and the treasury, he sent out another circular soliciting, in a personal manner, the support of his own friends. It is not certain to what number of members (or borough patrons) this letter was sent, and although it went to many, it certainly was not addressed to every one usually in receipt of the ordinary letters sent out before the opening of a session. Some of its copies at least read as follows:[2]

Sir,
The King has declared his intention to make me Secretary of State, and I (very unworthy as I fear I am of such an undertaking) must take upon me the conduct of the House of Commons: I cannot therefore well accept the office till after the first day's debate, which may be a warm one. A great attendance that day of my friends will be of the greatest consequence to my future situation, and I should be extremely happy if you would for that reason show yourself among them, to the great honour of,
Dear Sir, your etc., etc.

That this was not the ordinary 'circular letter', as is sometimes assumed, appears from the mere fact that it does not name the day on which parliament was to assemble, and does not mention the meeting at the Cockpit. It was a preliminary circular, unusual in character, and, as given here, even more unusual in its phrasing. The management of the house of commons was what Fox had been striving for and now hoped to obtain, and in some of the letters his zeal may have got the better of his discretion: he speaks of the conduct of the house, when the acknowledged constitutional functions of ministers were limited to the conduct of 'His Majesty's affairs in the House of Commons'. Next, the point about 'the first day's debate' and his own 'future situation' was so badly put as to lay him open to the imputation that he made his assumption of office depend on a vote in the house, which would indeed have been a constitutional innovation. In the debate of 21 November George Townshend suggested it in the sarcastic remark that 'he did not

[1] 32859, fo. 398.
[2] The text of the letter is printed in Horace Walpole's *Memoirs of the Reign of King George the Second*, second edition, 1847, ii. 64–7.

know that the first day of the Session he was electing a Minister'.[1]

On 12 October Newcastle wrote to Hardwicke that Lord George Sackville

> had receiv'd a letter from Mr. Fox, which Mr. Maxwel read to me, and the answer; they were both extraordinary in their kind. Mr. F. acquaints my Lord 'that the King intended to make him Secretary of State, and give him . . . the conduct of the House of Commons and *if your Lordship approves this, I hope, I shall have your assistance in my new station*'.[2]

Hardwicke replied the next day from Wimpole:

> The turn of Mr. Fox's letter to Lord George is remarkable, but I have been told that those words—*the conduct of the House of Commons*—are in all his letters. Some of them have been shewn in this country. He certainly has a meaning in it, but even in that view 'tis indiscreet, and there have been times, in which, I believe, such circulars would have been brought before the House.[3]

When Sir George Lee was approached through Hume Campbell with a view to taking office, he replied that he would not 'disgrace himself' by acting with Fox, and added 'that Mr. Fox would be attacked for his presumptuous letter, one of which he produced (as did the Princess of Wales to Munchausen).[4] The king, too, thought Fox's letter indiscreet.[5]

On 17 October Legge replied to Fox's original inquiry as to which of them was to issue the circular letters—the long delay in answering seems justified by the remark in Fox's letter of 2 October that he was going out of town and would not be back till the 12th—

> Dear Fox,
> I am very sensible of the tenderness you shew for my situation, which is to be sure a little delicate, but I really think it is much fitter that you should sign the circular letters than that I should do it. I take for granted the King's Speech must contain some intimation, and the words for the Address some approbation of the subsidies, and as I am so unfortunate as to dissent from the measure, I can with no propriety recommend to others what I cannot approve of myself. This being the case, it is certainly much better that I should not take a step, by signing the circulars, which would look as if I meant to

---

[1] Horace Walpole, op. cit., ii. 65.   [2] 32860, fo. 19.

[3] Ibid., fo. 33.   [4] Newcastle to Hardwicke, 18 October 1755; ibid., fo. 87.

[5] Ibid.; see also in the 'Register of Correspondence of the Earle of Bute', 36796, fo. 3, summary of a letter from Bute's brother, James Stuart Mackenzie, dated 5 October, and containing the sentence: 'Mr. Fox's circular letters to the Members in a different style to Mr. Pelham's.'

recommend subsidies; and had much rather you should sign them than do it myself.[1]

Of this formal circular letter I have so far failed to find a copy; but Fox's circulars were not the only summonses sent out by administration to its supporters. The duke of Newcastle wrote to his friends, to regional managers, group leaders, and individual members. Thus, for instance, to the duke of Argyll, on 27 September 1755:

We hear, we are to have great opposition in the House of Commons. May I presume to hope your Grace will have the goodness to send to such of the Members, as you may think proper, in time, to be in town the first day of the Session; for probably the great debate will be upon the Address.[2]

Whatever the justification of these letters as supporting Fox's request, Newcastle, no doubt, was glad to signify in this manner that he retained the management of the house. The following letter to Humphrey Morice, one among many, may serve as an example. It comes very near the usual circular, and offers a private statement on policy such as, in a more regular way, the friends of administration were usually given at the meeting at the Cockpit.

As business of the greatest consequence will probably come on the first day of the session, I hope from your goodness to me, that you will forgive my giving you this trouble to desire, that you would be in town before the Parliament meets. If you will do me the honor to call upon me, I will endeavour to explain to you, as well as I am able, the measures which have been taken for the support of the rights and possessions of His Majesty's Crown in North America.[3]

The joint labours of Newcastle and Fox, and the interest which attached to the forthcoming session, produced a favourable result. 287 members were present at the Cockpit, 'which was, by near thirty, a greater number than ever met there before,' wrote Henry Fox to Lord Hartington on 12 November 1755:[4] and Horace Walpole wrote to H. S. Conway, on 15 November: 'there were 289 Members at the Cockpit meeting, the greatest number ever known there'.

On 21 November George Townshend brought the question of Henry Fox's circulars before the house of commons:

---

[1] *Letters to Henry Fox, Lord Holland.* Edited by the Earl of Ilchester (1915), pp. 75–6.
[2] 32859, fos. 237–9.   [3] 32860, fo. 142.
[4] Quoted from the Devonshire MSS. by Lord Ilchester in his book *Henry Fox, First Lord Holland,* i. 281–2.

Our Ministers . . . had taken upon them to add to the usual respectable summons, not only the Ministerial invitation, but invitation of their own. . . . That this was an unconstitutional act of a Minister as desirous of power as ever Minister was.[1]

A similar report of the discussion appears in a letter from Welbore Ellis to Lord Hartington, quoted by Lord Ilchester from the Devonshire manuscripts:

He [Townshend] produced a letter from an enterprizing minister which he read and commented upon, in which there was this expression, viz., that His Majesty had committed *the conduct of the House of Commons* to his care, etc. Mr. Fox . . . confessed that he had written to some of the most considerable gentlemen of the House, those whom he thought his friends, an account of the station to which H.M. had advanced him. That some of those letters had been copied by his secretary, who had made a mistake by omitting a few words, but if he had been guilty of a negligence or imprudence in his expression in a letter written to a friend, he did not desire to be cured of it; as he should not wish to live when he must weigh the words he put on paper to a friend.[2]

That Fox's defence was not altogether disingenuous is proved by a copy of his impugned circular letter which is preserved among the Lonsdale manuscripts; it is dated 29 September 1755, and addressed to Mrs. (Katherine) Lowther, the widow of Governor Robert Lowther and mother of the well-known Sir James Lowther, who was as yet under age:[3]

I flatter myself you will not think me impertinent nor be sorry when I acquaint you, that the King has declared his intention to make me Secretary of State and give me charge of his affairs in the House of Commons. I must not take the seals till after the House meets because a debate is expected on the first day. You will immediately see the consequence of my having a numerous attendance of friends in this my first essay of Administration. I therefore beg, Madam, that you would be so good as to prevail upon your friends to shew themselves mine, the night before the Parliament meets, at the Cockpitt, to which place I shall have the honour to invite them.

---

[1] Horace Walpole, op. cit., ii. 64.

[2] *Henry Fox, First Lord Holland*, i. 287. The same allegation of a clerical mistake is mentioned in Walpole's report of Fox's defence: 'But indeed the objectionable part proceeded from a false writing; between the words *conduct* and the House of Commons other words which I will not name, were accidentally omitted.' See further a short account of the debate sent by James West to the duke of Newcastle, 32861, fos. 55–8.

[3] *Hist. MSS. Comm., MSS. of the Earl of Lonsdale*, p. 128.

The good opinion of persons of your character and rank is the only support I am ambitious of in my new station, and indeed I will endeavour to deserve it.

It will be noticed that this letter speaks of the king giving him the 'charge of his affairs in the House of Commons' and not of entrusting him with the 'conduct of the House of Commons', and that the reason why he delayed taking the seals is explained in a perfectly reasonable and unimpeachable manner: the assumption of office would have vacated his seat, whereas his presence in the house was required during the debate on the address.[1] The letter mentions, in express terms, that another more formal summons to the Cockpit would follow.

A year later, when parliament was about to meet, the duke of Devonshire was first lord of the treasury, Pitt secretary of state, and Legge chancellor of the exchequer. Legge seems to have thought of issuing the circular letters, as he had done under the duke of Newcastle in 1754; but the following letter from George Grenville to Pitt, published in the *Chatham Correspondence*,[2] shows that Pitt considered that it was for him, as leader of the house, to send out the letters and to preside at the Cockpit, and he naturally carried his point:

> Upper Brook Street. November 18, 1756.
> Past twelve o'clock.

Dear Pitt,

Lord Temple informed me late last night of the commission which you desired me to execute for you with Mr. Legge, about writing the circular letters, and convening the assembly at the cockpit. I saw him this morning, and had a long conversation with him upon that subject, in which I stated to him the great impropriety of such an idea; and I must do him the justice to say, that as soon as ever it was mentioned, which I did in the most friendly manner and expression, he absolutely declined any thoughts of it, and so fully, that one would scarcely believe he had ever entertained them. He assured me, in the strongest terms, that his most earnest wish was to see you take the lead in that and every other particular; that he was sensible how great an impropriety it would be for you to write the Speech . . . and for him to convene and open it at the cockpit; that for you to convene and open it at the cockpit, and him to write the circular letters to everybody to attend it, would be still more absurd, and not fit to be done, either for your sake or his own; that for his part he was clearly

---

[1] Previous to 1769 no writs for by-elections could be issued during a parliamentary recess. [2] i. 196–7.

of opinion you should do the whole yourself; that he would most certainly attend you there, and beg all his friends to do so too. We both
agreed that it would be of great consequence, and highly desirable to
have the meeting as numerous as it could be; and therefore, that as
little time as might be should be lost in giving the usual and proper
notices.

There are two sorts of summons upon this occasion. The first is, by
letters writ into the country, to desire gentlemen to come up. These
have always been writ by the secretary of the treasury, and signed by
the person that opens the assembly at the cockpit. The second are the
common circular letters writ and signed by the secretary of the
treasury, and sent about London the day before the meeting at the
cockpit is appointed. As the Parliament is so near, no time should be
lost in hastening the first; and as they have always been signed by the
minister of the House of Commons himself, it might occasion constructions, which, in the present state, may have an ill effect, if they
should be signed by the secretary of the treasury. Many might wonder
at the change, many be offended; if, therefore, you are well enough
(as I hope you are) in other respects, and the lameness is not in that
hand, it would be to be wished you should sign them, or as many as
you can.

Thus it appears that there was yet another circular, not mentioned
hitherto, a reminder, 'sent about London the day before the
meeting at the cockpit is appointed'.

Newcastle, who carefully watched every move of Pitt's in the
parliamentary game, obtained a copy of the 'Circular Letter intended to be sign'd by Mr. Pitt, to certain Members of the House
of Commons'; it runs as follows:[1]

Sir,
    The Parliament meeting on the [blank] day of December next,
and the state of publick affairs requiring the utmost assistance of the
Members of the House of Commons; I hope, you will pardon the
liberty, I take, in desiring your attendance at the opening of the
session; which will oblige your friends; and particularly, Sir, your
most obedient humble servant,

N.B. Intended to be sign'd
        by Mr. Pitt.

A year later Newcastle was again at the head of the treasury,
Legge chancellor of the exchequer, and Pitt secretary of state
and leader of the House of Commons. Naturally Pitt could not

---

[1] 32869, fo. 104. The letter seems on the whole modelled on that of Henry Pelham
quoted above; the copy is in the handwriting of H. V. Jones, Newcastle's private
secretary.

be treated as Sir Thomas Robinson had been in 1754, nor could his position in the house of commons be placed in a different light from what it had been the previous years. Still, Newcastle did not relish the idea of letting him muster the government forces, and West had to speak repeatedly to the duke about the matter before anything was done; nor was Pitt as eager to convene Newcastle's followers as he had been to summon his own in 1756. Newcastle wrote to Hardwicke on 5 November 1757:

> Mr. West had plagued me about the usual circular letters, and I at last gave him leave to speak to Mr. Pitt, as from himself upon them, which he did, and was snub'd for his pains.[1]

The story of what had passed with Pitt is told in full in letters from West to Newcastle. He wrote on 28 October:

> Mr. West asked Mr. Secretary Pitt, if he had any commands for him about letters for the meeting of the Parliament; he said very shortly, No, none at all; Mr. West begged his excuse for mentioning it, as he had been used to give orders for sending them about. Mr. Pitt hastily answered, I thank you but no, none at all.[2]

It was Pitt himself who next took up the subject. West reported to Newcastle on 2 November:

> Mr. Pitt sent to me to come to him, at four o'clock this day, when he returned from Kensington: he received me with great complaisance and told me he had thought of what I had mentioned to him on Friday last, about the circular letters, with great seriousness; that it was his opinion to waive them; he desired to know the form, which on my repeating to him what had been usual in Sr R. W. [alpole's] and Mr. P. [elham's] time; he said he could not say it was *particularly agreable to him* or *a pleasure to him* and therefore did not care to sign; that the only risque was the apprehension of its being looked upon as a slight, which he thought there was not much in, but however wished something like an advertisement, that the parliament would meet on such a day to do business, might be drawn up, dated from *the Treasury Chambers* and signed by *the Secretary of the Treasury*, and sent to the Members; that no time was to be lost. I represented to him that I doubted the slight would be much greater, for the Secretary to write to those who had been used to receive letters from the first man in the House of Commons in an affectionate manner: He then laughed and said jocularly, if I would write Secret Service it might be understood;[3]

---

[1] 32875, fo. 391.   [2] Ibid., fo. 307.

[3] At the time when Pitt made this remark, fifteen members, in a total of 558, were in receipt of secret service pensions (see my book *The Structure of Politics*, p. 217). Whether after a year in office he still entertained the current, vastly exaggerated ideas

that when those letters were wrote they were wrote by those who had
the parliament, that this was not *his Parliament*, but the D. of N——
Parliament; that tho' a great lord could not write such letters, yet he
thought an anonymous letter dated from the *Treasury Chambers* signi-
fying the day the parliament would meet for the dispatch of business,
might be right as a notification: he said he would sign the letters for
the meeting at his own house[1] and desired the usual notices for the
Cockpit might go from the Treasury. . . .
. . . When I asked Mr. Pitt to whom the letters should be addressed, he said to the usual persons only, for tho' very many will
vote for the publick supplies and the publick business, yet they cannot
all be reckoned friends to administration.[2]

The letters were finally sent without signature, as Pitt had
wished it, but also without the mark of *Treasury Chambers*, as can
be seen from the summons to attend the opening of parliament,
and the invitation to the meeting at the Cockpit, preserved among
the papers of Thomas Pelham of Stanmer:

Sir,
    The Parliament being to meet on Thursday the first day of Decem-
ber next your presence is then desired as it is expected they will
immediately proceed on business.[3]

    London,
24th Nov. 1757.

Sir,
    You are desired to be at the Cockpit, Whitehall, on Wednesday
next at seven o'clock in the evening.[4]

    Saturday,
26 Nov. 1757.

There is no trace in the Newcastle manuscripts of any circular
letters for the session of November 1758. Was the issuing of them
by now a matter of settled routine, in which the duke of Newcastle
did not interfere, or was it that Pitt, having established government
on a national basis, decided to dispense with them? The latter
seems indicated by a passage in the letter which, on 18 November

about the number of these pensions, or whether he simulated ignorance (as he did
with regard to the usual practice concerning the circular letters), may be left an open
question.
    [1] A preliminary meeting 'of the principal men in the House of Commons', usually
held the night before the meeting at the Cockpit. A meeting of that kind, on 1 November 1761, is mentioned by Horace Walpole in his *Memoirs of the Reign of George III*,
1894, i. 68; see also *Gentleman's Mag.*, 1742, p. 588, about those preliminary 'assemblies'.
    [2] 32875, fos. 376-7.   [3] 33087, fo. 355.   [4] Ibid., fo. 357.

1758, John Calcraft, the right-hand man of Fox, wrote to Lord Loudoun, then in America: 'None of the Members are to have summons's, Mr. Pitt says who wou'd you summons? The people of England are all of one mind.'[1]

In 1759 Parliament met for the winter session on 13 November, and again there is nothing in the Newcastle Papers about the circular letters. But in the correspondence of Thomas Pelham of Stanmer there is a letter sent from Pitt's house in St. James's Square:

Sir,
The favour of your company is desired at Mr. Secretary Pitt's on Sunday next, the 11th instant, at half an hour past seven o'clock in the evening.[2]

St. James's Square,
7th November, 1759.

There was no room in the house in which Pitt could have convened 200 members, the usual number at the meetings before the opening of the session, and the letter obviously refers to the different kind of gathering, of leading members of the house of commons, mentioned in Pitt's talk with West, when 'he said he would sign the letters for the meeting at his own house'.

Nor were apparently any summonses issued for the session of November 1760, the first of George III's reign, and the last of the house elected in 1754. But when the new parliament was to meet, in November 1761, after Pitt's resignation, Newcastle strained every nerve to bring up all those whom he considered his friends. 'It highly imports us, and all our friends,' he wrote to Lord Powis, the whig manager for Shropshire, on 15 October 1761, 'to have a great appearance at our first meeting; if ever the Whigs intend to show their strength in support of the King and the present Administration, now is the time; and the whole depends upon the appearance and attendance at first.'[3]

Newcastle now sent out his circular letter to those whom he reckoned 'Whigs' and friends of his own. George Grenville, who was to be the leader in the house of commons, and was therefore to preside over the meeting at the Cockpit, wrote no letters to Newcastle's friends, and none went from Newcastle to those who belonged to Bute. Administration was an uneasy coalition between

[1] See Letterbooks, vol. ii; 17494, fo. 49. No circular letter for that session is preserved among the papers of Pelham of Stanmer.

[2] 33087, fo. 388.

[3] 32929, fo. 281.

Newcastle and Bute, while Grenville was so full of doubts and
fears that at the last moment he desired 'Lord Barrington should
read the speech at the meeting' (at the Cockpit). Finally Newcastle persuaded Grenville to desist from that idea: 'I told him
plainly, that at once destroy'd the view and intention of his taking
the lead in Parliament.'[1]

The way in which the various members were grouped in the
summonses supplies a curious chart of the house. Newcastle's list,
marked 'Members to be wrote to, to attend the first day of the
Session, and by whom', and dated Claremont, 16 October 1761,[2]
contains the names of 342 members of parliament.[3] They are
arranged by counties, in the same order as they appear in the usual
parliamentary lists; against each member the name of the person
is marked who was to secure his attendance, for not all received a
direct summons from the duke of Newcastle. A paper, dated
26 October,[4] shows what lists of those summoned through the
intermediary of friends had been actually sent to these deputy-
conveners; 36 are given, containing 194 names.[5] Thus more than
half of the members on Newcastle's list were treated as primarily
or largely dependent on some group leader. Ninety-five of these
194 names, i.e. almost half, appear in the eight longest lists, each
containing ten names or more; they were those of the duke of
Bedford (ten names) and the duke of Devonshire (twelve), Lord
Powis (eleven) and Lord Rockingham (ten), Lord Anson (fifteen),
Lord Hardwicke (fourteen), Henry Fox (twelve), and Lord
Barrington (eleven).

Seven of the ten men whose attendance the duke of Bedford
was asked to secure largely or entirely owed to him their seats in
parliament; two others were distant relatives and close associates
of the duke's. Of the twelve members in the list of the duke of
Devonshire, four were Cavendishes, one was his nominee at Derby,
and two were men returned through his mediation; another one
was a Derbyshire man. These two lists represent aristocratic,
oligarchical groups.

Of the eleven members on Lord Powis's list seven were Shropshire and three Welsh members, and one lately a member for a
Welsh constituency. Of the ten on Lord Rockingham's list eight
sat for Yorkshire constituencies and the other two were Yorkshire

---

[1] 32930, fo. 104.   [2] 32929, fos. 303–11.
[3] There are actually 343 names, but one occurs twice.   [4] 32930, fos. 37–42.
[5] There are actually 205 entries, but in six cases these deputy-leaders, of whom eleven
sat in the house of commons, appear as asked to invite also themselves, and four
members occur twice in these lists.

men. These two lists represent groups under territorial managers.[1]

Of the fifteen men on the list sent to Lord Anson, first lord of the admiralty, two were admiralty officials (John Clevland and Philip Stephens, the secretaries) and nine naval officers;[2] two were near relatives of Anson's returned by him to parliament, and two civilian members for boroughs under admiralty influence. This can be described as a professional group. Lord Hardwicke's list is more of a family character though the legal profession still appears in it, a reminiscence of his chancellorship. The fourteen names in the list include four sons of Hardwicke and one son-in-law, and two nephews of his wife; and four lawyers: John Hervey, a Welsh judge, Dr. Simpson, dean of the arches and judge of the Cinque Ports, P. C. Webb, solicitor to the treasury, and Thomas Miller, lord advocate of Scotland.

The twelve members in Henry Fox's list were almost all personal friends, political associates or dependants for whom he had

[1] Rockingham found it quite natural to act as whip for all the Yorkshire members on his list, but seems to have felt shy of assuming such pre-eminence with regard to the two Yorkshiremen who sat for other constituencies: he obviously looked upon himself as the territorial manager, but not as the tribal chief of Yorkshire. He wrote to Newcastle on 29 October: 'I could not take the liberty of writing to Lord Downe [M.P. for Cirencester] on the occasion, for tho' we are exceeding well together I have not yet that degree of intimacy. As to Sir Lionel Pilkington [M.P. for Horsham, Sussex]—I have so little acquaintance with him that I could not write to him' (32930, fos. 158–9).

[2] Their number was so small because those away on active service were not included. The summoning of the naval officers through the first lord of the admiralty had the additional advantage of providing them automatically with leave of absence, if required. In November 1761 Captain Raby Vane, R.N., M.P., received Newcastle's summons through his brother, Lord Darlington, not through the admiralty; and here is the sequel:

32930, fo. 408.   Raby Vane to the Duke of Newcastle.
                                               Cleveland House. November 10, 1761.
'My Lord Duke,
    'In consequence of a letter your Grace wrote to my brother Darlington and one I received from him, I came up to town without leave of the Admiralty but wrote to their Lordships immediately saying my *private affairs* had brought me hither but that I was desirous of returning before my ship could be ready to sail, and hoped they would not be displeased as I had no time to make my request of leave of absence. As it was your Grace's commands solely which brought me to town I hope you will not let me suffer in their good opinion. As it is I must return to my ship.'
[Enclosure.]
Ibid., fo. 410.   John Clevland to Raby Vane.
                                               Admiralty. November 10.
    'I have communicated to my Lords Commissioners of the Admiralty your letter of the 9th inst., informing them that your private affairs requiring your presence in London, you was come to town without their Lordship's leave, and desiring their permission to remain here till Friday; and I am to acquaint you, that their Lordships are extremely surprized and displeased at the liberty you have taken, in coming to town without leave; and they direct you to return to the ship you command, without a moment's loss of time, and carry into execution Captain Buckle's orders.'

negotiated seats; he owned no pocket boroughs in which to accommodate his men but he had his political 'pack' which he provided for, both in parliament and in offices. This is not an oligarchical, territorial, professional, or family group, but a parliamentary 'faction', i.e. political in the eighteenth-century sense of the term.

Lord Barrington's list is a mere jumble, and, as likely as not, contains men with whom he had little acquaintance or influence. When Newcastle did not exactly know what to do about certain members, he assigned them to one of his political or official drudges, Barrington or Kinnoull, James West or Andrew Stone. Barrington had for six years been secretary at war, and, although in March 1761 he was made chancellor of the exchequer, there are still three army officers in his list. For in 1761 Newcastle was in a difficult position with regard to army officers: he had no one to put in charge of them in parliament. A friendship was now growing up between him and the duke of Cumberland, but as Cumberland no longer commanded the army, his secretary, Lord Albemarle, who gradually came to replace Fox as his political representative, was asked to summon only those army officers who held places in the duke's household, four in all. Lord Ligonier, the commander-in-chief in Great Britain, though himself in the house of commons, did not dabble in politics; while Newcastle knew that Charles Townshend, the new secretary at war, could not be trusted—a year ago he 'had sworn allegiance' to Bute, '*for a time*' as Bute himself put it after having received Townshend's homage.[1]

Another professional group, which was contemplated in the sending out of circular letters, was to have been that of the treasury in its financial, not its political, character. The double mark of the duke of Newcastle, its first lord, and James West, its secretary, was put at first against the names of twelve merchants, most of them government contractors, of two small men in receipt of secret service pensions, and of some others who were in various ways financially connected with the treasury. But this scheme, resembling Pitt's suggestion about the *Treasury Chambers*, seems to have been dropped, and West was left with only four stray members, with whom Newcastle did not know what to do, and against whom West's name alone had been placed.

The smaller lists are based mainly on family or territorial influence, two things which naturally often coincided: George Onslow, the son of Speaker Onslow, had to secure the attendance

[1] See Dodington's *Diary* under 16 January 1761.

of his relatives and of a few Surrey members; the list of Lord Sandwich can be labelled Huntingdonshire and the East India Company; Lord Darlington was to manage Durham, Lord Buckinghamshire Norfolk, etc. Lord Lincoln, Newcastle's nephew, was to summon six boon companions, and John Roberts whom he had inherited from his father-in-law, Henry Pelham; and even the old duchess of Newcastle had to write letters inviting the attendance of four members of parliament, of her nephew Lord Villiers, and three distant cousins.

From other correspondence it appears that some more lists were sent out, not mentioned in the paper of 26 October,[1] and that some of the members who were in the lists of group leaders received also direct summonses from Newcastle. Thus T. Whichcot, M.P. for Lincolnshire, was summoned through the duke of Ancaster, the first magnate in the county,[2] but as a member of standing was also written to directly by Newcastle; he replied on 28 October that he had not intended to be in town at the opening of parliament, but having received the duke's letter would try to be.[3] Indeed, a good deal of diplomacy was required to reconcile in the summonses the regard which was due to a patron conscious of his influence, with the courtesy expected by a member attentive to his own importance.

The duke of Bedford, in political and social standing the greatest of all the group leaders to whom Newcastle turned for support, received from him the most elaborate letter:

Never did the situation of the publick require more attention than the present; or make it more necessary for all the friends to their King and Countrey to give early attendance in Parliament: for that purpose, I shall take the liberty to apply, in the best way I can, to my friends, to be at the meeting at the Cockpit, Monday November 2. Your Grace is so good to me as to encourage me to ask the favour of you to send to your friends. I have put down a few names, which I take the liberty to enclose to you; and hope you will pardon me.

Mr. George Grenville will preside at the Cockpit.[4]

[1] Thus a list seems to have been sent to John White, M.P. for East Retford, enjoining him to secure the attendance of John Hewett, M.P. for Nottinghamshire, Plumptre, M.P. for Nottingham, and Sir George Savile, M.P. for Yorkshire; see his reply of 24 October, 32930, fos. 22–3, and to Roberts, who was to try to secure Lord Verney and through him presumably Verney Lovett; see his reply of 30 October, ibid., fo. 190.

[2] See letter from Newcastle to Ancaster, 19 October; 32929, fo. 373.

[3] 32930, fo. 122. When John Page, M.P. for Chichester, an old whig and close associate of Newcastle's, was asked by him to write to Henry Knight, M.P. for Grimsby, a nephew of his first wife, Page did so, but remarked in a postscript: 'If your Grace can find time to write two lines to Mr. Knight I dare say it will please him' (32930, fo. 132).

[4] 17 October 1761; 32929, fo. 324.

Lords Sandwich, Northumberland, Darlington, and Buckinghamshire, and the dukes of Bolton and Ancaster, received letters of almost identical contents; the letter to Lord Sandwich may serve as example:

Claremont. October 17, 1761.

The Duke of Newcastle sends his compliments to my Lord Sandwich, and begs the favor of his Lordship to send to all his friends; and particularly to those here mentioned, to attend, without fail, the first day (November 3) of the Session; and to be at the general meeting at the Cockpit, the night before, Monday November 2.[1]	Lord Carysfort Edward Montagu Robert Jones Thomas Ducket John Stevenson

To most of these letters favourable replies were received. Thus Lord Sandwich wrote from Hinchingbrooke on 22 October:

I have the honour of your Grace's commands, which I shall immediately obey by desiring all the gentlemen (except one) to appear at the Cockpitt the day before the meeting of the Parliament, and I should imagine they will very readily follow my advice.

As to my cousin Mr. Montagu, I much fear he never will (as he never yet has) give his countenance to any administration.[2]

Lord Northumberland wrote on 18 October:[3]

I hope I can answer that the gentlemen mentioned in the list your Grace sent me will be in town against the meeting of Parliament, and will attend at the Cockpitt the preceding evening.

To give another example—one among many—Lord Buckinghamshire wrote on 24 October:

I . . . immediately spoke to Mr. Harbord and my brother who will both be at the Cockpit on Monday sennight. Col. Hotham will not I fear be in England. I shall see Mr. Bacon at Norwich tomorrow and will then mention your Grace's desire to him.[4]

The letters to individual members seem to have been mostly of a very simple and standardized type, and so were the replies of

[1] Ibid., fo. 338.

[2] Ibid., fo. 452. This was Edward Montagu (the husband of Mrs. Elizabeth Montagu), who, though he was Lord Sandwich's nominee at Huntingdon, maintained a complete independence, both towards his patron and the government, so much so that in Bute's list of the parliament of 1761 he was at first described as a tory.

[3] Ibid., fo. 363.

[4] 32930, fo. 16. Harbord and Bacon were members for Norwich, a very large and independent constituency, where, none the less, Lord Buckinghamshire held a preeminent position. George Hobart, his brother, sat for Beeralston, a pocket borough which the Hobarts shared with the Drakes of Buckland. Charles Hotham was Buckinghamshire's brother-in-law and sat on his interest for St. Ives.

those who were accustomed to the procedure. Only a few among the new members, especially of the merchant class, seem to have thought that any letter from his grace the duke of Newcastle called for a long and elaborate reply. Thus George Prescott, a man of almost fifty, who had spent many years in trade in Italy and had become there the banker of the English nobility, and who now first entered parliament, wrote to the duke on 27 October:

> I will certainly attend at the Cockpit and the first day of the Sessions, and your Grace may depend on my attendance on any future day when business of moment may be supposed to come on. If I have not appear'd at your levée it has not been from want of respect, but it is my opinion that the publick and your Grace may be better served by a close attention to my commercial affairs and a regular conduct of them, and I wish some of my brethren had followed this rule.[1]

Henry Shiffner, one of the 'brethren' who had not done so, and was now nearly bankrupt, sent a no less elaborate reply to the circular letter:[2]

> I endeavoured to pay my duty to your Grace this morning at Newcastle House, not to trouble your Grace with any matter relative to myself, but purely on the letter I had the honor of receiving from your Grace, and relative to the meeting at the Cockpitt.
>
> I shall always, my Lord, with the greatest alacrity be ready to shew my devotion to your Grace, begging at present the indulgence of only five minutes to represent to your Grace the present crisis of my affairs in order to submitt the propriety or impropriety of my appearing at the Cockpitt to your determination.
>
> I hope in eight days to settle all matters; my separate estate and qualification for setting in Parliament remaining vested in myself.

By the autumn of 1762 Newcastle had been driven from office, and had refused the overtures made to him in the summer of that year for resuming it under Bute. He had by no means decided on the line he was to adopt in the forthcoming session, but a good

---

[1] 32930, fo. 118. Prescott seems to have prided himself on the character of a bluff, straightforward city man; and on the very day on which Newcastle and Barrington left the treasury (26 May 1762) he promptly wrote to Sir Francis Dashwood, the new chancellor of the exchequer: 'As it never was my custom to augment the levées of the great, you'll excuse me if I take this method of sincerely congratulating you and my country on your late appointment in the Treasury; persons like you of resolution, ability, and honesty are more than ever necessary in the first departments of the State, to extricate us from the labyrinth of wild expence and politicks we are got into. You may relye, Sir, that without any pecuniary view to myself I shall most heartyly concurr to second in my sphere of life all measures the New Ministry may adopt towards the attainment of such a desirable end.' (Eg. MS. 2136, fo. 33.)   [2] 32930, fo. 246.

D

time beforehand started computing the lists of his friends and considering whom to summon for the opening of the session; no longer parliamentary manager for the government, he continued the practice as leader, not of the opposition—for this part he still repudiated—but of a 'connexion' of his own. A paper is preserved among his manuscripts, dated Claremont, 27 September 1762, and marked 'List of Members to be sent to to attend'.[1] It is a monument of his amazing naivety and ignorance. No less than 317 members of the house of commons, i.e. nearly three-fifths of it, appear on that list, so high did he rate his personal influence; and, as Lord Anson was dead, Newcastle, though himself already in semi-opposition to the government, proposed to summon nine naval officers and two admiralty officials through John Clevland, a regular civil servant and senior secretary to the admiralty! Of army officers nineteen were to be summoned through the duke of Cumberland, while the duke of Devonshire had thirty-four names placed on his list and Rockingham fifteen.

On 3 October 1762 Newcastle drafted a paper under the heading 'Substance of a very material conversation, which I had the honor to have with H.R.H. the Duke of Cumberland, at Windsor Great Lodge, on Friday last, the 1st inst.: and some few observations of my own upon it.'[2] These remarks include the following reflections:[3]

A true zeal for the interest of this countrey, in the terrible situation it is now in; and that regard which many profess for those, who have been driven, by my Lord Bute, out of the Administration, should be sufficient to engage every single man, in either House of Parliament, who pretends or desires to be thought a friend, to be present the first day of the Session.

It is to be consider'd, and that soon, whether our friends of both Houses, should be encouraged or dissuaded from attending the meetings upon the Speech, either at my Lord Egremont's or my Lord Bute's, for the House of Lords; or Mr. Grenville's at the Cockpit, for the House of Commons.

On 9 October Newcastle wrote to the duke of Devonshire:

I hope, we shall all agree, in getting *all* our friends to attend, the first day of the session. His Royal Highness has been so good as to take a list of the names of some persons to be spoke to. I have also given one to my Lord Hardwicke; and another to our Marquess [Rockingham]. . . . I take the liberty to send your Grace a list for yourself, of which you will make such use, as you may think proper,

[1] 33000, fos. 129–35.   [2] 32943, fos. 28–46.   [3] fo. 45.

when occasion offers. I don't propose that any of us should write *circular letters*.[1]

The next day he wrote again to the duke of Devonshire:

I wish your Grace would let me know your thoughts, as to the attendance of our friends, Lords and Commons, at the meetings upon the Speech.

To be sure, I could wish that there should not be great numbers; that would strike them more than any thing; but, whether it is right to attempt to prevent it, or, whether *curiosity* or some *management* for the Court, may not render any such attempt vain, I can't say; for myself, I am determined not to go; as to your Grace and my Lord Hardwicke, I could wish, you would do alike; and then I am very indifferent what you do, in that respect.[2]

The duke of Devonshire replied from Bath on 15 October:

A strong attendance is certainly to be wishd at the first meeting of Parliament, I will take all the care I can about those contain'd in the two lists you sent me. Those that are in office can not well avoid attending at the reading the King's Speech, those that are not in employment may do as they please and it will undoubtedly be a symptom of their disposition.[3]

On 19 October Newcastle was again on a visit to the duke of Cumberland at Windsor, and the next day put down notes on what had passed between them. Cumberland had raised a new point with regard to attendance at the Cockpit:

We talk'd of preventing our friends from going to the meetings of both Houses the night before the Parliament. That would undoubtedly have the greatest effect, and strike the greatest terror of anything; but the Duke fear'd (without being able to determine anything) that the absence of our friends in place, upon that occasion, would give my Lord Bute an occasion to closet every man early, to know what his future conduct would be with regard to the Administration; and to make early examples of those who would not give him satisfaction; that will follow sooner or later, but perhaps there may be some objection to the stirring or giving rise to it so soon.

I proposed to the Duke, as a middle way, to let those in employment, who chuse to be absent, be so; (and many, or some, of those there are;) and to contrive, that all our countrey, independant friends should know, that their not appearing at the meeting would, in our opinion, have a very good effect.

For my own part I shall be surprized to see an inclination in our friends to compliment Mr. Fox with their attendance upon this

---

[1] 32943, fo. 134. [2] 32943, fos. 143-4. [3] Ibid., fo. 217.

occasion, after the strong declarations they have made against him.
Nothing but mean submission to power can engage them to do it.
And, if that is so, perhaps the sooner it is known the better, and we
shall give ourselves no farther trouble. I am sure, that is the case with
me, for one.[1]

Fox, Bute's new parliamentary manager, was meantime giving
out—which Newcastle as yet refused to believe—that many of
Newcastle's friends were coming over to the government.

H. V. Jones, Newcastle's late private secretary, wrote to him on
the morning of 21 October:

> The circular notes were sent out yesterday from the Treasury, in
> the usual manner, for the meeting at the Cockpit, the evening before
> the Parliament assembles. I have not been able to get a sight of the
> list. But, by what I have hear'd, I should think it probable, that the
> invitation has been pretty general. It does not yet appear, *where* the
> Lords are to meet.[2]

Newcastle, in the afternoon of the same day, added in a postscript to the letter he had written to Hardwicke:

> You see by Jones's note, that the summons for the meeting is going
> out. I hope, our friends will have the wisdom not to go; if they do,
> they declare, they will go to any body who has power; for nobody can
> be more obnoxious to them than Mr. Fox.
> A friend of mine upon whom I can depend; and who, by his living
> with them, has means of knowing many things, told me they were in
> good spirits; that Mr. Fox was to sound all our friends; they brag'd,
> that Mr. Fox had *had* (and I believe it after my Lord Bute's) a great
> levée; that they had sure friends 260, or 280, in the House of Com-
> mons; they still brag of my friends.[3]

It is not clear what Newcastle had meant, when on 9 October
he wrote to Devonshire that he did not propose that any of them
'should write *circular letters*', as on the same day he started writing
letters to friends to secure the attendance of various members. Did
he merely mean that he would not write to any individual members (which in fact he did very soon), or did he mean that they
would not issue the last whip which, on the day before the session,
was circulated by the treasury in London?

---

[1] Ibid., fos. 312–13.   [2] Ibid., fo. 345.
[3] Ibid., fo. 339. But on the morning of 22 October H. V. Jones reported that he had
not heard of Fox having had a levée, 'only that some of his friends had call'd on him,
upon the late occasion' (ibid., fo. 358); and on 23 October he again remarked that
'it does not appear, that Mr. Fox has had, or intends to have, any levées' (fo. 387).

On 9 October Newcastle wrote to James West:

I should be sorry that in these circumstances, any of my friends should be absent the first day of the session. I am sure you will speak to your particular acquaintance, my Lord Archer, his sons, etc.[1]

West replied from Alscot in Warwickshire on the 12th:

I . . . can answer both for his [Lord Archer's], Mr. Archer, and Lord Winterton's attendance the first day of the session, which I hear from all quarters will be full.[2]

On 16 October Newcastle wrote to Thomas Thoroton, the business manager of the Manners group, to secure the attendance of its various members,[3] assuming that, if in their places, they would certainly be with him; Thoroton replied on the 20th that Lord George Manners and Mr. John Manners 'will certainly be in town by the meeting of Parliament', but that he had not yet seen Lord Robert Sutton: he naturally said nothing about the line they would take. On 23 October Newcastle addressed the following earnest appeal to Lord Ashburnham:

They give out industriously that they have made great impression upon the Duke of Newcastle's friends; and that many of them are gone over to my Lord Bute. They name some of my nearest relations, and particularly our friend Offley,[4] for which, I am persuaded, there is no real foundation; tho' I am afraid, our friend has been a little indiscreet in his discourse.—Those, who keep company of different complexions, should be very much upon their guard, or reports of this kind will be made from things, that are really trifles in themselves: but, to shew the falsity of these reports, it is absolutely necessary that all our friends shall be at the House, the first day of the session; and I beg your Lordship to speak to Mr. Ashburnham to be there.—I don't insist upon their graceing Mr. Fox's meeting, at the Cockpit, the night before.[5]

On 23 October further letters were written to John Page, Thomas Pelham, Lord Sondes, John White, and Lord Rocking-

---

[1] Ibid., fo. 138. Andrew Archer, M.P. for Coventry, the son and heir of Lord Archer, was married to West's daughter.

[2] Ibid., fo. 177.   [3] Ibid., fo. 244.

[4] M.P. for Orford; he was a groom of the bedchamber to the king, and 1758–62 had been in receipt of a secret service pension of £400 p.a. (see *The Structure of Politics*, pp. 217 and 220), and this was probably still continued to him. He remained, however, faithful to Newcastle.

[5] 32943, fo. 398.

ham to secure the attendance of various friends.[1] Some of those mentioned in the lists, like on previous occasions, were sent in addition direct summonses from Newcastle, and a number of independent members received them in that way only.

On 31 October Jones reported to the Duke:

> The prorogation of the Parliament to the 29th November is strongly talk'd of. The circular notes to the Commoners were stop'd, after having been wrote.[2]

Does this refer to the notes which on 21 October were reported to have been sent out the previous day or to a further circular?

At the end of the month the storm broke over the duke of Devonshire's dismissal, but while Newcastle expected that this would raise a flame among the whigs and tried his best to fan it, it merely served to show how strong the position of Bute and Fox had become and how many of the friends he had counted on had already gone over to the government. By 13 November, when he compiled a new list of the house of commons under the headings of 'Pro', 'Doubtful', and 'Contra',[3] he had given up the idea of still having 317 'friends' in the house: 214 only were now listed as 'pro', 88 as 'doubtful', and 256 as 'contra'. And a week later Newcastle wrote to the duke of Devonshire: 'I am sorry to acquaint your Grace, that appearances do not mend. Threats and offers begin to find their weight—more than I thought to have been possible.'[4]

The meeting at the Cockpit took place on Tuesday, 24 November, and Lord Barrington, who, though still in office, tried to preserve his old friendship and connexion with Newcastle by supplying him with confidential information, sent him immediately the following report marked 'Tuesday night, 3/4 after ten':

> I am this moment come from hearing the Speech and Address; and in obedience to your Grace's commands I have the honour to acquaint you, that the Speech is long and historical, with a general account of the peace. It commends in the strongest terms the conduct of the officers and men employ'd this campaine; but the first and strongest commendations are given to Prince Ferdinand by name, and the

---

[1] The letter to Pelham names John Butler, Sir Francis Poole, Thomas Sergison, John Thomlinson, William Ashburnham, and Rose Fuller (all Sussex men), and asks whether Mr. Frankland, Thomas Pelham's father-in-law, could not influence Admiral Thomas Frankland. In the letter to Sondes Newcastle asks him to write to his brother Lord Monson 'to speak to Mr. Whichcote, Mr. Chaplin, and all our Lincolnshire *friends* to be at the House the first day'. White was asked to secure the attendance of John Hewett and Sir George Savile, and, if possible, of Frederick Montagu.

[2] 32944, fo. 177.   [3] 33000, fos. 153–61.   [4] 32945, fos. 88–9.

forces under his command. The Address in this as well as other parts corresponds with the Speech; but every thing which relates to the Peace, seems to me very guarded, very general, and such as will not preclude any censures from passing on the Treaty, or those concern'd in making it, whenever it shall be communicated to the House. Mr. Fox said it was so intended, and wished gentlemen to object if they thought the Address convey'd approbation. I am not accurate enough to attempt acquainting your Grace with the expressions, but the company thought them unexceptionable.[1]

A day later Barrington supplemented his report by a note dated 'Wednesday Even., near nine':

The numbers at the Cockpit were 248, but among these is counted Mr. Wilks, and several others not supposed to come here as friends. Nothing unusual happen'd, except that the person who presided is not a Member of Parliament.[2]

Ld. Charles Spencer seconds: No notice is taken in the Address of the *particulars* of the Peace mention'd in the Speech: among the rest, what concerns the King of Prussia and his dominions, is past over in silence.[3]

There is, moreover, a curious list among the Newcastle Papers docketed 'List of Persons at the Meeting at the Cockpit. Wednesday, 24 November 1762',[4] and arranged to contain 248 names; but only 97 numbers are filled in with 95 names (two being repeated twice), while the remaining numbers are left blank: obviously an attempt was made to compute a list of those present, but this was never completed. Lastly, there is a paper marked 'Memorandums, November 25, 1762',[5] but its contents cannot be satisfactorily explained until further information is forthcoming from other sources. For, while the Newcastle manuscripts supply a good picture of the way in which the opposition tried, and finally failed, to prepare for the impending muster, the story on the government side remains to be told. The materials for it are neither in the Liverpool Papers nor in the Bute manuscripts, and all that can be gathered from those two collections is that Bute himself did not engage in circularizing members of parliament or

---

[1] Ibid., fo. 127.

[2] Henry Fox's seat had been vacated by his accepting the sinecure of writer of the tallies and clerk of the pells in Ireland; Barrington wrote to Newcastle in his note of the previous night: 'Mr. Fox's writt will be moved so soon as the House meets, the lawyers being of opinion that he has accepted his reversionary grant by paying fee; for it, &c.'

[3] Ibid., fo. 139.   [4] 33000, fos. 169–71·   [5] 33000, fo. 175.

group leaders with a view to securing attendance at the opening of the session.[1]

A year later George Grenville was at the head of the treasury, and the draft for his circular is preserved among the Newcastle Papers:[2]

Downing Street. October 1763.

Sir,

As business of great importance is expected to come on at the opening of the ensuing Session of Parliament, which is now fixed by Proclamation for the 15th of next month, I persuade myself that your zeal for the public service at this critical conjuncture will induce you to give your attendance as early as possible: I flatter myself therefore that I shall have the pleasure of seeing you[3] [here before the day of the meeting which I shall look upon as an obliging mark of your regard and attention. I am with great truth] in Town before that time and am with great truth & regard,

Sir,

your most obedient, humble servant

By 1763 the procedure of the 'circular letter' was firmly established, and it even seems that the withholding of that 'whip' was considered a slight. Henry Fox wrote to Lord Sandwich,[4] on 12 November 1763:

Lord Temple has courted Lord Verney extremely, and he thinks Mr. Gr[enville] has neglected him, because he had no letter, and because I suppose Lord Temple tells him so.

[1] An isolated letter to Sir James Lowther, his son-in-law, does not prove the contrary: the relation in which Lowther stood to Bute fully explains his doing so. Bute wrote to him on 17 November 1762: 'I hardly know how to desire you to take so long a journey at such a season and yet the presence of a person of your character and great consideration joined to the relation we stand in cannot fail to have the best effects, and be in a peculiar manner acceptable to me' (38200, fo. 112).

[2] 32952, fo. 162.

[3] The passage in brackets is crossed out and replaced by the following sentence.

[4] Sandwich MSS., in the possession of the earl of Sandwich, at Hinchingbrooke.

7
THE FORD LECTURES, 1934

INTRODUCTORY NOTE

SIR LEWIS NAMIER delivered the Ford Lectures in the University of Oxford in the Hilary Term of 1934. He chose as his title 'King, Cabinet, and Parliament in the early years of George III'. The lectures attracted a large and interested audience, and their publication was eagerly awaited. As his foreword to the Lectures makes clear, however, a good deal of further work remained to be done to make them ready for publication, and it was not till 1938 that he was able to arrange for leave of absence from his professorial duties at Manchester to undertake this work. The coming of war held up these plans for five years; and then first the preoccupation of the post-war years and next the beginning, in 1951, of his work on the *History of Parliament* pushed the project into the background. But he never abandoned it and, only a few weeks before his death, he spoke of his wish to see the lectures published.

After his death Mr. John Brooke and I, at Lady Namier's request, went through the drafts and notes he had preserved of the lectures. We found them reasonably full and coherent for two of the six lectures and for part of a third, as also for the foreword with which he introduced the course, though the texts of all of them were in an unpolished and uncorrected form as he had dictated them to an often puzzled typist. For the rest of the course no material remained which could be used by anyone but Sir Lewis himself. Particularly regrettable is the absence of any material on the lecture on the King's Friends, and on Sir Lewis's treatment of the role in politics of the eighteenth-century 'man of business'.

Incomplete though these sections are, we consider them worthy of publication both for their intrinsic merit and as an illustration of the views of their writer as formulated in 1934. No attempt has been made to bring the text up to date, and in consequence the comparisons with contemporary practice apply to 1934 and not to 1962, and views are occasionally advanced which he later considerably modified. Where this is so, attention is drawn to the fact in a footnote placed in square brackets. The text has been reproduced with the minimum of change; but a few references of ephemeral interest have been omitted, and the wording has been emended where this is necessary in the interest of clarity or accuracy. We are much indebted to Lady Namier for her assistance in this process. Footnotes have been added where their presence was indicated.

L. S. SUTHERLAND

FOREWORD

WHEN choosing the subject of these lectures, I was faced with the need to make a decision: was I to draw on work finished by me some time ago, or try to put before you that on which I now am engaged? In other words, should I offer you the fruit of my past research as a still-life, carefully arranged and with a decorative—dead—piece of salmon on top; or should I invite you into my workshop—with its unavoidable untidiness—and put before you the very incomplete results of my current efforts? I have chosen the second course because to me the sense of lectures such as these is in their subject still being alive in the lecturer's mind, not set, not yet in its final form, still subject to revision. I am told that before a mineral can express itself as a crystal, the substance must be absolutely dead because the slightest vestige of life would interfere with the process of crystallization. To my feeling, historical research should not—barring obvious exceptions—be put into print until it has crystallized. But once it has done so there it should remain, in the best shape its author was able to give it. And then its place is in the libraries, the universally accessible repositories of our past work and thoughts. In the lecture-room the unavoidable confusion of life seems to me preferable to the tidiness and decorum of the graveyard.

But I have also another, more grave excuse for putting before you a work in its becoming; a work which I may even have to print in its half-finished, only partly crystallized state. Previously I had concentrated to a large extent on the nature of Parliament in the early years of George III's reign: on members, constituencies, and the subtler connexions with government. In the first volume of my work *England in the Age of the American Revolution*, the only piece of consecutive historical narrative was centred round the puzzling fact of Newcastle being so easily overthrown in the Parliament of 1761, of which he himself had largely had the choice. You will appreciate that even in this part of that book I still dealt with the House of Commons. And (I come now to the crucial point) for all that former work the most important materials were in the Newcastle and Hardwicke Papers at the British Museum, and in the Bute MSS. to which their owner, Lord Bute, has kindly given me unrestricted access.

If my work is to be continued in its logical and chronological sequence I must next deal with the nature of the government at the centre as shown in the seven years of confusion, 1763–70, when Cabinets used themselves up very quickly and changed frequently till a new stabilization was reached under Lord North. In other words, I ought to deal with the Administrations of Grenville, Rockingham, Chatham, and Grafton; with those of Grenville and Rockingham coming first, not only in time but also as the most interesting and important for the study of constitutional theory and practice during a period the later years of which are to such an extent dominated by Chatham's abnormal personality —above the norm in greatness and prestige but also abnormal in the sense of being pathological—that it is difficult to trace in them what might be described as typical.

Obviously, for the years 1763–6 the three essential collections of MSS. are the papers of King George III, of Grenville, and of Rockingham. The correspondence of George III, now at the Windsor Archives, has been published practically in full by Sir John Fortescue; moreover, any serious student can obtain access to the originals. But the printed Grenville and Rockingham Papers are mere selections, and the Grenville Papers from Stowe have been dispersed, the best part of them having gone to America;[1] while the owner of the Rockingham MSS., Lord Fitzwilliam, is unwilling to allow scholars access to his papers.[2] Most of the Stowe MSS. that have gone to America are in the Huntington Library in California; I am told they have there 800,000 items from that collection, so far unsorted. Still, we know that there any serious student will be welcome, the difficulties for us being only the minor ones of time and distance.

None the less for the present, in dealing with this period, I could only draw on printed material and the originals at Windsor; the Newcastle, Hardwicke, and Liverpool MSS. at the British Museum; the Chatham Papers at the Record Office; and certain auxiliary collections for these years—the Bute, Holland, Sandwich, and Grafton MSS., whose owners have very kindly allowed me full access to them.

[1] Sir Lewis was not at this time aware that there were also Grenville MSS. in various English collections.
[2] Since deposited in the Sheffield Public Library and in the care of the Northamptonshire Record Office at Delapré Abbey.

(i)

The King and his Ministers

WILLIAM BLACKSTONE in his *Commentaries on the Laws of England*
(published 1764–9) describes the King as

> not only the chief, but properly the sole, magistrate of the nation;
> all others acting by commission from, and in due subordination
> to him. . . .[1]

The passage, of which this sentence forms the kernel, is singled
out for criticism by Dicey in his lectures on the *Law of the Constitution* (published 1886) as an example of Blackstone's habit

> of applying old and unapplicable terms to new institutions, and
> especially of ascribing in words to a modern and constitutional
> King, the whole and perhaps more than the whole of the powers
> actually possessed and exercised by William the Conqueror.[2]

Dicey goes on to say,

> The language of this passage is impressive. . . . It has but one
> fault . . . the statements it contains are the direct opposite of the
> truth. The executive of England is in fact placed in the hands of a
> committee called the Cabinet. If there be any one person in whose
> single hand the power of the State is placed, that one person is not
> the Queen, but the chairman of the committee known as the Prime
> Minister. Nor can it be urged that Blackstone's description of the
> royal authority was a true account of the powers of the King at the
> time when Blackstone wrote. George the Third enjoyed far more
> real authority than has fallen to the share of any of his descendants.
> But it would be absurd to maintain that the language I have cited
> painted his true position.[3]

Mark the sequence of the argument: it starts with a flat denial
of Blackstone's statements, then broadens out into an account
of the constitutional position in the fiftieth year of Queen Victoria's
reign coupled with an admission that things may have been
somewhat different in 1760, yet ends with the implied assertion

---

[1] Twenty-first edition (1844), vol. i, p. 250.
[2] Eighth edition (1923), p. 7.   [3] Ibid., pp. 8–9.

that fundamentally they must have been very much the same as in 1886. To Dicey, George III was obviously 'a modern and constitutional King'.[1] In reality Blackstone's definition was as exact as it could be in his time, given its being put in one single short sentence. The royal authority is not described in terms reminiscent of Stuart claims; but in terms admittedly applicable to the position of a modern Prime Minister; and still more to that of the President of the United States—which in itself is *prima facie* evidence in favour of Blackstone. For America is, in certain ways, a refrigerator in which British ideas and institutions are preserved long after they have been forgotten in this country.

In 1760 the King of Great Britain was the actual head of the Executive, as the President of the United States is today; he was expected to take an active part in Government, and, by universal agreement, had the right to choose his Ministers. This was the constitutional theory consciously held by contemporaries, and usually acted upon in practice.

What then was the nature of that contest which took place in the early years of George III's reign, and in which the extent of the Royal power is supposed to have been at issue? A deliberate and persistent attempt was alleged to have been made by the King to stretch his authority beyond its established limits, and the outcry was raised that the standard of prerogative had been hoisted once more in Great Britain; this was answered by counter-cries of oligarchical confederacies formed to enslave the Crown; and the two cries seemed to bear each other out in creating the semblance of a clash of principles. But neither charge was ever formulated in clear constitutional terms, still less was it substantiated; there, a void remained—subsequently to be filled by conceptions belonging to a later age. And I ask myself: can we find in the first ten years of George III's reign a real, fundamental difference of ideas concerning the nature and extent of the Royal power; or was the dispute a logical outcome of an inherently incongruous arrangement, aggravated by personal factors and fortuitous circumstances?

Both cries are embedded—unexplained—in Horace Walpole's *Memoirs of the Reign of King George III*, one of the most remarkable works of contemporary history, and the most important repository of accurate facts, shrewd observations, and current cant and nonsense, for the first ten years of George III's reign. The theme of prerogative runs through these memoirs, only to give place to

[1] Ibid., p. 7.

the other cry when Walpole's friend Conway is in office and in danger of being displaced.

Prerogative became a fashionable word.[1]

the torrent which soon carried everything in favour of prerogative[2]

a plan had been early formed, of carrying the prerogative to very unusual heights.[3]

The almost universal aquiescence to the favourite's influence persuaded both him and his dependents that . . . prerogative would master all opposition.[4]

These are but a few examples of dozens that could be quoted from the *Memoirs*.

Occasionally an even more sinister turn is given to the allegations, and Walpole speaks of 'a new prospect of arbitrary power',[5] 'the arbitrary measures of the Court'[6], 'the strides I had seen made towards arbitrary power',[7] etc. Yet nowhere are these allegations explained in concrete terms.

What then were the measures of prerogative and the strides towards arbitrary power? Were, perhaps, General Warrants one of them? When dealing with these on their merits, Walpole himself gives, perhaps, the best description of the case ever penned, and admits that all merely amounted to 'the rashness' of the King's servants which 'contrived to involve the Crown and themselves in inextricable difficulties'.

> I do not mean to lead the reader through the maze of vague and barbarous law proceedings, which sprang out of this transaction. It did but lay open the undefined or unmeaning magazine of terms which the chicanery or contradictions of ages had heaped together, and it proved that the Crown and the subject might be justified in almost any excesses. The right hand of Nonsense armed the King, and her left defended the subject. The lawyers on either side were employed in discovering springs or loop-holes[8]

—an admirable description of a technical legal controversy whose ghost was finally and appropriately laid in the law courts. To it I would add the striking remark made in the debate of 17 February 1764 by Richard Hussey, one of the most upright lawyers in the House of Commons. Walpole reports that

---

[1] Horace Walpole, *Memoirs of the Reign of George III*, re.-ed G. F. Russell Barker (1894), vol. i, p. 13.
[2] Ibid., vol. i, p. 9. [3] Ibid., vol. i, p. 14. [4] Ibid., vol. i, p. 110.
[5] Ibid., vol. i, p. 133. [6] Ibid., vol. i, p. 268. [7] Ibid., vol. i, p. 269.
[8] Ibid., vol. i, pp. 218–19.

he [Hussey] wished to have General Warrants condemned because
to some there stood the names of men of virtue, which seemed to
authorize so bad a practice.[1]

In other words, as generally admitted, the measure was not without precedent.

Were, perhaps, the dismissals of officers for voting against
Government in the House of Commons the symptoms of prerogative and arbitrary power? As far as Horace Walpole is concerned, he admits the difficulties of his own position,

> Nor hurt as I was by the treatment of my friend, could I myself
> wish to have the matter discussed in Parliament, where by voting
> against the measure of dismissing officers for their conduct in the
> house, I must in fact have condemned my father. . . .[2]

Again there were precedents in the previous highly constitutional
reign. Nor could the Stamp Act, nor the Townshend Duties, nor
the Printers' Case be adduced as basis for the allegations against
George III. In all these measures he was closely joined to Parliament.

And the tone of Horace Walpole's remarks during the period
when his friend Henry Seymour Conway was in office and in
danger of being displaced changed remarkably. According to his
own report Walpole, when urging Conway not to resign, thus
described to him the position of the country:

> That the nation was now quiet and satisfied; and that all sober
> men, not ranked in any faction, would not bear to see the King taken
> prisoner; that all danger of arbitrary power was over . . . but that
> another danger was growing upon them, a danger I had always
> feared as much as the power of the crown; danger from aristocracy,
> and from those confederacies of great lords.[3]

But who were these great lords so dangerous to the Crown and
the nation? The Duke of Newcastle, petty, shuffling, inefficient
—the 'greatest coward of the age'—determined 'never to be a
minister, or a bit of a minister again'?[4] A man whose fears, in
Walpole's words, 'had surmounted his passion for the first rank
in power'.[5] A man of whom Bute had written to Grenville on
13 October 1761, 'Shall this feeble old man, decaying both in
mind and body . . . attempt to fetter him [the King] in either
House? To me the very idea appears both absurd and impossible.'[6]

---

[1] Ibid., vol. i, p. 295.   [2] Ibid., vol. ii, p. 47.   [3] Ibid., vol. iii, p. 55.
[4] Newcastle to Rockingham 19 June 1765. 32967, f. 69v.
[5] *Memoirs*, vol. ii, p. 164.   [6] Bute MSS.

Or the Duke of Devonshire, whom Walpole described after his dismissal as 'though grievously insulted, and provoked, ... of so decent and cautious a nature, that he was the last man on earth to think of exciting his friends to violent measures; and, indeed, after the first sally of passion, bore his affront with too much patience'?[1] Or the Duke of Bedford about whom Walpole writes in a passage suppressed by his editors: 'I acquit his Grace ... of malice; but his Duchess ... and Rigby seldom acquainted the Duke of the true grounds on which he acted'?[2]—a description which seems to voice the view of those who knew him best. Or, finally, the Marquess of Rockingham, whom Walpole himself describes as 'that nothing Rockingham', a man who 'had so weak a frame of person and nerves, that no exigences could surmount his timidity of speaking in public.'[3] This characterization is borne out by Rockingham's own letters to the King. On 17 December 1765, he wrote,

> Lord Rockingham is ashamed to inform His Majesty that he did not attempt to speak upon this occasion.[4]

And when at last on 21 January 1766 he had to attempt it, the King wrote to him in encouraging terms,

> I am much pleased that opposition has forced you to hear your own voice, which I hope will encourage you to stand forth in other debates.[5]

He did, and on 28 May 1766 reported to the King,

> Lord Rockingham found the necessity of attempting, and though indeed extremely confused, got better through than he expected[6]

—hardly a man to enslave the Crown, certainly one who did not try to.

In groups and when in office men frequently act out of character as though driven by an extraneous force. Almost they appear as puppets subject to a power hidden behind the circumstances; a power which uses the contradictions of a situation to pull about these puppets, or men, this way and that. And if the nature and development of the conflict with which I am concerned is to be determined, the fundamental factors of the constitutional position in 1760 must first be made clear. Inquiry

---

[1] *Memoirs*, vol. i, p. 269.

[2] It should occur at p. 321 of vol. i of the *Memoirs*. Lord Holland wrote of him to Lord Sandwich on 15 September 1763, 'The Duke of Bedford (never, you know, thoroughly let into his own secrets.)' Sandwich MSS.   [3] *Memoirs*, vol. ii, p. 140.

[4] J. Fortescue, *The Correspondence of King George III*, (1927) vol. i, No. 163.

[5] Ibid., vol. i, No. 244.   [6] Ibid., vol. i, No. 342.

into the meaning of the word 'prerogative' and into the allegations of 'aristocratic faction' fails to yield useful results; but there
was at that time a widespread constitutional theory generally
accepted by statesmen and politicians. Summed up as the Independency of the Crown, it stressed the right of the King to choose
his ministers, and condemned any attempt on the part of candidates for office to force themselves upon the Crown. Let us
examine, one by one, the attitude to these matters of the leading
contemporary statesmen.

In the reign of George II, which we have been taught to look
upon as an early conception of mid-Victorian constitutionalism,
during the Cabinet crisis of April 1757 the Duke of Newcastle
himself put down in a memorandum a resolution. He would not

> attempt by force, in Parliament, to remove or replace ministers;
> or in any degree to force the King contrary to his inclinations to add
> any persons into his administration.[1]

When two years later, Bute, on behalf of the Prince of Wales,
inquired with Newcastle and his friends what part they would
take on the death of the King, Newcastle replied that they

> wished the Prince of Wales may succeed to the crown . . . in such
> a situation as shall leave his opinion free and enable him to form his
> plans of Government with advantage,

and further that they

> have nothing more at heart than . . . to prevent his being overruled
> or constrained by any faction or combination of men whatsoever.[2]

The point of this declaration was aimed at the Duke of Cumberland and Henry Fox—for at that time Cumberland was expected
to rely on Henry Fox as leader of a dynastic opposition at the
accession of George III, and not on Newcastle and Rockingham
as it in fact turned out to be.

When George III succeeded to the throne, during the war and
at a time when Pitt's popularity and prestige had reached their
highest point, circumstances and Pitt's refusal to serve under Bute
forced the King to continue the previous administration; but
when in September 1761 the first break occurred in that administration and Pitt found himself out-voted by the Whig pacifists,
the Duke of Devonshire, whom Walpole describes as head of the
Whig party[3] ('No man would have disputed that pre-eminence

---

[1] 32997, f. 135.   [2] 32889, ff. 136-7.
[3] *Memoirs*, vol. ii, p. 15. Walpole also wrote that the Princess of Wales 'had more
than once termed him ironically the *Prince of the Whigs*'. (Ibid., vol. i, p. 159.)

with him') commended Newcastle for the stand he took against Pitt's City supporters.

> It is very plain [what] . . . is their view . . . to induce you to retire imagining by that means to get the better more easily of Lord Bute and then take possession of the King.[1]

And Devonshire, in his diary preserved at Chatsworth, notes having told the King that if only Bute and Newcastle united cordially, Pitt

> would be of no consequence, but that if they differed he would get the better of them and take possession of His Majesty, as they had done of his grandfather, which I should be very sorry to see.[2]

This, recorded by Devonshire himself in his private diary, constitutes a declaration in favour of the independency of the Crown which recent historians would hardly have made us expect from the head of the Whigs.

But when, a year later, the same Duke was dismissed from office and Newcastle tried to raise a hue and cry among the Whigs, Bute, in seeking to secure support for the King, alleged in circular letters that 'the most factious combination of soi-disant great men had been formed against the lawful right and liberty of the King, that ever happened in this country', and that they tried to give the law to the King.[3]

And when on 1 April 1763 Bute wrote to Grenville about a talk he had with Egremont and Halifax, he said,

> They . . . entered thoroughly into the necessity of strict union, not only among yourselves, but that of the other parts of the defenders of Government, and this as the only means of supporting the King's Independency.[4]

Newcastle rightly foresaw what the slogan of the new administration would be. He wrote to Hardwicke on 9 April 1763,

> I hear that the language now given out, is, that now the Scotchman and favourite has resigned, there remains no other question but whether the King shall chuse his ministers, or suffer others to impose them upon him. I always thought that this would be the turn the new ministers would give it. . . .[5]

Clearly both Newcastle and the ministers thought that the use of this slogan would strengthen the administration.

[1] 24 October 1761. 32930, f. 5. [2] Chatsworth MSS. [3] 38200, ff. 89–90.
[4] *The Grenville Papers*, ed. W. J. Smith (1852), vol. ii, p. 40. [5] 32948, f. 99.

When in August 1763 George III appealed to Pitt to form an administration, Grenville, when asked by his colleagues what attitude they should adopt towards the King, replied,

> We entered into the King's service . . . to hinder the law from being indecently and unconstitutionally given to him. We have continued in his service upon these principles; let us leave it with the same, and let us not be *complained of* as the authors of that very measure of which we have so much right *to complain*, and have sacrificed so much to prevent.[1]

In the negotiations between the King and Pitt, the Crown was faced with the plan of a complete and united administration of Pitt's choice. Still, when taking leave from the King, he said,

> Sir, the House of Commons will not force me upon Your Majesty, and I will never come into your service against your consent.[2]

The authority for this statement might be considered, at first sight, insufficient. Walpole records having heard it from Lord Hertford, to whom the King is alleged to have told it. But there is plentiful evidence to bear it out. Thus Newcastle writes to John White on 19 June 1764, that Pitt, in a conference with Lord Lyttelton, stated 'that for one he would never force himself upon the King'.[3] And Newcastle in a memorandum of a conference, of August 1764, with Monsieur Michel, the Prussian Minister, represents him saying that 'Mr. Pitt talked in the usual style, that he would never come in by force; or without the King's good will. . . .'[4] There is a good deal more evidence to that effect.

Even when the King, unwillingly, had to take back the Grenville Administration, and they felt strong enough to enforce Bute's removal from Court, George Grenville—in circular letters sent out to his friends—still repeated the old formula that they continued 'to prevent any undue and unwarrantable force being put upon the Crown',[5] and he appealed even for Bute's brother's support 'for the honour and independence of the Crown'.[6] In fact the King was now between the upper and the nether millstone: those whom he had a year earlier accused of trying to give him the law, and those who claimed to have rescued him from such oppression. Indeed Charles Jenkinson, in a memorandum on relations between Bute and Grenville preserved among his

---

[1] *Grenville Papers*, vol. ii, p. 86. [2] Walpole, *Memoirs*, vol. i, p. 231.
[3] 32960, f. 17. [4] 32961, f. 187.
[5] *Grenville Papers*, vol. ii, p. 106. [6] Ibid., pp. 122–3.

MSS., records that great pains were taken to dissuade Bute from acting against the Grenville Administration, as it would have been impossible for the King

> to carry on his Government by the assistance alone of those who were attached to himself and that he would be thereby obliged to put himself and his Government into the hands of some of those leaders of faction who meant to give him the law.[1]

In the course of the next two years the Grenvilles had however so far established their influence in Parliament, and had come to feel to such an extent secure, that in the words of George III, 'their whole attention was confined, not to the advantage of their country but to making themselves masters of the closet . . .'[2] while the King made attempts (in April and May 1765) to free himself of saviours who had acquired such preponderance as practically to dictate to him in public.

Now came the turn of the wheel—'Everything comes round in this country" said Lord Rockingham to Horace Walpole on a suitable occasion. In a letter to the Duke of Cumberland, 12 June 1765, the King refers to

> Those worthy men Lord Rockingham, Duke of Grafton, Newcastle, and others, for they are men who have principles and therefore cannot approve of seeing the Crown dictated to by low men . . .[3]

And indeed, Newcastle himself looked upon it as a great advantage that the opposition could now enter office

> without being liable to the trite, common objections of forcing the Crown—coming in without the King's approbation—being not sure of the King's support etc.[4]

And Lord Temple in February 1766 informed the King (as Grenville noted in his Diary)

> that he should esteem himself happy to be the instrument to rescue the King out of the hands of those who wanted and meant to take him prisoner.[5]

A year later the Rockingham Government collapsed under the weight of its own inefficiency. Pitt was invited by the King to form a new administration; and in their conference on 12 July 1766 he is reported by the King to have said,

---

[1] Printed by N. Jucker in *The Jenkinson Papers, 1760–1766* (1949), p. 395.
[2] Fortescue *Correspondence*, vol. i, No. 139.   [3] Ibid., vol. i, No. 118.
[4] M. Bateson. *A Narrative of the Changes in the Ministry, 1765–1767, told by the Duke of Newcastle in a Series of Letters* (1898), p. 2.
[5] *Grenville Papers*, vol. iii, p. 360.

That no man was an honest man that recommended none but his own friends, as that must be to form a phalanx to disable the Crown from dismissing them when it judged it proper.[1]

And here again, though the authority for this statement might seem open to doubts and objections, its accuracy is borne out by Pitt's pronouncements and his general attitude to parties or factions. For instance, in his letter to the King of 25 July 1766 he writes

Permit me Sir, most humbly to add that if Lord Rockingham's being *quiet* . . . depends on no other motive than Mr. Dowdeswell continuing Chancellor of the Exchequer, I must humbly advise that a resolution be finally taken that Mr. Dowdeswell . . . is not to remain in that office.[2]

And when the negotiations about Lord Edgcumbe and Lord Bessborough were going on in November 1766, Pitt, now Lord Chatham, sent a haughty answer 'that he would not suffer connections to force the King.'[3]

Such examples could be multiplied, but to what purpose? The doctrine of the Independency of the Crown—that is the right of the King to choose his ministers—was asserted over and again in the most explicit terms. Some may think, perhaps, that Horace Walpole at least—the son of the man who is (quite wrongly) reputed to have been the first modern Prime Minister in this country—did see far into the future, and held on this matter a point of view that differed from his contemporaries. But no, not even he did. When in July 1767 negotiations were on foot, between the much weakened Chatham Administration and the Rockinghams and Bedfords, with a view to broadening the administration's bottom—as it was then termed—Walpole reports having said to Conway that

There were many independent men who would not sit still and see the closet taken by storm.[4]

And when about the same time the Duke of Richmond, discussing with Walpole the scheme of a new administration, objected to Lord Camden as 'the King's man', Walpole's retort was pointed,

I asked if they expected that every man should depend on King Rockingham and nobody on King George.[5]

---

[1] *Correspondence of King George III*, ed. Sir John Fortescue, vol. i, No. 143 (misdated).
[2] Ibid., vol. i, No. 363. [3] Walpole, *Memoirs*, vol. ii, p. 270.
[4] *Memoirs*, vol. iii, p. 41. [5] *Memoirs*, vol. iii, p. 47.

There is no doubt that in theory, about 1760, the right of the King to choose his ministers stood uncontested; but in practice disagreement about this choice lay at the basis of all the political conflicts of the period—with the cries of independency on the one hand and of prerogative and oligarchic faction on the other —and pointed to a fundamental ill-adjustment in the constitutional machinery. But before entering into the discussion of this problem I propose to consider the matter from a different angle, and prove that the right of the King to choose his ministers at that time was more than a current assumption, or a constitutional convention, and that it was both inherent in the political situation of that time and its inevitable logical result—much as the limitation of the powers of the Crown in that choice a hundred or a hundred and fifty years later was again no constitutional convention but the logical outcome of a new situation. Here I should like to join issue with Dicey on a matter of terminology which is of far-reaching importance. In his book on the *Law of the Constitution* he regrets that certain maxims (the conditions of tenure of office by ministers being one of them) 'must be called conventional', for the word 'suggests a notion of insignificance or unreality'. For my own part I object to the word 'convention' even because of its more fundamental meaning: it might imply that these maxims are the result of an understanding, an agreement which, as a rule, the contracting parties are free to shape according to their own choice. In reality, the basic power of the King to choose his ministers in 1760, and his basic duty to accept them from Parliament in 1910, was, and is, the inevitable outcome of a situation which no single individual could control.

What then was it that in time placed the Prime Minister at the head of the executive in this country? It was the evolving system of big, closely knit and well-disciplined parties, a system that clearly singles out men, or a group, able to command a majority in the House of Commons. If there were a multitude of small parties in the House, as there is for instance in France, or were the allegiance of members to their party uncertain, the Crown as the one fixed element in Government would regain considerable latitude in the choice of the Prime Minister.

What then is it that exercises the greatest constraining force on the Member and binds him to his party? In other words what is the main factor in party discipline? It is dependence of the Member on his party for his seat in Parliament, and—viewed from this angle—it is indifferent whether his success is due to the goodwill of his constituents or to the strength of the party machine. The more the Members depend for their seats on the party organization and its leaders, the greater the inner coherence of the party and the strength of its leaders against all and sundry.

But so long as politics were local in character, there could be no real party discipline. Members sat in their own right or else on the influence of private patrons; and, most important of all, so long as the Crown, through a system of patronage, controlled the disposal of certain posts, it exercised considerable influence both in elections and in the House.

About 1760, even in the freest constituencies, politics still bore a local character to a remarkable degree. In my book *The Structure of Politics*, I have given numerous examples of it, and here I shall only illustrate the matter with one telling example: in 1774, in the populous free constituency of Newcastle-upon-Tyne, the question of the right to graze cows on the castle leas played a greater part in the election of Members to Parliament than the entire, colossal, problem of America.

But most important of all at that time was the influence exercised by the Crown. From it, only Members sitting for private or pocket boroughs, or boroughs practically devoid of voters, could be wholly free. Research into the matter shows that the number of seats really controlled by the Treasury, or other government departments, was relatively small; but that the cost to a private patron of cultivating an interest in an average borough would have been almost prohibitive without access to government patronage.[1] Thus beside the patronage handed out directly to members in the form of places and favours to themselves and their relatives, the Crown also had a hold over them through the preferments it conferred on their constituencies. Though the Crown's control of Members was far less complete or wide than the hold of parties is over individual Members today (because of the party-trained electorate) it still was the largest electoral influence in the eighteenth-century House of Commons. And from this situation there was no escape, and could be none so long as appointments to the Civil Service were not removed altogether from the sphere of politics and submitted to definite rules and competitive examinations. Furthermore, so long as a certain limited number of people could determine elections even in large constituencies, there had to be a controlling electoral influence at the centre (in

---

[1] [As a result of his later work on the History of Parliament, Sir Lewis substantially modified his opinion on this question.]

the Treasury) and the question only was who exercised it, the King or his ministers. Fundamentally the position was this; had a set of ministers obtained exclusive control of that electoral influence, they would indeed have become kings. Whereas if the King was to hold the balance between the parties, or factions, in Parliament he was bound to have the choice of ministers. And should he have wished to attach himself absolutely to one individual or minister, and delegate his own power to that individual, the cry of 'Favourite' was bound to go up from all the other, thwarted, aspirants. In the case of Lord Bute it did so.

Originally—and not in England alone—the King was head of the executive, and his ministers were his tools and servants bound to carry out his policy, as ministers in the United States are to this day bound to carry out the policy of the President. The legislature, under those conditions, was like an audience watching the performance of actors with enough approval or disapproval to influence—and even direct—the performance up to a point, but without playing an active part in it. The next development was reached when the English realized that the work of governing was easier if the servants of the Crown were chosen from among the leading members of the legislature. But since the legislature was divided into parties or factions, a curious—indeed, a paradoxical—position arose; the system functioned best when one side was definitely tainted with disloyalty to the Crown—in the first half of the eighteenth century, if they were either Jacobites or adhered to the undutiful heir to the throne. For then the King was induced to work with the chiefs of one party, and did so more or less harmoniously. But as the parties became extinct, the position grew inherently more difficult; until, about 1760, almost all men in both Houses were, as far as loyalty to the Crown was concerned, fit to enter the King's service. And from then on, there was something inherently illogical in the King constituting himself—as he was bound to do so long as he had the choice of ministers—the chief of the 'ins' as against the 'outs'. This is not to say that there was no friction between the King and his ministers. A certain amount of it there always was, and the King's desire to choose his ministers from among the best men of any party was not based on high principles alone. Thus, at the very time when Bute was preaching 'strict union' to Grenville, Egremont his brother-in-law, and Halifax his friend, letters were passing between Bute and the King on the desirability of avoiding too strong a union among them. 'Nothing can be more true', wrote George III to Bute about 17 March 1763, 'than my dear friend's sentiments with regard to having men not too much ally'd in the active posts of Government that my independency may be preserved.'[1] Still, the opposite factor must not be overlooked either—the desire of the King not to constitute himself the chief of one party in the State was much more congruous with the fundamental conception of royalty than the acceptance of a party by him when he was contributing considerably, even in Parliament, to their securing a majority. It is when thus regarded that the constitutional and Parliamentary position in Great Britain about 1760 appears to contain the inherent contradiction I have spoken of. And you will concede that it was bound to continue until both the King and the Civil Servants were taken out of party politics.

When the discovery of the system of party government is hailed by 'Whig' historians as a great achievement of eighteenth-century Britain, insufficient regard is usually paid to the contradictory position in which that system was bound to place the King. Personalities (the King, Bute, and Pitt) did add considerably to the confusion and difficulties of the first ten years of George III's reign; but the fact remains that while George III never really transgressed the limits of authority set for him by the constitutional customs of the time, he came over and again into conflict with the leading statesmen or with political factions. Yet those conflicts of the period which seem to be about the constitution itself, should really be described as the result of inevitable maladjustments in the constitutional machinery; and during the period of transition from purely Royal to purely Parliamentary government, these maladjustments were inevitable.

A somewhat similar position can be seen in France under the July Monarchy when Louis Philippe tried to uphold the French tradition of a strong and independent executive coupled with a Parliamentary system copied from Great Britain. And the French, with their genius for definition, coined during that period a number of fine terms closely applicable to the problems of George III's early years. Prerogative they called *pouvoir personel*, corruption—*conquête individuelle* and for them the whole doctrine of the position of the King turned on whether Thiers's definition— *le roi règne et ne gouverne pas* should be accepted or not. Guizot passionately denied the theory, and asserted that the throne was not an empty chair and that the King was *un être intelligent et libre*.

[1] R. Sedgwick, op. cit., No. 284.

As for the King's advisers, he considered it their task to mediate between the King and Parliament, and to establish harmony between them by obtaining the King's consent for the policy which they thought it their duty to defend before Parliament. In other words they were to form a buckle between the legislature and the prominent head of the executive, a buckle which, even at the best of times, was bound to bear much strain; and it was always with a view to gaining the ready acquiescence of Parliament and the public that a wise King was to choose his ministers. Chatham, too, once gave a definition of the Cabinet as it should be constructed. He wished 'to see the best of all parties in Employment, that that was the only means of carrying on affairs with any degree of utility'.[1] And Walpole's rhetorical question to the Duke of Richmond, about the desirability of everybody depending on King Rockingham and no one on King George, echoed in its own way the theory that the Cabinet should be a compromise between a party, or group, in Parliament and the Crown. Curious expressions on the part that a popular minister could play are to be found in a correspondence between Henry Fox and a small dependant of his, John Luke Nicholl (they are among the Holland House MSS.). On 19 October, Fox wrote to Nicholl criticizing Pitt's famous letter to the City, in which he explained his resignation on the ground that he had no longer been allowed to 'guide' the policy of the country. 'Surely Mr. Pitt's letter can do him no service', wrote Henry Fox, '. . . sole Prime Minister used to be thought an abomination in a free country.' To which Nicholl replied,

> These are surely the most extravagant times my little reading or experience ever knew. Mr. P. the man best fitted for them—Hanover; Continental German measures; and a prime sole Minister, were formerly held in horror and the promoters in detestation. But *he* was the Prime Minister of the people not the Sovreign—and thereby enabled to do more for the latter, than all the most abandon'd Court Ministers since the Conquest ever could or dared attempt to do. . . .[2]

Note how this letter also points to another disturbing element in the situation. Pitt was a Prime Minister neither of the Sovereign nor of the Parliament, but of the people and therefore, at the height of his power, carried out with ease for the King measures that no other minister could have achieved.

[1] Fortescue, op. cit., vol. i, No. 143.   [2] Henry Fox MSS.

Let us now look at the relations between the ministers and the King from another angle. Once he had placed them in office and if he continued to support them, their tenure was practically unlimited, unless they were overthrown by some national disaster. Such relative permanency produced, naturally enough, a form of disloyalty, innocuous yet personally galling: I have in mind the gathering of an opposition round the Prince of Wales which was based on the conflict between fathers and sons, typical in the House of Hanover, and which was bound in its turn to embitter that family conflict. Clearly, if the support of the King was sufficient to keep more or less well-chosen ministers in office, the chances of the 'outs' to come in were meagre until the King's death. And yet if he dismissed his ministers without some obvious and overwhelming reasons, or without the ministers themselves giving up their offices in despair at their own incapacity to cope with a situation, he could not but give the impression of being whimsical or even arbitrary, and was certain to create enemies for himself. In fact, in the early years of George III's reign, the unsteadiness of the Parliamentary situation was aggravated by there being no Prince of Wales capable of leading an opposition to the Sovereign. And so Bute, and the legend which soon gathered round him, and the whole problem of the so-called 'King's friends', became the chief disturbing elements, and endured for the first ten years of the reign.

What then were the restrictions on the King's choice of ministers? In the first place they resulted from the material—its availability. When on 1 November 1760 Devonshire urged Bute to have management for Pitt as administration would be impossible without him, Bute replied,

> 'My Lord, I would not for the world the King should hear such language, he would not bear it for a moment.'
> I answered 'not bear it! He must bear it. Every King must make use of human instruments to attain human ends or his affairs will go to ruin.'[1]

Furthermore, the men who could be simultaneously placed in office were to some extent already in the habit of working together or, to put it in eighteenth-century language, were grouped in factions; and the King as a rule had to accept this fact. Lastly— a very important point—the number of men fit to hold office was by no means great, which is proved, for instance, by the failure

---

[1] Chatsworth MSS. Devonshire Diary.

of the Newcastle-Rockingham group to form an administration in May 1765, or to carry on effectively in 1766. These failures point a significant difference between the 1760s and our own time. A great statesman requires much the same qualities today as he then did, though these qualities will, possibly, express themselves somewhat differently; but from the middling rank and the working ministers much more was then required than is now. Today, for their political work in Parliament, ministers can call on the help of a party system which efficiently eases the running of the machinery of government. Then, not even the worst corruption could have achieved anything like such easing. Equally, in the administrative work of the departments, working ministers now enjoy the support of a highly trained Civil Service. Such assistance was almost entirely lacking to the eighteenth-century minister. The junior lords at the various boards and one or two secretaries in each department (frequently themselves sitting in the House of Commons) composed between them what might be called the first-division staff, and the burden on them, and the ministers they served, was heavy indeed. I have been through the correspondence of Lord Sandwich as Secretary of State—it is preserved at Hinchinbrooke, in the Record Office, and in the Stowe Papers in the British Museum—and there is hardly a draft which is not in the handwriting of Sandwich's under-secretary, Richard Phelps, or of Sandwich himself.

It is almost inconceivable with what trifles not only the Under-Secretary but ministers and even the King had to deal personally all the while. Small wonder that the choice of ministers open to the Crown was never great.

(ii)

The Cabinet

BETWEEN 1912 and 1919 several important studies on the eighteenth-century Cabinet appeared in *The English Historical Review*; and recently[1] a book by the late Professor Turner[2] was

---

[1] [Written in 1934.]

[2] E. R. Turner, *The Cabinet Council of England in the Seventeenth and Eighteenth Centuries, 1622–1784*. Two vols. (Baltimore, 1930).

published on the same subject. The latter publication may be of
some use to students as an index of printed works on the Cabinet
and a guide to some collections of MSS. But the author lacks the
minute knowledge and the supreme care needed for correct inter-
pretation of the various Cabinet meetings, and—outside its
narrow field of usefulness as an index of material—his book should
be read with the utmost caution. Here is one example of his slap-
dash method. Cumberland, he says vaguely, attended Cabinets
in 1762; actually, in George III's reign, Cumberland attended no
Cabinet before July 1765. What happened in 1762 was that the
ministers met at the Duke of Cumberland's 'late lodgings'. There
are also other equally gross mistakes, amusing only to those who
know how wrong they are. In contrast, we have Mr. Temperley's[1]
essay published in 1912. Here, as in much else, Temperley was a
pioneer and still is worth reading, though his statement that the
'nominal' Cabinet was used to check the 'efficient' Cabinet, and
that this led the North-Fox coalition to dispense with it, is wrong.
Sir William Anson's essay, published in 1914,[2] contains valuable
definitions and, like all his writings on the eighteenth century,
shows an understanding that verges on intuition; but he, unfortunately, lacked intimate knowledge of the people and conditions
discussed. And from this point of view, the best of a whole group
of essays is Mr. Sedgwick's, published in 1917,[3] shortly after he
took his degree at Cambridge. His essay is limited to the last two
or three years of Walpole's administration but is so thorough in
the use of materials that his conclusions can be accepted as final,
so far as they go.

I would add a word of caution on the whole bulk of the work so
far done on the eighteenth century: it has left us a dangerous
terminological legacy or, more precisely, has bequeathed to us a
bad misnomer. 'Inner Cabinet' and 'Outer Cabinet' have become
accepted terms for the eighteenth-century situation, whereby a
false analogy with similar bodies in our own time has been established. Even now there is good ground to demur against using the
term 'Inner Cabinet', because it tends to endow that fleeting
shadowy group with a too formal and wellnigh official character.
Some expression like 'inner ring' or 'directing group' would seem

[1] H. W. V. Temperley, 'Inner and Outer Cabinet and privy council, 1679–1783',
E.H.R., vol. xxvii (1912), pp. 682–99.

[2] W. R. Anson, 'The Cabinet in the seventeenth and eighteenth centuries', *E.H.R.*,
vol. xxix (1914), pp. 56–78.

[3] R. R. Sedgwick, 'The inner cabinet from 1739 to 1741', *E.H.R.*, vol. xxxiv
(1919), pp. 290–302.

preferable. To make my reasons for this statement more clear, I would like you to follow me in examining how the present official Cabinet and that inner ring compare with the two 'Cabinets' of the eighteenth century.

Today the Cabinet[1] consists of about twenty members, of whom only two are at present free of departmental duties, the Prime Minister and Mr. Baldwin—the two leaders. That the 'first digestion of business'—as the eighteenth century termed it—is not possible in so large an assembly is, I presume, clear. And in fact, by now, for that specific work the custom has grown up of forming official or semi-official Cabinet Committees in which the minister most directly concerned prepares the business together with colleagues whose departments are affected by it or who, for one reason or another, are chosen to do the work with him. The most important work of the leader, by whatever name he goes (for quite a while he has been known as the Prime Minister), is to determine the general policy of the Government; and since early on, the Prime Minister has mostly done so with the help of a few friends whom he may, or may not, have put in charge of the most important Government departments. For this group, consisting of the Prime Minister and his intimate advisers, in the last twenty-five years, the name of 'Inner Cabinet' has become current. Considering the situation more closely we see that, strictly speaking, no such group is necessary but whenever it forms, it is by far the most important committee of the Cabinet, although never officially acknowledged or fixed. The chief thing about it is its altogether independent composition, I mean a composition detached from the departmental position of its members. And when for a short time during the war, a real inner Cabinet was officially established under the name of 'War Cabinet' and with the purpose of its directing our policy, its members were altogether free of departmental duties.

One thing is equally true of the present Cabinet and of that in the eighteenth century. As the one is, so the other was, an instrument used for the most delicate and difficult work; strong, it yet is supremely supple, and subject to continual readjustments and changes determined by the purposes it serves. Furthermore, as soon as any part (of either) acquires a fixed formal existence, it is apt to wither away—because it soon loses that adaptability which is essentially necessary for its existence. And therefore the Cabinet's living core, its heart, is at all times to be found by tracing the

[1] [Written in 1934.]

heartbeat, the actual workings, rather than by examining its known and acknowledged forms.

About 1760 there were two kinds of Cabinet—the one most commonly known as the 'nominal' Cabinet or 'Cabinet Council', the other usually described as the 'efficient' or 'effective' Cabinet; but bearing also a multitude of names—'conciliabulum', 'the King's principal servants', 'the lords who are consulted upon His Majesty's secret affairs', 'the lords whom the King entrusts with his private correspondence', etc.; and sometimes, this narrower efficient Cabinet is also called the 'Cabinet Council.'

Taking the two in their most perfect form they can be described as follows: the first man on the list of the full nominal Cabinet was the Archbishop of Canterbury; next came the Lord Chancellor, the Lord President of the Council, and the Lord Privy Seal; four great court officials were included—the Lord Chamberlain, the Lord High Steward, the Groom of the Stole, and the Master of the Horse; also the First Lord of the Treasury and the two Secretaries of State; the First Lord of the Admiralty and the Commander-in-Chief; and a certain number of leading peers, elder statesmen, and important politicians. The whole bears a striking resemblance to the scheme of a narrower reformed Privy Council as it was proposed by Charles II in 1679 (you will find the documents quoted by Mr. Temperley from the Privy Council Register in his article in the *English Historical Review*, 1912). It is again obvious that a body so numerous and heterogeneous could hardly be expected to transact the ordinary daily work of government, and therefore another body was bound to evolve, consisting of the working ministers. This was the 'efficient Cabinet'. Anyone acquainted with eighteenth-century administration could guess its membership. Three ministers had always and invariably to be of it, forming the absolutely irreducible minimum: the First Lord of the Treasury and the two Secretaries of State—the men in charge of finance, home affairs, and foreign affairs. As a rule, the efficient Cabinet also included the Lord Chancellor—the great lawyer whose advice ministers would naturally seek when transacting the work of the government. And the last of the 'Big Five'—as I may perhaps call them—was the Lord President of the Council, the surviving link with the matrix of all Cabinets, and the only person in the efficient Cabinet who was not, strictly speaking, a working minister. Besides this, always in war-time but at other times too, the First Lord of the Admiralty was a member of the efficient Cabinet; while the Army was represented, if at all, by, the

Commander-in-Chief or the Master of the Ordnance, never by the Secretary at War, who almost to the end of the eighteenth century was merely a kind of civilian Under-Secretary to the other two.

Note how unfortunate the application of the terms 'Outer' and 'Inner' Cabinet is for the eighteenth century, even if considered proper for our own time. True, the nominal Cabinet approximated to the size of the Cabinet of our day, and the efficient Cabinet was a ring within it, as the so-called 'Inner' Cabinet is now in the full body. But here the resemblance ends. The present full Cabinet is the descendant of the efficient Cabinet —practically all its members sit in it on the strength of their departmental position. The nominal Cabinet of the eighteenth century has by now disappeared altogether, while growth in the number of departments and the volume of business has led to the formation of various Cabinet Committees which form the real counterpart to the efficient Cabinet. In the eighteenth century the scope of Government work was so narrow that one single committee was sufficient. As for the inner ring which is now described as the 'Inner Cabinet', it did have its counterpart in the eighteenth century but seldom included all the members even of the narrow efficient Cabinet: for there almost always was somebody whom the leading minister had to place in charge of an important government department but whom he did not trust sufficiently to take into his most intimate councils.

The above picture of the two types of Cabinet in the eighteenth century gives them in their purest form; but over and again intermediate forms developed to suit the circumstances of the time and the business in hand. Mr. Sedgwick has definitely established that an efficient Cabinet existed in the closing years of Sir Robert Walpole's Administration. Apparently there was none in the first few years after his fall, not for the reasons put forward by Professor Turner[1]—that the high attendance during 1744 is to be explained by the anxiety of ministers in respect of the dangers that threatened—but because these were years of a Coalition Cabinet, without a real leader or a leading group, and in which the various parts did not trust each other. Therefore, even if small meetings perhaps were occasionally held by ministers in charge of the working departments, many problems had to be decided in what might best be described as a coalition conference. Thus the minutes surviving of twenty-three meetings held between 2 February and

[1] Loc. cit., p. 684.

30 March 1744, show that average attendance amounted to something like fourteen or fifteen members. So that these gatherings very nearly coincided with the nominal Cabinet, except for the Archbishop of Canterbury and two or three other members not attending these meetings as a rule. Towards the end of the forties, and still more in the beginning of the fifties, the supremacy of the Pelhams came to be established and various coalition branches were lopped off. Then, the narrow efficient Cabinet once more emerged; and also, even more definitely, an inner ring—more narrow than the efficient Cabinet—consisting of the Duke of Newcastle, Henry Pelham, and Lord Chancellor Hardwicke. Nor did the Coalition of 1757 revive the large Cabinet conference. It was dominated by Pitt, and the surviving Cabinet minutes usually show a strict business attendance by ministers in charge of important departments. Hardwicke, though he had resigned the position of Lord Chancellor in 1756, continued a member both of the nominal and the efficient Cabinet; while Henley, the new holder of the Great Seal, had to content himself with the office of Lord Keeper. In other words, the office of Lord Chancellor was in abeyance and split, and Hardwicke the ex-Chancellor continued its political work while Henley performed its judicial and administrative duties. As this was war-time, Anson and Ligonier usually attended for naval and military business; and others also attended if and when required. For instance, the Lord Keeper was present at the meeting on 17 July 1758 for Dr. Hensey's examination—a meeting of a semi-judicial character—and in the list of those present he was conceded the first place. Or again, when the Cabinet had to discuss the question of whether Lord George Sackville could be tried by court martial after having been dismissed from the army, both the law and the army were fully represented—the Lord Keeper, Lord Hardwicke and Lord Mansfield, Lord Ligonier and Lord Barrington, Secretary at War, were all there, 'present'.[1] Anyone could be summoned to the efficient Cabinet if required, and if he was a member of the other Cabinet he seems to have sat in the efficient Cabinet as a full member; but I have nowhere found this practice put down in so many words, as a rule. With regard to other statesmen, in certain minutes a distinction is drawn between those described as 'present' and those mentioned as 'attending'.

It is astonishing how little we know about the transformation of the efficient Cabinet during the month following the accession

[1] Op. cit., vol. ii, p. 76.

of George III. On 7 November Pitt and Bute talked to Newcastle about a future Cabinet, Bute saying that

> the King would have everything go on for the present as it was in
> his grandfather's time, and till the several officers are appointed
> after the expiration of the six months; but when the new appoint-
> ments are made the King will then declare whom he would call to
> his Cabinet Council[1]

and we know that Bute entered the efficient Cabinet even before
he became Secretary of State. But by the summer of 1761, when
peace negotiations were carried on with France, there was again
something like a Cabinet committee within an efficient Cabinet;
in size it came somewhere between the efficient and the nominal
Cabinets, and it included all the working ministers with a number
of leading statesmen added to them. What would have been in
that summer of 1761 the membership of the efficient Cabinet
constructed on orthodox lines? It would have consisted of Newcastle as First Lord of the Treasury, Pitt and Bute as Secretaries
of State, Henley as Lord Chancellor, and Granville as Lord
President of the Council; in other words, of a triumvirate—Newcastle, Pitt and Bute—and a nonentity, a shadow, and not always
a sober shadow at that. But in fact, neither Newcastle nor Bute
would have dared to transact business unattended by their
friends; Newcastle was cowardly and ineffective, Bute was
cowardly and inexperienced. Therefore Newcastle had to be
attended by his political nurse, Hardwicke who held no office,
and by Devonshire who was Lord Chamberlain; Bute hoped to
find support in Bedford and Mansfield; while Pitt had his 'second'
in Temple; these alone would have made a Cabinet of eight. But
when so many who held no office were included, Anson and
Ligonier—as heads of the fighting services—could not be kept
out. And so the number rose to twelve. Once more we have a
formation which cannot be described either as a nominal or as an
efficient Cabinet, yet was the British Cabinet in the summer of
1761.

Immediately after Pitt and Temple had resigned on 2 October
1761, Bute pointed out to Newcastle that the Cabinet Council
was too large, and suggested that 'the first concoction' of business
should be limited to a committee of four, consisting of Newcastle
as First Lord of the Treasury, Bute and Egremont as Secretaries
of State, and George Grenville who on the resignation of Pitt had

[1] 32914, f. 171v.

become leader of the House of Commons. Newcastle saw from the very outset, as he wrote to Devonshire on 9 October, that it was

> Lord Bute's view, by confining the concert about business to himself, his two friends, My Lord Egremont and Mr. Grenville and myself . . . to get the whole power and disposition of business as well as all employments, to himself. I am now fully convinced of it . . . the point indeed is to make me as weak in the council as possible.[1]

And some ten days later Newcastle wrote to Sir Joseph Yorke, about a dispatch to Madrid, that he supposed it had been agreed between Lord Egremont and Lord Bute 'for not withstanding the Cabinet Council of us four *I know nothing of the matter*'.[2] Thus we have a whole chain of Cabinet formations—the nominal Cabinet of about twenty; the surviving committee without Pitt and Temple, presumably of about ten members; the council of four, formed by Bute to isolate and reduce Newcastle; and lastly the inner ring of Bute and his two assistants. Very few Cabinet minutes are extant for the period 2 October 1761–26 May 1762, that is for the months intervening between the resignation of Pitt and that of Newcastle; but those known to me, for instance those of 29 March and of 8 and 30 April 1762, all refer to the larger committee, including each time nine members (the formal ten, plus George Grenville now leader of the House, but without Granville and Anson who were absent).

How uncertain and ill-defined the rules of Cabinet membership as yet were, can be seen in the correspondence and discussions in which were asserted points that would now be taken for granted and not mentioned at all; certain logical results of what had occurred were construed into grievances; suggestions were made which no one even distantly acquainted with the normal procedure would now put forward; in fact, the famous conflict which ended in the resignation and disgrace of Devonshire was the result of such uncertainties. On 1 June 1762 George III wrote to Bute

> As to the Cabinet, the D. of Newcastle by saying he retir'd of course goes off, therefore would it not be best only to summon those at present able to attend, and afterwards to consider whom of the others ought still to be nominal.[3]

Possibly the last words refer to Newcastle's friends Hardwicke and Devonshire. The case of Hardwicke was especially puzzling

[1] 32929, ff. 139–42.   [2] Ibid., f. 426.   [3] Sedgwick, op. cit., p. 113.

as he had held no office of any kind since 1756, and therefore could not possibly resign; and it was difficult to express in words that he had been the political nurse of Newcastle and should still push the pram. As to Devonshire, he retained his office of Lord Chamberlain which entitled him to a seat in the nominal Cabinet but had asked to be excused from attending the efficient Cabinet.

No sooner had Newcastle resigned than he, who always wished at the same time to be and not to be a minister—to enjoy all the advantages of office without sharing in its responsibilities—began to complain of the neglect and disregard shown to him and his friends. On 30 May 1762 he wrote to Andrew Stone complaining that Devonshire, Hardwicke, and he himself, though they had

> entirely concurred in the orders which were sent by my Lord Egremont, relating to the terms of peace, not one of us . . . know in the least the orders that have gone since, or the contents of what may have been since received. This shows either an indifference amounting near to a contempt or suspicion of us none of us can deserve.[1]

Hardwicke took a more sober view of the matter, and in a letter to Newcastle, 17 June, wrote that he did not think 'it was to be *expected* that, after having left the Cabinet Council, such communications should be made. They would embarrass both sides.'[2] But even he was uncertain as to what his position would be, and in a letter to Newcastle, 19 June, written after an interview with Bute, remarked,

> He said not one word about me being summoned to meetings or not, nor about the discontinuing of the circulation of letters to me, and Your Grace may be sure I did not give the least hint tending to it.[3]

In fact Hardwicke was not summoned to the Cabinet meeting on 21 June, and Newcastle, who always loved to expatiate on the wrongs done to his friends by people who, he felt, had aggrieved him, wrote to Devonshire on 23 June

> I think the not summoning my Lord Hardwicke, as usual, especially as my Lord Mansfield was summoned was as great an affront to him as could be; and I see my Lord H[ardwicke] takes it so.[4]

In reality, Hardwicke did not quite take it so, but does appear to have been slightly piqued,

> . . . I have so much sang froid as not to look upon it in quite so strong a light as your goodness for me makes you do . . . but I will never

---

[1] 32939, f. 102.   [2] Ibid., f. 386.   [3] Ibid., f. 419v.   [4] 32940, f. 48.

talk of this affair in such a style as to bring explanations upon myself which might lay me under greater difficulties. In truth, I am heartily glad they have taken this part. . . .[1]

The members present at the Cabinet meeting on 21 June (as far as Newcastle and Hardwicke could find out, and both were curious to know) were Bute, Bedford, Egremont, Halifax, George Grenville, Ligonier, Mansfield, and Melcombe.[2]

When the difficulties and dangers involved in peace-making became apparent and the leading ministers though wishing to make peace felt some anxiety lest its terms be criticized as insufficient, they naturally wished to get as many politically important people as they could to set their hands to the treaty and commit themselves and their followers to its terms. On 29 September 1762 Henry Fox wrote to the Duke of Cumberland that Grenville had told Bute, in the morning, about his having

talked of sending for everybody that could be got to the Cabinet Council, *nommément*, the Duke of Newcastle, Lord Hardwicke, and the Duke of Devonshire. 'You have no right to send to the two first,' says Lord Bute, 'and neither of the three would come.'[3]

From our point of view it is a matter of comparative indifference whether Grenville had really made the suggestion of summoning Newcastle and Hardwicke, or whether Bute or Fox had wrongly reported him. That such an idea could at all have been entertained or imputed to a man of the standing and experience of Grenville is sufficient to show the fundamental difference between the Cabinet of those days—the Council of the King's Advisers to which the King could, in theory, summon every Privy Councillor and, in practice, any man who was in his service—and the clearly defined party committee of today.

However, as far as Devonshire was concerned, the suggestion was carried out. He was summoned by Egremont to the Cabinet meeting convened for 4 October to consider the French peace terms; and replied that, being desirous of obeying the King's commands, the letter he had received laid him under the greatest difficulties,

I must hope that His Majesty's goodness will excuse my not attending at a Council where it is impossible for me to give any opinion in the uninform'd situation I am in; the King is I am sure too just to

---

[1] Ibid., f. 80.   [2] Ibid., ff. 49–51v.
[3] Printed by Albemarle in *Memoirs of the Marquis of Rockingham and his Contemporaries*, 2 vols. (1852), pp. 129–30.

expect that I should make myself responsible for measures that I have had no share in and that I am in a manner unacquainted with.[1]

Ten days later in a letter to Cumberland, of which the draft is preserved at Chatsworth,[2] he confessed to the uneasiness he felt at having to disobey the King's commands, and his intention to resign the court office which he still held. But on 4 October George III wrote to Bute

> I have just received the D. of Devonshire's refusal to attend Council, this I believe is [an] unheard of step, except when men have meant open opposition to the Crown; this is a personal affront to my person, and seems to call for the breaking his wand.[3]

The incident throws some light on the relations of the nominal to the efficient Cabinet, the nominal Cabinet being a kind of reserve on which the King and his leading ministers could draw for their inner councils when a wider attendance was required. In fact, as far as I know, the nominal Cabinet sat for the last time with the Archbishop of Canterbury present on 16 February 1763, to approve the preliminary peace terms signed by the Duke of Bedford on the 10th.

On Bute's resignation in April 1763 there appeared a Cabinet group perhaps unique in British history, the so-called triumvirate of Grenville as First Lord of the Treasury, and Egremont and Halifax as the two Secretaries of State. I hardly know what to call it—a split Premiership, or a Premiership in commission, or the narrowest efficient Cabinet on record. Its formation was facilitated by the fact that the Presidency of the Council was vacant since the death of Granville in January 1763; that Henley the Lord Chancellor, and Sandwich the First Lord of the Admiralty, were as yet politically insignificant; and that peace having been concluded, the general problem concerning the fighting services was, as is usual in Great Britain on such occasions, how to economize on them. Lastly the fact that Grenville was married to a sister of Egremont, bound those two ministers more closely together. The reason why I suggest that the Triumvirate was to some extent the premiership in commission is that the patronage of the Treasury which was the most distinctive perquisite of the premiership at that time seems, as it appears from later discussions, to have been filled by the three. Was there an efficient

[1] 32943, ff. 48–9. Cf. Namier, *England in the Age of the American Revolution*, p. 370.
[2] Chatsworth MSS.   [3] Sedgwick, op. cit., No. 195.

Cabinet besides?[1] Or were there no minutes taken of the meetings of the Triumvirate? These questions I can merely formulate; I cannot answer them. The Triumvirate lasted altogether only four months—to the death of Egremont on 21 August 1763; and the Grenville Papers are now at the Huntington Library, in California, eight hundred thousand items so far unsorted and of which I do not know what percentage may relate to our period.

When, after the crisis of August 1763, Grenville's administration was reconstructed with an addition from the Bedford group, the normal efficient Cabinet seems to have consisted of Grenville, First Lord of the Treasury; Sandwich and Halifax, Secretaries of State; Bedford, Lord President of the Council; Henley, Lord Chancellor—in 1764 raised to an earldom with the title of Northington; and usually Egmont, First Lord of the Admiralty. But again, on various occasions others were added according to the business of the day—thus at the Cabinet meeting of 5 April 1765, which considered the King's proposals for a Regency Bill, Mansfield—Lord Chief Justice—was present, probably to strengthen the legal element and because he alone had taken an active part in drafting the previous Regency Bill.[2] But, gradually, a certain differentiation took place even within the efficient Cabinet. In January 1764 Sandwich suggested that Grenville, Bedford, Halifax and himself, should 'dine together once a week to talk upon business'. Here we have what is now described as the inner Cabinet, and in the eighteenth century would have been called a 'junto'. Sandwich rather carelessly mentioned the idea to the King, who, according to Grenville's Diary,

> when he saw Mr. Grenville asked him about it, and advised him to treat of nothing there but public business only, and not to come upon the arrangements for offices, in which he would be overpowered by the other three. Mr. Grenville assured his Majesty that it was his intention to do so, knowing that the Duke of Bedford and Lord Sandwich would always join upon that head against him. The King said he thought he would do well to join the Chancellor into this weekly meeting.[3]

Thus even that junto were not yet perfectly at one, and the King was able to influence them and play the one against the other, as when he warned Grenville not to let the premiership be placed

---

[1] At the formal meeting of the Cabinet called for 18 April 1763 to hear the King's Speech the Chancellor and Lord Mansfield were present. Sedgwick, op. cit., p. 317. For this meeting see also *Grenville Papers*, vol. ii, pp. 45–6.

[2] *Grenville Papers*, vol. iii, p. 15.   [3] Ibid., vol. ii, p. 489.

into commission between them. But from all the evidence we have, he failed to persuade them to accept into their midst Northington who, by that time, had become something like the King's observer in the Cabinet. By the beginning of 1765 the cleavage in the Cabinet became even clearer; Northington and Egmont, perhaps to some extent because of being excluded from the inner ring, having become entirely 'King's men'.

About that time one of 'Bute's men' said to Horace Walpole that 'Grenville was grown too powerful in the House of Commons'; to which Walpole added the remark,

> I own I did not think the Constitution quite ruined when the House of Commons could make a Minister formidable to the crown.[1]

The King, worn out by Grenville's endless and tedious discourses, by his insistence on nominating to even the smallest court offices, and by the growing power of the ministers whom he had only unwillingly accepted after the failure of the negotiations with Pitt in August 1763, appealed to his uncle, the Duke of Cumberland, the dynastic leader of the Opposition, to rescue him from the previous saviours of his independency. And now comes probably the most curious Cabinet group in British history —but the magic influence of Burke's verbose eloquence and of the 'Whig' tradition seems to have been such that except for a remark by Sir Willian Anson, in a footnote to the Autobiography of the Duke of Grafton,[2] no one has apparently, so far, paid proper attention to the exotic character of the first Rockingham Administration—the reputed pattern of constitutional government. It is wrong to describe Rockingham during the months July to October 1765 as that Administration's Prime Minister. That Cabinet was formed and presided over by the Duke of Cumberland, a Prince of the Blood, a man holding no office and with no definable constitutional responsibilities. It was he who selected for First Lord of the Treasury Rockingham, one of his younger rising companions (his older companions, Bedford, Sandwich, and Henry Fox, he had lost when they joined Bute in October 1762). It was he who negotiated the formation of the Government with the King and continued to serve as intermediary between them. It was at his house that all the most important meetings of the Cabinet took place; and even when he was not present, the minutes embodying the decisions of the

---

[1] *Memoirs*, vol. iii, pp. 69–70.
[2] *Autobiography and Political Correspondence of Augustus Henry Third Duke of Grafton, K.G.*, ed. W. R. Anson (1898), p. 61, no. 1.

Cabinet—if they contained matters of first-class importance—
were submitted to him before being acted upon. If ever in the
reign of George III supreme influence was exercised by a man who
had no proper place within the four corners of the British constitution, it was by the Duke of Cumberland in the first four
months of the Rockingham Administration.

The position of the King in the Government of Great Britain
at the time was still such, as I have pointed out in my books, that
even the opposition still always gathered round a royal person,
usually the Prince of Wales. But while no King could receive into
office an Opposition under the leadership of his undutiful son—
without practically abdicating the Crown perhaps for the rest of
his life—the situation was different when the dynastic head of the
Opposition was a senior man, a loving uncle, a man of greater
experience of life. It was not necessarily degrading for the King
to accept such help, especially from the Duke of Cumberland who
acted with great consideration and much tact. Thus it was that
Great Britain received a Viceroy, a prince somehow introduced
between the responsible ministers and the ruling King. And this
paradox has been handed down to us by the 'Whig historians'
as the pattern for a constitutional government!

Who then were the men in the efficient Cabinet at this time?
Newcastle no longer wanted to hold any responsible office, but
still wished to be in the inner councils. He wrote to Rockingham
on 14 July 1765,

> As to myself I can be of as much use to you *all* without it [office]; and
> I am very desirous of being so . . . if I am treated with friendship
> and confidence and consulted . . . in the first concoction of things.[1]

On 17 July Rockingham asked Newcastle to come to town 'in
order that H.R.H. and your Grace and us may consider who are
to be of the conciliabulum'.[2] So far I have found no record of
that meeting, if it ever took place; but in a memorandum for
Lord Rockingham dated 21 July 1765 Newcastle writes:[3]

Cabinet Council and Conciliabulum	Are the persons named by the King to attend the Conciliabulum?
	Q. His Royal Highness the Duke
	Q. Is my Ld Mansfield to be summon'd to either?
	Q. Lord Egmont
	Q. Is Lord Huntingdon to be of the Cabinet, and Conciliabulum?

[1] 32967, f. 389.   [2] 32968, f. 34.   [3] Ibid., ff. 183-4.

For the next three months very few Cabinet minutes can be traced in the collections of MSS. accessible to me. Yet Newcastle specially urged Conway, now Secretary of State, to keep such minutes,

> ... from experience I know to be essential to the carrying on business with success and precision ... that the resolution of every meeting of the King's servants should be reduced into a minute; which you did one night, very ably. Without that, there is no security for the execution of what is agreed.[1]

Conway replied in a letter, which I remember seeing but have at the moment been unable to trace, that he was doing so but considered these things of too confidential a nature to put immediately into the hands of a clerk and copied for circulation.[2] Anyway there are very few among the Newcastle MSS.; but these suggest that the efficient Cabinet was of a normal composition. It consisted of Rockingham, First Lord of the Treasury; Grafton and Conway, Secretaries of State; Northington, Lord Chancellor; Winchelsea, Lord President; Egmont, First Lord of the Admiralty; and Newcastle, Lord Privy Seal.

Some meetings I can trace through summonses or references: eight were held in the presence of Cumberland, and four without him. But even at this time a certain distinction is noticeably made between Rockingham, Conway and Grafton, and the others. On 18 September Conway writes with a touch of resignation to Newcastle,

> The Lord Chancellor is now in town and I suppose must be summoned.[3]

Clearly Conway would have preferred not to. And on 28 October Newcastle addressed a letter to Albemarle, Cumberland's political secretary, wishing to lay his 'distress' before his Royal Highness,

> the total want of confidence and communication in the two young Lords and particularly in the Marquis of Rockingham makes my present situation most uncomfortable to me.[4]

On 31 October a meeting of the efficient Cabinet was to have been held at Cumberland House—the question of the repeal of the Stamp Act was to have been discussed. Among Northington's few surviving papers I have found his notes for what he intended to say at the meeting; they may have remained unopened since he folded them up, on that day.[5] At night Cumberland died of

[1] 32969, f. 321.　　[2] Ibid.　　[3] Ibid., f. 429.
[4] 32971, f. 177.　　[5] Northington MSS.

a stroke, and Newcastle immediately went to the King. Here I must digress, to give you an amusing latter-day detail: according to the next letter as published by Miss Bateson, Newcastle told the King that now 'there was a charm which must be supplied'.[1] No such suggestion to apply magic was really made—Miss Bateson misread 'charm' for 'chasm'. To fill this void Pitt was to be persuaded to join the Government. But the headstrong boys, as Newcastle called Rockingham, Grafton and the other young men, or the 'young troup', to use Walpole's description, went their own way; and in a paper marked 'Considerations to be laid before my Lord Rockingham only', and dated 9 November 1765, Newcastle makes a characteristic remark about himself,

> Considering the very long experience he has had in all the offices where the centre of business is, it may be reasonable and necessary for him to expect different confidence and different and previous communication from that which is made to my Lord Chancellor or my Lord Egmont, who have never at any time been in the secret of affairs.[2]

The explanation is lame; the idea behind it appears in a simpler and truer form in a memorandum dated 25 September 1765,

> No confidence, no friendly concert or previous communication from my Lord Rockingham. . . . called to meetings with Lord Chancellor and Lord Egmont.[3]

The point is that a new junto had arisen; and the Cabinet was once more a compromise between a political group and the King; with Rockingham, Grafton and Conway representing the group, while Northington and Egmont acted as observers for the King. It was because of this new situation that Newcastle complained he was not taken into the confidence of party councils but treated as an outsider.

When discussions started on the most important problem of the repeal of the Stamp Act, the Cabinet or the committee dealing with it assumed unusual forms. On 1 January 1766 Newcastle wrote to Rockingham complaining of a meeting which had been held at Rockingham House on 27 December,

> . . . Lord Egmont, Mr. Conway, Lord Dartmouth, Mr. Attorney General, and, I am not sure, if there was not Sir Wm. Baker; Mr. Dowdeswell was there, several resolutions were proposed to be taken in both Houses by Mr. Attorney Genl., relating to the proceedings

---

[1] Bateson, op. cit., p. 39.　　　[2] 32971, f. 317.　　　[3] Ibid., f. 63.

in America; and agreed to; and one strong motion made by Mr. Yorke, for an Act of Parliament, declaring the right of the Parliament of England; and also an Address to the King, promising to support His Majesty to the utmost extent; the last, or the two last, I hear, were strongly objected to, by my Ld. Egmont, and Mr. Conway.[1]

Rockingham replied,

I consider'd that meeting merely as taking an opportunity of bringing persons together to talk over their ideas, and as preparatory to coming to some fixed plan.[2]

And with this peculiar committee Rockingham continued. On 20 January Newcastle again wrote to him,

My dear Lord,
I, this moment, hear that your Lordship has a meeting, tomorrow night, of the Duke of Grafton, Mr. Conway, Lord Dartmouth, the Chancr. of the Exchequer, Mr. Charles Townshend, the Atty. General, Mr. Hussey; that Lord Hardwicke was spoke to but does not go; to settle the Parliamentary proceedings upon the American affairs. I hear also that you are all like to differ widely amongst yourselves. My informer was uncertain, whether Lord Egmont was to be there, or not.
I say nothing as to this meeting; the manner and composition of it; but I hope Your Lordship will think proper, to have one, or more meetings, this week, *of Lords*, otherwise, we shall none of us know, what is proposed to be done; and consequently shall follow our own ideas.[3]

That Newcastle's information was correct can be seen from a letter written by Rockingham to Charles Yorke and dated 17 January.[4] On 2 February Newcastle himself wrote to the Archbishop of Canterbury,

I hope . . . that the measures agreed upon by the administration, will be approved by your Grace. I have had very little to do in the settlement of them; which, I understand was done, at the meeting of the three ministers [Rockingham, Grafton, and Conway] Mr. Charles Yorke, Mr. Dowdeswell, and Mr. Charles Townshend.[5]

In other words the most important decision regarding the most important action of the Rockingham Administration was settled by the three chief ministers, the Chancellor of the Exchequer, the Attorney General, and a man who though merely holding the

[1] 32973, f. 3. [2] Ibid., f. 11. [3] 32973, f. 202.
[4] 35430, f. 258. [5] 32973, f. 342.

office of Paymaster-General of the forces was one of the most brilliant speakers in the House of Commons; while on other occasions, leading merchants such as Sir William Baker, Barlow Trecothick and Aufrère, or leading lawyers such as Richard Hussey were consulted. It is not clear at what point in those rather chaotic times Dowdeswell, the Chancellor of the Exchequer, came to be a member of the efficient Cabinet, but in the minutes of the last meeting of the Rockingham Cabinet (of which I have a copy) the following are put down as present on 4 July: Rockingham, Winchelsea, and Conway; the Duke of Richmond, who had replaced Grafton as Secretary of State; Lord Dartmouth, the President of the Board of Trade, who came to participate in the meeting during the many months of discussions on America; young Lord Hardwicke who had joined the efficient Cabinet in May; and Dowdeswell; while the Attorney and the Solicitor-General were noted as 'assistants'. Egmont had gone into the country, and Northington had declared that he would no longer attend Cabinet Councils. The two representatives of the King had withdrawn, and on 12 July the King opened negotiations with Pitt for the formation of a new government.

In this new administration the efficient Cabinet consisted of Chatham, who now merely held the Privy Seal; Grafton, First Lord of the Treasury; Conway and Shelburne, Secretaries; Camden, Lord Chancellor; Northington, Lord President; Saunders, First Lord of the Admiralty; and Granby, Master of the Ordnance. Before the end of the year Charles Townshend, Chancellor of the Exchequer, was added to their number and, later on, Hillsborough, as third Secretary for Colonies. The number of government departments represented in the efficient Cabinet was growing. Lord North, as Chancellor of the Exchequer, held a prominent place in the efficient Cabinet because both Grafton, the First Lord of the Treasury, and Conway, the Secretary of State, were all the while more or less on the point of resigning; and from 1767 he acted as the leader of the House of Commons.

In the North Administration of 1770 we get once more a larger efficient Cabinet, all of one hue, without any separate party ingredients. There is no evidence of an inner ring, while the greater size of the efficient Cabinet by itself led gradually to the extinction of the nominal Cabinet.

(iii)

The Prime Minister

WHEN George II told Hardwicke that 'Ministers are the Kings in this country', Hardwicke replied, in effect, that this would be so if there were a Prime Minister;[1] and when on the death of Casimir Périer, in 1832, Louis Philippe tried to do without a Prime Minister, he declared that he did not want a viceroy. A 'sole minister' if effective as chief of a group of leading politicians, was bound to be a potential check on the 'Independency of the Crown': he welded the prominent men into a faction and thereby narrowed down the King's freedom of choice. Indeed, in view of the shortage of men fit to hold office, he could in that way replace to some extent the party organization of which there was none as yet either in the country or in the House of Commons. For the same reason he was bound to become odious to individual politicians who were out of office—to them he appeared as intercepting the favour of the King. Whereas to the entire Opposition he was odious because it was he who gave coherence to the governing group. And all turned on to him the batteries which would otherwise have had to be directed against the King himself. This shifting of their hostility also enabled the disgruntled or disappointed to accuse the leading minister of unlawfully encroaching upon the rights of the Crown. Yet at times a need was felt for ordered and unified leadership in the Government, and a closer inquiry shows that the attitude of men towards the idea of a First, or Prime, Minister varied with circumstances.

When Bute became Secretary of State in March 1761, Henry Fox sent him through Lord Fitzmaurice a message, adding that since from

> Robert Walpole's time there has been no ministry in this Kingdom he hopes this will be the beginning of a durable and honourable one to both King and State[2]

[1] Quoted P. C. Yorke, *The Life and Correspondence of Philip Yorke Earl of Hardwicke* (Cambridge, 1913), vol. i, p. 383.
[2] Bute MSS.

which did not prevent him from writing in the opposite strain
after Pitt, his enemy, in a letter to the City had raised the claim
to Primacy in the Cabinet. Fox told Nicholl on 19 October 1761
that Pitt had explained his resignation on the grounds of his
being unable to stay

> if over-ruled by the united opinion of all the rest of the King's ser-
> vants. A sole Prime Minister used to be thought an abomination in a
> free country.[1]

According to Dodington, Beckford said to Bute on the accession
of George III 'that he wished to see the King his own minister';[2]
but in the debate of 11 December 1761, after Pitt's resignation,
he declared that 'it was necessary to have *one* minister';[3] while
Grenville on this occasion replied to Beckford that

> He had heard with surprise that *one* man ought to direct. What had
> been the constant charge against Sir Robert Walpole, but his acting
> as sole Minister? . . . Prime Minister was an odious title. . . .[4]

But a few years later Grenville, when himself First Lord of the
Treasury, bitterly complained if the King neglected his Primacy
among the ministers. And Pitt who in the days of Sir Robert
Walpole had attacked the idea of a premiership, clearly aimed at
it, yet tried politely to explain away his claim by professing that
his friend Beckford 'had thought more of him than he had done
of himself', and that 'if present questions tended to make one
individual minister, he should be against it'.[5]

Gradually the functions of a Prime Minister were emerging;
but it still took a certain time before they were clearly fixed in
one man, and before their scope came to embrace the total range
of government.

It is indeed often difficult to say who in those years was the
Prime Minister or, to use the contemporary expression—*the*
minister. In the last three years of George II's reign it is impossible
to assert if it was Newcastle or Pitt. And after the accession of
George III, before Bute assumed the Treasury, it is equally impossible to make any definite assertion. Newcastle emphatically
denied being *the* minister of the new reign; nor could Pitt have
made any claim to being him. And who was Prime Minister
between July and October 1765; and from 1766 to 1768—Pitt or
Grafton; and who, again, between 1768 and 1770? As late as 1786,

[1] Henry Fox MSS.
[2] *The Diary of the late George Bubb Dodington*, ed. H. P. Wyndham (1784).
[3] Walpole, *Memoirs*, vol. i, p. 89.   [4] Ibid.   [5] Ibid., vol. i, p. 92.

Beatson in his *Political Register* published a list, curiously headed as 'Prime Ministers or Favourites from the time of Henry VIII to this day', and placed these men before the peerage, baronetage, etc., quite apart from all the other holders of ministerial office. His classification is odd, yet truly points to the double function of the ideal mid-eighteenth-century First Minister, whose task it was to mediate between the Crown and Parliament, and whose distinguishing mark was to possess the confidence of the Crown and have the management of the House of Commons. When this dual distinguishing mark was stamped on one man, you had a Prime Minister—Bute in 1762-3, and North after 1770.

When Cumberland's negotiations with Pitt and Temple had broken down on 25 May 1765, Newcastle wrote to the Bishop of Oxford,

> The result was, that the Duke offered my Lord Temple the Treasury, and Mr. Pitt the Secretary of State; whereby the one was set at the head of the finances and the home affairs; and the other of the foreign affairs.[1]

'Home affairs at the Treasury'? Surely the present Home Office has branched out of the Office of the Secretaries of State? But then, this quaint description springs from Newcastle's idea of 'Home Affairs'. To him it meant patronage and the management of the House of Commons; and these, for historic and technical reasons, were centred in the Treasury.

The original functions of the House of Commons were primarily financial; therefore the Treasury was the department with which the House was more immediately concerned. The connexion continued, and in a certain sense continues to this day. Further, though various Government offices like the Admiralty and the Post Office, had their own patronage, the greatest amount of Government patronage centred in the Treasury. And once the principle was accepted that the First Lord of the Treasury should have the management of the House of Commons, the patronage of other departments under the Crown—in so far as it could be used for electoral purposes—came to be subordinated to the Treasury. But this was not achieved without considerable resistance from the other ministers. The one branch of the services which the Hanoverians, with their predilection for soldiering, managed, to some extent, to keep out of the hands of their chief ministers was the Army. And a constant grievance of Newcastle, even more

---

[1] 32966, ff. 463-6.

than of Sir Robert Walpole, was George II's refusal to allow
either of them to subordinate the interests of the Army to Parliamentary considerations. It was in his double character of guardian
of the national finance and maker and manager of the House of
Commons that the First Lord of the Treasury came to be looked
upon, more often than not, as the first man in the Cabinet.

In these circumstances it was logical that the First Lord of the
Treasury should be in the Commons. Sometimes the fact is stressed
that between 1721 and 1801 there were about twice as many First
Lords of the Treasury in the Upper House as in the Commons.
But consider how long peers held the Treasury, rather than how
often they were appointed to it. While Sir Robert Walpole held
it for twenty-one years, his successor, Lord Wilmington, only did
so for something over a year; Pelham held it for eleven years, till
his death in 1754, but the Duke of Newcastle spent two most
uncomfortable years casting about for a deputy in the Commons,
and then gave up the attempt. During the next four years Devonshire and Newcastle were mere figureheads for Pitt. Bute held
the Treasury for one year. George Grenville, though at first considered hopelessly weak, steadily gained strength in the House,
and succumbed only at the third attempt of the King to overthrow him. Lord Rockingham spent one uneasy year at the
Treasury; and even the mighty name and shadow of Chatham
could not secure the smooth working of government after he had
gone to the House of Lords. But when, in 1770, Lord North,
another Commoner, was placed at the head of the Treasury, it
required the disasters of the American Revolution to overthrow
him; and even so he had a twelve-years' run. Next, three peers,
Rockingham—who died after a few months—Shelburne, and the
Duke of Portland, carried on for a joint twenty months; while
their successor William Pitt lasted seventeen years.

Even allotting to the peers the four years when Pitt—rather
than Devonshire or Newcastle—was the first minister, during the
period 1721–1801 the average life of administrations presided over
by peers ran into about as many months as that of Commoners
ran into years.

Whenever the First Lord of the Treasury was in the House of
Commons, he was also Chancellor of the Exchequer. To this there
is not one exception during that period. And in official reports
he is often described as Chancellor of the Exchequer, and not by
his higher title of First Lord of the Treasury. But whenever the
First Lord of the Treasury was in the Upper House, there had to be

a Chancellor of the Exchequer to represent the Treasury in the
Commons. However, as the First Lord of the Treasury still took
an active part in the financial work of the Treasury, the Chancellor of the Exchequer was something of an Under-Secretary to
him. Yet, since the Chancellor of the Exchequer, when there was
one in the Commons, naturally was the chief representative of the
Treasury in the House, he ranked far above the other ministers.
Nonetheless, he was not as a rule deemed of Cabinet rank. Even
when a man of the political standing of Charles Townshend had,
in 1766, been browbeaten by Chatham into accepting the office,
he 'was not called to the Cabinet'; and only managed to worm
himself in a few months later. The Duke of Grafton wrote in his
Autobiography, 'On the night preceding Lord Chatham's first
journey to Bath, Mr. Charles Townshend was, for the first time,
summoned to the Cabinet.'[1] His successor Lord North was included in it not as Chancellor of the Exchequer, but rather as
leader of the House of Commons.

During the eighty years from 1721 to 1801, whenever the First
Lord of the Treasury was in the Commons, both Secretaries of
State were in the Lords; but whenever the First Lord of the
Treasury was in the Upper House, one Secretary of State was in
the Commons—with very few exceptions, and none of these
lasting for more than a few months. Since the other two of the
'Big Five' who completed the core of the efficient Cabinet—the
Lord Chancellor and the Lord President of the Council—were
invariably peers, it seldom happened that more than one minister
of first rank sat in the Commons. For even when the First Lord
of the Admiralty or the Commander-in-Chief happened to be
Commoners and were included in the efficient Cabinet—like
Ligonier, Granby, Saunders, or Hawke—such a minister's function in the Cabinet and in the House was that of an expert rather
than of a politician.

A Secretary of State who was in the Commons had, therefore,
always an obvious claim to the leadership of the House. But could
the leadership of the House be separated from its management,
and hence from patronage, the lubricant of that management?
Here we touch one of the great inherent difficulties in the position
of a Prime Minister who was a peer. Foreign Affairs and the Army
were always considered to some extent the special personal
domain of the King, and it was an accepted rule that the Secretaries
of State could directly discuss questions of foreign policy with the

[1] *Autobiography*, pp. 92 and 105.

King. But the position of the First Lord of the Treasury, with regard to the King, was based on his management of the House of Commons—as understood by Newcastle, 'home affairs'. Were the First Lord to cede this management to the Secretary of State, he would have been left with nothing but revenue business.

In 1754, Newcastle offered Fox the Secretaryship of State but without the management of the House of Commons, and Fox refused. When a year later they came to an understanding, Newcastle still tried to have the circular letters, summoning Members of Parliament to the opening of the session, sent out by his Chancellor of the Exchequer, H. B. Legge, rather than by Fox.[1] With Pitt, in 1757, a peculiar *modus vivendi* was established, Newcastle being the 'minister of men', in charge of patronage, while Pitt was the 'minister of measures'—the leader in the House of Commons and master in the Cabinet. Still, judging by the bitter remarks which Pitt threw out to James West when, in November 1757, he was asked for orders concerning the circular letters, he was perhaps not quite so happy in that position as is sometimes supposed; and this may have been the reason why in 1765 he insisted on having Temple at the Treasury. In fact during this period, hardly a case can be quoted of a truly happy partnership between a First Lord of the Treasury in the Upper House, and a Secretary of State leading the Commons. It was while Bute was at the Treasury and George Grenville led the Commons, as Secretary of State in the summer of 1762, that the first rift in their relations occurred—Grenville being rather reluctant to do on Bute's behalf work in the Commons in which he excelled later, when doing it for himself. Even the mild and indolent Rockingham seems to have had his jealousies, towards Conway; and to have tried to work through Dowdeswell, his Chancellor of the Exchequer, in order to retain the management of the House while in the Treasury. Horace Walpole, when trying in the spring of 1767 to persuade Conway to take the Treasury, said

> He could not be Minister of the House of Commons without power; had Lord Rockingham imparted any to him before?

and added that he himself

> would propose nothing so ridiculous as Rockingham and Dowdeswell over again.[2]

---

[1] See preceding essay in this volume.
[2] *Memoirs*, vol. iii, p. 10.

The limit of absurdity was, however, reached in the first year of Chatham's administration when, on certain important measures, the two Cabinet ministers in the Commons—Conway, Secretary of State, and Townshend, Chancellor of the Exchequer —opposed Government measures which had to be carried through in the House by men of second rank, such as Jeremiah Dyson Commissioner of Trade, and Thomas Bradshaw Secretary to the Treasury.

In 1770, with Lord North First Minister in the House of Commons, normality was once more reached. And Horace Walpole thus summed up the general sense of relief,

It was obvious how much weight the personal presence of the first minister in the House of Commons carried with it.[1]

[1] *Memoirs*, vol. iv, p. 51.

8

THE END OF THE NOMINAL CABINET

On 14 February 1921, King George V presided over a Cabinet Council, attenuated and atrophied, held to hear the Speech with which Parliament was to be opened on the 15th. But no one present seems to have known that this was a Cabinet meeting, and when in July 1921 the King was leaving for Scotland before the text of the Speech could be conveniently fixed, it was decided to dispense with a formality of which the origin and meaning were forgotten—the Speech was to be 'sent to Balmoral in a box'. The last vestige of a Cabinet held in the presence of the Sovereign was being extinguished, apparently without anyone realizing it.

While the outlines of the eighteenth-century Cabinet have by now been drawn, the detail, which in parts is of decisive importance, has still to be filled in; and the subject calls for a film, perhaps, rather than a picture to render the quick, fleeting changes. No schematic pattern can do justice to the history of the Cabinet, even in reference to short periods. The last trace of life has to be removed from matter before crystallization becomes possible; but the Cabinet is a living organism, governed by the purposes which it serves, and has therefore always been essentially pragmatic in its nature. Whatever part of it is fixed tends to become ornamental, and in time passes into pageantry and folklore.

The story which ascribes the King's withdrawal from the Cabinet to an accident—George I's ignorance and George II's imperfect knowledge of English—is a crude and, by now, exploded legend. George II talked English to his Ministers, and notes in his own hand testify to his having had quite a satisfactory command of the language; while the thirteen years of George I's reign would not have wrought such a change had not deeper forces been at work, one of them being the gradual transference of the real business of the Cabinet to a new body. From the Cabinet Council over which the King had once presided he never completely withdrew, but that Council itself gradually faded away, till it sank into an anonymous grave, on which this essay is intended to place a commemorative inscription.

Early in the eighteenth century the Cabinet Council consisted of the Archbishop of Canterbury, the Lord Chancellor, the Lord President of the Council, and the Lord Privy Seal; the four great Court officers—the Lord High Steward, the Lord Chamberlain, the Groom of the Stole, and the Master of the Horse; the Lord Chief Justice; the First Lord of the Admiralty and the Commander-in-Chief (or the Master-General of the Ordnance); the Lord Lieutenant of Ireland; the First Lord of the Treasury and the Secretaries of State; and a few more peers or statesmen summoned because of their personal weight. This was a Council of State rather than an Administration; it represented the Church, the Law, the Court, the Services, and (at the tail-end) the chief departments of State. Even when fundamental problems of policy were still debated and settled by this body, the working Ministers had to meet apart for the handling of current business—diplomatic correspondence, dispositions of the Fleet or Army, Colonial or trade affairs, and so on. This smaller Cabinet necessarily included the First Lord of the Treasury, the Secretaries of State, and almost invariably the Lord Chancellor and the President of the Council, with others added according to requirements—for example, naval business could hardly be discussed without the Navy being represented. But its composition was extremely elastic and pragmatic, and curious hybrid forms were developed at times. The one person who never joined the Ministers sitting, as it were, in their shirt-sleeves was the Sovereign; he never dropped out completely from the original Cabinet, but he never entered the one from which the present Cabinet is lineally descended.

By 1760 the original Cabinet had declined so much that it came to be called the 'Nominal Cabinet'; while the smaller body of working Ministers was known as the 'Efficient' or 'Effective Cabinet', its members being referred to by names such as 'the King's principal servants', 'the King's confidential servants', or 'the lords whom the King entrusts with his private correspondence' (they alone had the 'circulation of papers', which is always the distinctive mark of the directing body).

The Nominal Cabinet seems to have retained only two regular functions, both performed in the presence of the King. It met some days before the opening or prorogation of Parliament to hear the King's Speech, and was occasionally summoned to advise the King on death sentences (this is why, in July 1766, Lord Temple, in a moment of irritation, contemptuously dubbed it 'the hanging Committee'). As a special decision had to be taken to hold a meeting for hearing a criminal case, there is more material about this kind of Cabinet than about meetings for the King's Speech, which were apparently a matter of routine; moreover, as the King was present, a Cabinet minute, which usually took the form of a communication to him, was not required. Still, there is sufficient evidence to prove the existence of the custom.

To give a few examples. On 23 April 1755, Lord Hardwicke wrote to the Duke of Newcastle:

> Lord Chancellor sends his compliments to the Duke of Newcastle, and begs the favour of his Grace to make his humble excuse to the King for his not being able to attend the Council for the Speech.

On Thursday, 13 November 1760, before the first opening of Parliament in the new reign, Newcastle wrote to Hardwicke: 'When is the Council to be for the Speech?' Hardwicke replied: 'The Cabinet for the Speech may be to-morrow, if there is to be one without the King. That, in His Majesty's presence, need not be before Monday.' On Sunday 16 November, Newcastle received, from Bute, George III's famous addition to the Speech: 'Born and educated in this country, I glory in the name of Britain'; and wrote to Hardwicke that these words had to be inserted in the Speech, 'which is to be laid before the King to-morrow in Cabinet Council'. Again, on 10 January 1766, Newcastle, having received a summons from the office of the Secretary of State 'to attend His Majesty, this day, in his Closet', wrote to Rockingham:

> As I know, it was only for the Speech; and as I had told the King, that I had seen, and approved the Speech, I was sure, His Majesty would be so good, as to excuse me.

A few days before Parliament assembled the Speech was read also at another gathering—by the Leader of the House of Commons to its 'efficient men' or 'men of business'—that is, the frontbenchers (at that time usually not more than one or two members of the Efficient Cabinet were of the House of Commons). These were, in fact, parallel meetings—at least four-fifths of the members of the Nominal Cabinet were peers, and it included almost all the leading men on the Government side in the House of Lords; it would therefore have been sheer pedantry to have had another meeting of the front-bench peers for the same purpose. But that no particular constitutional significance attached to this meeting of the Nominal Cabinet is shown even by the fact that in November 1760 the Speech was read by Pitt to the front-benchers of the House of Commons on the night before the Cabinet Council met for it in the presence of the King.

At a later date, a dinner began to be held for the Speech, attended by the Cabinet, the Speaker, the junior Ministers, and the Under-Secretaries, lords and commoners alike; also by the movers and seconders of the Address. It was discontinued in 1931 for reasons of economy. Now a cup of tea and a bun take its place, and, as this treat is not sufficiently attractive for Cabinet Ministers, who are acquainted with the Speech, they have dropped out, the tea-party changing into a 'children's party'.[1]

In time the Cabinet Councils for the Speech came to be tacked on to meetings of the Privy Council, but although the memory of their origin, meaning, and character seemed to have been lost they were kept distinct from the others. The question, however, who was entitled to attend the reading of the Queen's Speech and, still more, what constitutional importance attached to it seems at times to have puzzled Presidents of the Council and other Ministers.

On 29 November 1852, Lord Exeter, then Lord Chamberlain, wrote to the President of the Council (this document, as well as the next, is in the Privy Council Office, and is now published with the permission of that department):

> I have had the honour of communicating the contents of your letter of the 15th inst to the Queen, and I have received Her Majesty's commands to inform your Lordship that in future it is Her Majesty's pleasure the Clerk of the Council shall upon all occasions when the ordinary business has been concluded and Her Majesty's Speech is about to be read desire the Gold Stick to retire with himself, and that the only persons who have the privilege of remaining in the Council Chamber with the Ministers, are the Great Officers of State and the Groom of the Stole to His Royal Highness Prince Albert.

Again, on 13 September 1884, Sir C. L. Peel, clerk of the Privy Council, wrote to Mr. Gladstone:

> With reference to our conversation at Balmoral, I cannot find any trace in the records of this Office of the Sovereign's Speech to Parliament having been ever treated as Privy Council business. . . .

---

[1] In November 1938, the Prime Minister being detained by urgent business, the Speech was, very appropriately, read to the junior Ministers by the Chief Whip.

There is no mention of the Speech itself in any list of Business or in the Minutes of the Privy Council.

I imagine that the Royal Assent is signified by the fact that the Speech is always delivered either by the Sovereign in person, or by the Lord Chancellor 'in the Sovereign's own words' under authority of a Royal Commission. . . .

When in 1921 the difficulty arose of fixing the King's Speech before he left for Scotland, Sir Almeric FitzRoy, Clerk of the Privy Council, submitted the following memorandum (which is printed in his *Memoirs*):

There is nothing to show that any constitutional sanction attaches to the approval of the King's Speech after a Council.

It is certain, on the other hand, that such approval is no part of the business of the King in Council, and it appears probable that the practice is the result of convenience hardening into custom.

In the old days Councils were usually attended by a large number of Cabinet Ministers, and the moment, therefore, was favourable for a formal act of the Crown in combination with Ministers; but now, in normal circumstances, the Lord President is the only Cabinet Minister present, and, so far as the presence of a second is concerned, it has been due to my efforts to secure it, in order that the Lord President should have the countenance of a colleague if any alteration is required at the last moment.

It was only in my time that the authentication of the approved document by the Sign-manual was introduced, and, now that the practice is formalized, it is clear that the King's approval can be as regularly obtained in that way as for any other Act of State for which it is requisite.

On these grounds, I submit that, at the dictate of convenience, the King's approval of the Speech could be signified upon the document being sent to Balmoral in a box if Parliament has to be prorogued while he is there, the Prorogation Commission having been passed at the last Council His Majesty holds before his departure to take effect upon the day upon which the Royal Assent is given to the last Act of the Session in being.

To this Sir Almeric adds that Mr. Balfour accepted his view, 'pronouncing very firmly upon the folly of Ministers tying themselves up with conditional formulæ in matters where practice was merely dictated by convenience'; and that the King himself emphatically agreed,

so that all difficulty disappears, and the King's Speech will be approved on despatch to Balmoral in a box, without the preliminary of a Council: a step which years ago Queen Victoria denounced as 'revolutionary'.

Perhaps Queen Victoria was right, after all, when she described the step as 'revolutionary', but probably even she did not fully understand what it was that was to be buried, unceremoniously, in a red dispatch-box.

9

KING GEORGE III:
A STUDY OF PERSONALITY

THERE were three large pictures of George III at the exhibition of Royal Portraits arranged by the Academy of Arts in the spring of 1953. Looking at the first, by Reynolds, painted when the King was 41, I was struck by the immaturity of expression. The second, by Lawrence, painted in 1792 at the age of 54, depicts him in Garter robes; face and posture seem to attempt in a naive, ineffective, and almost engaging manner to live up to a grandeur which the sitter feels incumbent on him. The third, by Stroehling, painted in November 1807 at the age of nearly 70, shows a sad old man, looking dimly at a world in which he has no pleasure, and which he soon will not be able to see or comprehend.

A picture in a different medium of the King and his story presents itself to the student when in the Royal Archives at Windsor he surveys the papers of George III. They stand on the shelves in boxes, each marked on a white label with the year or years which it covers. The eye runs over that array, and crucial dates recall events: 1760, '65 and '67, '74 and '75, '82 and '83, 1789, '93, '96, 1802, 1805—the series breaks off in 1810; and brown-backed volumes follow, unlabelled: they contain the medical reports on a man shut off from time, which means the world and its life.

Fate had made George III ruler when kings were still expected to govern; and his active reign covered half a century during which the American conflict posed the problem of Imperial relations, while at home political practice constantly ran up against the contradiction inherent in the then much belauded 'mixed form of government': personal monarchy served by Ministers whose tenure of office was contested in Parliament. Neither the Imperial nor the constitutional problem could have been solved in the terms in which the overwhelming majority of the politically minded public in this country considered them at the time; but George III has been blamed ever since for not having thought of Dominion status and parliamentary government when ✓ constitutional theory and the facts of the situation as yet admitted of neither.

In the catalogue, *Kings and Queens*, on sale at the exhibition, the introduction dealing with the reign of George III gave the traditional view of his reign:

> Conscientious and ambitious, he tried to restore the political influence of the Crown, but his intervention ended with the humiliating American War of Independence.

Conscientious he certainly was, painstakingly, almost painfully, conscientious. But was he ambitious? Did he try to exercise powers which his predecessors had relinquished, or claim an influence which was not universally conceded to him? And was it the assertion of Royal, and not of Parliamentary, authority over America which brought on the conflict and disrupted the First British Empire?

Let us place ourselves in March 1782. Dismal, humiliating failure has turned public opinion, and the House of Commons is resolved to cut losses and abandon the struggle; it is all over; Lord North's government has fallen; and the King is contemplating abdication. He has drafted a message to Parliament (which was never sent); here are its first two paragraphs:

> His Majesty during the twenty-one years he has sate on the throne of Great Britain, has had no object so much at heart as the maintenance of the British Constitution, of which the difficulties he has at times met with from his scrupulous attachment to the rights of Parliament are sufficient proofs.

> His Majesty is convinced that the sudden change of sentiments of one branch of the legislature has totally incapacitated him from either conducting the war with effect, or from obtaining any peace but on conditions which would prove destructive to the commerce as well as essential rights of the British nation.[1]

In the first paragraph the King declares his unswerving devotion to the British Constitution, and shows himself conscious of his difficulties in America having arisen through 'his scrupulous attachment to the rights of Parliament'; the second paragraph pointedly refers to the Commons as 'one branch of the legislature', and gives the King's view of the American war; he is defend-

---

[1] Fortescue, op. cit., vol. v, No. 3061.

ing there the vital interests and essential rights of the British nation.

A year later, in March 1783, when faced by the necessity of accepting a Government formed by the Fox-North coalition, George III once more contemplated abdication; and in a letter (which again was never sent) he wrote to the Prince of Wales:

> The situation of the times are such that I must, if I attempt to carry on the business of the nation, give up every political principle on which I have acted, which I should think very unjustifiable, as I have always attempted to act agreeable to my duty; and must form a Ministry from among men who know I cannot trust them and therefore who will not accept office without making me a kind of slave; this undoubtedly is a cruel dilemma, and leaves me but one step to take without the destruction of my principles and honour; the resigning my Crown, my dear Son to you, quitting this my native country for ever and returning to the dominions of my fore-fathers.
>
> Your difficulties will not be the same. You have never been in a situation to form any political system, therefore, are open to addopt what the times may make necessary; and no set of men can ever have offended you or made it impossible for you to employ them.[1]

Alongside this consider the following passage from a letter which George III wrote on 26 December 1783, after having dismissed the Coalition and while he was trying to rally support for the newly formed Administration of the younger Pitt:

> The times are of the most serious nature, the political struggle is not as formerly between two factions for power; but it is no less than whether a desperate faction shall not reduce the Sovereign to a mere tool in its hands: though I have too much principle ever to infringe the rights of others, yet that must ever equaly prevent my submitting to the Executive power being in any other hands, than where the Constitution has placed it. I therefore must call on the assistance of every honest man . . . to support Government on the present most critical occasion.[2]

Note in these two passages the King's honest conviction that he has always attempted to do his duty; that he has been mindful not to infringe the rights of others; but that it would be equally wrong in him to submit 'to the Executive power being in any other hands, than where the Constitution has placed it'. And while I do not for a moment suggest that these things could not

[1] Windsor MSS.   [2] Windsor MS. 5709.

have been done in a happier manner, I contend that the King's statements quoted above are substantially correct.

In the eighteenth century, a proper balance between King, Lords, and Commons, that is, the monarchical, aristocratic, and representative elements of the Constitution acting as checks on each other, was supposed to safeguard the property and privileges, the lives and liberty of the subjects. Single-Chamber government would have been no less abhorrent to the century than Royal autocracy. The Executive was the King's as truly as it is now of the President in the United States; he, too, had to choose his Ministers: but from among Parliamentary leaders. And while aspirants to office swore by the 'independency' of the Crown and disclaimed all wish to force themselves on the King, if left out they did their level best to embarrass and upset their successful rivals. The technique of Parliamentary opposition was fully established long before its most essential aim, which is to force a change of government, was recognized as legitimate; and because that aim could not be avowed in its innocent purity, deadly dangers threatening the Constitution, nay the life of the country, had to be alleged for justification. Robert Walpole as 'sole Minister' was accused of arrogating to himself the powers of both King and Parliament; the very tame Pelhams of keeping George II 'in fetters'; Bute, who bore the name of Stuart, of 'raising the standard of Royal prerogative'; and George III of ruling not through the Ministers of his own choice whom he avowed in public, but through a hidden gang of obscure and sinister 'King's friends'. It is obviously impossible here to trace the origin and growth of that story, or to disprove it by establishing the true facts of the transactions to which it has become attached—it was a figment so beautifully elaborated by Burke's fertile imagination that the Rockinghams themselves finished by believing it, and it grew into an obsession with them. In reality the constitutional practice of George III differed little from that of George I and George II. William Wyndham was proscribed by the first two Georges as a dangerous Jacobite, and C. J. Fox by the third as a dangerous Jacobin; while the elder Pitt was long kept out by both George II and George III on personal grounds. But for some the Royal veto and Royal influence in politics lose their sting if exercised in favour of successful monopolists in Whiggery.

I go one step further: in the eighteenth century the King had to intervene in politics and was bound to exercise his political influence, for the party system, which is the basis of Parliamentary government, did not exist.[1] Of the House of Commons itself probably less than half thought and acted in party terms. About one-third of the House consisted of Members who looked to the King for guidance and for permanency of employment: epigoni of earlier Courts or forerunners of the modern Civil Service; and if they thus pursued their own interest, there is no reason to treat them as more corrupt than if they had done so by attaching themselves to a group of politicians. Another one-fifth of the House consisted of independent country gentlemen, ready to support the King's Government so long as this was compatible with their conscience, but averse to tying themselves up with political groups: they did not desire office, honours, or profits, but prided themselves on the disinterested and independent line they were pursuing; and they rightly claimed to be the authentic voice of the nation. In the centre of the arena stood the politicians, their orators and leaders fighting for the highest prizes of Parliamentary life. They alone could supply the façade of governments: the front benches in Parliament. But to achieve stability a Government required the active support of the Crown and the good opinion of the country. On matters about which public opinion felt strongly, its will would prevail; but with the House constituted as it was, with the electoral structure of the unreformed Parliament, and an electorate which neither thought nor voted on party lines, it is idle to assume that modern Parliamentary government was possible.

I pass to the next point: was George III correct in saying that it was 'his scrupulous attachment to the rights of Parliament' which caused him the difficulties in America? Undoubtedly yes. It was not Royal claims that the Americans objected to, but the claims of 'subjects in one part of the King's dominions to be sovereigns over their fellow-subjects in another part of his dominions'.[2] 'The sovereignty of the Crown I understand,' wrote Benjamin Franklin; 'the sovereignty of Britain I do not understand. . . . We have the same King, but not the same legislature.' Had George III aspired to independent Royal Power nothing could have suited him better than to be Sovereign in America, the West Indies, and possibly in Ireland, independent of the British Parliament; and the foremost champions of the rights of Parliament, recalling the way in which the Stuarts had played off Ireland and Scotland against England, would have

---

[1] For a fuller discussion of this point see below, pp. 220–29.
[2] Benjamin Franklin to the Rev. Samuel Cooper of Boston, 8 June 1770.

been the first to protest. But in fact it would be difficult to imagine a King simultaneously exercising in several independent countries executive powers in conjunction with Parliamentary leaders. It will suffice to remember the difficulties and jealousies which Hanover caused although itself politically inert. The two problems which George III is unjustly accused of having mismanaged, those of Imperial and constitutional relations, were inter-connected: only after responsible government had arisen did Dominion status within the Commonwealth become possible. Lastly, of the measures which brought on the American conflict none was of the King's making: neither George Grenville's Stamp Act, nor the Declaratory Act of the Rockinghams, nor the Townshend Duties. All that can be said against him is that once the struggle had started, he, completely identifying himself with this country, obstinately persevered in it. He wrote on 14 November 1778:

> If Lord North can see with the same degree of enthusiasm I do the beauty, excellence, and perfection of the British Constitution, as by law established, and consider that if any one branch of the Empire is alowed to cast off its dependency, that the others will infalably follow the example . . . he . . . will resolve with vigour to meet every obstacle . . . or the State will be ruined.[1]

And again on 11 June 1779, expecting that the West Indies and Ireland would follow:

> Then this island would be reduced to itself, and soon would be a poor island indeed.[2]

On 7 March 1780:

> I can never suppose this country so far lost to all ideas of self importance as to be willing to grant America independence, if that could ever be universally adopted, I shall despair of this country being ever preserved from a state of inferiority and consequently falling into a very low class among the European States. . . .[3]

And on 26 September 1780:

> . . . giving up the game would be total ruin, a small State may certainly subsist, but a great one mouldering cannot get into an inferior situation but must be annihilated.[4]

When all was over, Lord North wrote to the King on 18 March 1782:

[1] Fortescue vol iv, No. 2451.   [2] Ibid., No. 2649.
[3] Fortescue vol v, No. 2963.   [4] Ibid., No. 3155.

F

Your Majesty is well apprized that, in this country, the Prince on the Throne, cannot, with prudence, oppose the deliberate resolution of the House of Commons . . . Your Majesty has graciously and steadily supported the servants you approve, as long as they could be supported: Your Majesty has firmly and resolutely maintained what appeared to you essential to the welfare and dignity of this country, as long as this country itself thought proper to maintain it. The Parliament have altered their sentiments, and as their sentiments whether just or erroneous, must ultimately prevail, Your Majesty . . . can lose no honour if you yield at length . . .

Your Majesty's goodness encourages me . . . to submit whether it will not be for Your Majesty's welfare, and even glory, to sacrifice, at this moment, former opinions, displeasures and apprehensions (though never so well-founded) to . . . the public safety.[1]

The King replied:

I could not but be hurt at your letter of last night. Every man must be the sole judge of his feelings, therefore whatever you or any man can say on that subject has no avail with me.[2]

What George III had never learnt was to give in with grace: but this was at the most a defect of character.

2

Lord Waldegrave, who had been Governor to the Prince of Wales 1752–6, wrote in 1758 a character sketch of him so penetrating and just that it deserves quoting almost in full.[3]

The Prince of Wales is entering into his 21st year, and it would be unfair to decide upon his character in the early stages of life, when there is so much time for improvement.

A wise preamble; yet a long and eventful life was to change him very little. Every feature singled out by Waldegrave finds copious illustration in the fifty years that followed (in one case in a superficially inverted form).

His parts, though not excellent, will be found very tolerable, if ever they are properly exercised.

He is strictly honest, but wants that frank and open behaviour which makes honesty appear amiable. . . .

---

[1] Ibid., No. 3566.   [2] Ibid., No. 3567.
[3] James, 2nd Earl Waldegrave, *Memoirs* (1821), pp. 8–10.

His religion is free from all hypocrisy, but is not of the most charitable sort; he has rather too much attention to the sins of his neighbour.

He has spirit, but not of the active kind; and does not want resolution, but it is mixed with too much obstinacy.

He has great command of his passions, and will seldom do wrong, except when he mistakes wrong for right; but as often as this shall happen, it will be difficult to undeceive him, because he is uncommonly indolent, and has strong prejudices.

His want of application and aversion to business would be far less dangerous, was he eager in the pursuit of pleasure; for the transition from pleasure to business is both shorter and easier than from a state of total inaction.

He has a kind of unhappiness in his temper, which, if it be not conquered before it has taken too deep a root, will be a source of frequent anxiety. Whenever he is displeased, his anger does not break out with heat and violence; but he becomes sullen and silent, and retires to his closet; not to compose his mind by study or contemplation, but merely to indulge the melancholy enjoyment of his own ill humour. Even when the fit is ended, unfavourable symptoms very frequently return, which indicate that on certain occasions his Royal Highness has too correct a memory.

Waldegrave's own endeavour was to give the Prince 'true notions of common things'.[1] But these he never acquired: which is perhaps the deepest cause of his tragedy.

The defect Waldegrave dwells upon most is the Prince's 'uncommon indolence', his 'want of application and aversion to business'. This is borne out by other evidence, best of all by the Prince's own letters to Bute:[2]

July 1st, 1756: I will throw off that indolence which if I don't soon get the better of will be my ruin.
March 25th, 1757: I am conscious of my own indolence . . . I do here in the most solemn manner declare, that I will throw aside this my greatest enemy. . . .
September 25th, 1758: . . . . that incomprehensible indolence, inattention and heedlessness that reigns within me . . .

And he says of his good resolutions: 'as many as I have made I have regularly broke'; but adds a new one: 'I mean to attempt to regain the many years I have fruitlessly spent.'

December 19th, 1758: . . . through the negligence, if not the wickedness of those around me in my earlier days, and since perhaps

---

[1] Ibid., p. 64
[2] See *Letters from George III to Lord Bute* (1939), edited by Romney Sedgwick.

> through my own indolence of temper, I have not that degree of
> knowledge and experience in business, one of my age might reason-
> ably have aqcuir'd . . .
> *March* 1760: . . . my natural indolence . . . has been encreas'd by
> a kind of indifference to the world, owing to the number of bad
> characters I daily see. . . .

By shifting the blame on to others, he tries to relieve the bitter
consciousness of failure: which is one source of that excessive
'attention to the sins of his neighbour' mentioned by Waldegrave.
Indeed, George III's letters, both before and after his accession,
are full of it: 'the great depravity of the age', 'the wickedest age
that ever was seen', 'a degenerate age', 'probity and every other
virtue absorb'd into vice, and dissipation'; etc. 'An ungrateful,
wicked people' and individual statesmen alike receive castigation
(*in absentia*) from this very young Old Testament prophet. Pitt
'is the blackest of hearts', 'the most dishonourable of men', and
plays 'an infamous and ungrateful part'; Lord Temple, an
'ungrateful arrogant and self-sufficient man'; Charles Townshend is 'a man void of every quality', 'the worst man that lives',
'vermin'; Henry Fox, a man of 'bad character', 'void of principles'; Lord Mansfield is 'but half a man'; the Duke of Bedford's
character 'contains nothing but passion and absurdity'; etc. As
for George II, the Prince felt ashamed of being his grandson.
And on 23 April 1760, half a year before his accession, aged
twenty-two he wrote to Bute: '. . . as to honesty, I have already
lived long enough to know you are the only man who possesses
that quality . . .'

In Bute he thought he had found the tutelary spirit who would
enable him to live up to his future high vocation. Here are further
excerpts from the Prince's letters to him:

> *July* 1*st*, 1756: My friend is . . . attack'd in the most cruel and
> horrid manner . . . because he is my friend . . . and because he is
> a friend to the bless'd liberties of his country and not to arbitary
> notions . . .
> By . . . your friendship . . . I have reap'd great advantage, but
> not the improvement I should if I had follow'd your advice . . .
> I will exactly follow your advice, without which I shall inevitably
> sink.
> *March* 25*th*, 1757: I am resolved . . . to act the man in everything,
> to repeat whatever I am to say with spirit and not blushing and
> afraid as I have hitherto . . . my conduct shall convince you that
> I am mortified at what I have done and that I despise myself . . . I

hope this will persuade you not to leave me when all is at stake, when nobody but you can stear me through this difficult, though glorious path.

In June 1757 Leicester House were alarmed by rumours of an alliance between the Duke of Newcastle and Henry Fox, and were ascribing fantastic schemes to the Duke of Cumberland. The Prince already saw himself compelled to meet force by force or to 'yield up the Crown',

> for I would only accept it with the hopes of restoring my much beloved country to her antient state of liberty; of seeing her . . . again famous for being the residence of true piety and virtue, I say if these hopes were lost, I should with an eye of pleasure look on retiring to some uninhabited cavern as this would prevent me from seeing the sufferings of my countrymen, and the total destruction of this Monarchy . . .
>
> *August 20th*, 1758: . . . by . . . attempting with vigour to restore religion and virtue when I mount the throne this great country will probably regain her antient state of lustre.

Was this a Prince nurtured in 'arbitrary notions', ambitious to make his own will prevail? or a man with a 'mission', striving after naively visionary aims? No doubt, since early childhood it must have been rammed into him, especially when he was being reproved, to what high station he was born; and disparaging comparisons are said to have been drawn between him and his younger brother. He grew up with a painful consciousness of his inadequacy: 'though I act wrong perhaps in most things', he wrote on one occasion. Excessive demands on a child, complete with wholesome exhortations, are fit to reduce it to a state of hebetude from which it is not easy to recover. A great deal of the pattern of George III's behaviour throughout life can be traced back to his upbringing.

He spent his young years cut off from intercourse with boys of his own age, till he himself ceased to desire it. Bubb Dodington notes in his *Diary* on 15 October 1752 that the Princess Dowager of Wales

> did not observe the Prince to take very particularly to anybody about him, but to his brother Edward, and she was glad of it, for the young people of quality were so ill-educated and so vicious, that they frightened her.

And so they did him for the rest of his life. Isolation by itself would be apt to suggest to a child that there was something wrong with those he had to shun; but this he was probably told in so many words. On 18 December 1753, Dodington records another talk with the Princess:

> I said, it was to be wished he could have more company. She seemed averse to the young people, from the excessive bad education they had, and from the bad examples they gave.

So the boy spent joyless years in a well-regulated nursery, the nearest approach to a concentration camp: lonely but never alone, constantly watched and discussed, never safe from the wisdom and goodness of the grown-ups; never with anyone on terms of equality, exalted yet oppressed by deferential adults. The silent, sullen anger noted by Waldegrave was natural to one who could not hit back or speak freely his mind, as a child would among children: he could merely retire, and nurture his griefs and grievances—and this again he continued through life. On 3 May 1766, during a political crisis, he wrote to Bute: 'I can neither eat nor sleep, nothing pleases me but musing on my cruel situation.' Nor could he, always with adults, develop self-reliance: at nineteen he dreamt of reforming the nation, but his idea of acting the man was to repeat without blushing or fear what he had to say.

For the pious works which were 'to make this great nation happy' Bute's 'sagacious councils' were therefore indispensable. When in December 1758 Bute expressed doubts whether he should take office in the future reign, the Prince in a panic searched his own conscience:

> Perhaps it is the fear you have I shall not speak firmly enough to my Ministers, or that I shall be stagger'd if they say anything unexpected; as to the former I can with great certainty assure that they, nor no one else shall see a want of steadiness either in my manner of acting or speaking, and as to the latter, I may give fifty sort of puts off, till I have with you thoroughly consider'd what part will be proper to be taken. . . .

George III adhered to this programme. On his grandfather's death he waited to hear from Bute what 'must be done'. When expecting Pitt at a critical juncture: 'I would wish to know what I had best say. . . .' With regard to measures or appointments: 'I have put that off till I hear my Dear Friend's opinion'; 'If this [is] agreeable to my D. Friend I will order it to day . . .'; 'I desire my D. Friend to consider what I have here wrote, if he is of a contrary opinion, I will with pleasure embrace it.' And when in

November 1762 Bute declared he would retire on conclusion of peace:

> I had flattered myself [wrote the King] when peace was once established that my D. Friend would have assisted me in purging out corruption . . .; . . . now . . . the Ministry remains compos'd of the most abandon'd men that ever had those offices; thus instead of reformation the Ministers being vicious this country will grow if possible worse; let me attack the irreligious, the covetous &c. as much as I please, that will be of no effect . . . Ministers being of that stamp . . .

Two years on the throne had worked little if any change in his ideas and language; nor did the next twenty. The same high claims on himself, and the same incapacity to meet real situations he was faced with: hence his continued dependence on others. By 1765 he saw that Bute could not help him, by the summer of 1766 he had written off Bute altogether. In the spring of 1765 he turned to the Duke of Cumberland, the bugbear of his young years: 'Dear Uncle, the very friendly and warm part you have taken has given me real satisfaction. . . .'[1] And to Pitt, 'the blackest of hearts': 'My friend for so the part you have acted deserves of me. . . .'[2] In July 1765 Cumberland formed for him the Rockingham Administration and presided over it a quasi-Viceroy; but a few months later Cumberland was dead. In July 1766 Chatham formed his Administration; but a few months later his health broke down completely. Still George III clung to him like a molusc (a molusc who never found his rock). 'Under a health so broken', wrote Chatham, 'as renders at present application of mind totally impossible . . .'[3] After nearly two years of waiting for his recovery, the King still wrote: 'I think I have a right to insist on your remaining in my service.'[4] Next he clung to the ineffective Grafton who longed to be relieved of office; and when Grafton resigned, the King wrote to him on 27 January 1770:

> My heart is so full at the thought of your retiring from your situation that I think it best not to say more as I know the expressing it would give you pain.[5]

Then came North. Totally unequal to the difficulties of the American crisis, in letter after letter he begged the King to let him resign. Thus in March 1778:

[1] Fortescue vol. i, No. 74.   [2] Ibid., No. 94.
[3] Ibid., No. 538.   [4] Fortescue vol. ii, No. 669.   [5] Grafton MSS.

Lord North cannot conceive what can induce His Majesty, after so many proofs of Lord North's unfitness for his situation to determine at all events to keep him at the head of the Administration, though the almost certain consequences of His Majesty's resolution will be the ruin of his affairs, and though it can not ward off for a month that arrangement which His Majesty seems to apprehend.[1]

But the King would not hear of it. 2 July, 1779: 'no man has a right to talk of leaving me at this hour. . . .'[2] 25 October, 1780: he expects North 'will show that zeal for which he has been conspicuous from the hour of the Duke of Grafton's desertion.[3]

George III's attitude to North conformed to the regular pattern of his behaviour. So did also the way in which after a while he turned against North in bitter disappointment. By the '70s the King spoke disparagingly of Bute and Chatham; and in time his imagination enabled him to remember how on the day of his accession he had given the slip to them both. A month after Grafton had resigned, George III wrote to him: 'I . . . see anew that the sincere regard and friendship I have for you is properly placed. . . .'[4] Somewhat later his resignation changed into 'desertion'. When North resigned: 'I ever did and ever shall look on you as a friend as well as a faithful servant. . . .'[5] But incensed at the new situation he soon started attacking North, and treated him niggardly and unfairly over his secret-service accounts. George III's attachment was never deep: it was that of a drunken man to railings—mechanical rather than emotional. Egocentric and rigid, stunted in feelings, unable to adjust himself to events, flustered by sudden change, he could meet situations only in a negative manner, clinging to men and measures with disastrous obstinacy. But he himself mistook that defensive apparatus for courage, drive, and vigour, from which it was as far removed as anything could be. Of his own mental processes he sometimes gave discerning though embellished accounts. Thus to Bute in 1762: 'I . . . am apt to despise what I am not accustom'd to. . . .' And on 2 March 1797, to the younger Pitt when criticizing the way measures were weakened in passing through Parliament:

> My nature is quite different I never assent till I am convinced what is proposed is right, and then . . . I never allow that to be destroyed by after-thoughts which on all subjects tend to weaken never to strengthen the original proposal.[6]

[1] Fortescue vol. iv, No. 2241. [2] Ibid., No. 2696.
[3] Fortescue vol. v, No. 3165. [4] 2 March 1770, Grafton MSS.
[5] Fortescue vol. v, No. 3593. [6] Windsor MSS.

In short: no after-thoughts, no reconsideration—only desperate, clinging perseverance.

Still it might be said: at least he broke through his indolence. Yes, indeed: from pathologically indolent he turned pathologically industrious—and never again could let off working; but there was little sense of values, no perspective, no detachment. There is a legend about a homunculus whose maker, not knowing what to do with him, bid him count poppy-seed in a bag. That George III was doing with his own busy self. His innumerable letters which he copied in his own hand, or the long documents transcribed by him (he never employed an amanuensis till his eyesight began to fail) contain some shrewd perceptions or remarks, evidence of 'very tolerable parts if . . . properly exercised'. But most of his letters merely repeat approvingly what some Minister, big or small, has suggested. 'Lord A. is very right . . .'; 'General B. has acted very properly . . .'; 'the minute of Cabinet meets with my fullest concurrence . . .'; 'Nothing can more deserve my approbation than'—whatever it was. But if a basic change is suggested, his obstinacy and prejudices appear. On 15 March 1778, in a letter to Lord North, he makes an unusual and startling admission:

> I will only add to put before your eyes my most inmost thoughts, that no advantage to this country nor personal danger can ever make me address myself for assistance either to Lord Chatham or any other branch of the Opposition. . . .[1]

As a rule he would sincerely assert, perhaps with somewhat excessive ostentation, that first and foremost he considered the good of the country. When told by Bute that it would be improper for him to marry Lady Sarah Lennox, he replied: 'the interest of my country ever shall be my first care, my own inclinations shall ever submit to it' (and he added: 'I should wish we could next summer . . . get some account of the various Princesses in Germany'—and he settled down to 'looking in the New Berlin Almanack for Princesses'). When considering withdrawal from the German war, he wrote (with a sidelong glance at the late King) about the superiority of his love 'to this my native country over any private interest of my own. . . .' He was 'a King of a free people'; 'I rely on the hearts of my subjects, the only true support of the Crown', he wrote in November 1760. They will not desert him—

---

[1] Fortescue vol. iv, No. 2221.

if they could be so ungrateful to me who love them beyond anything else in life, I should then I realy believe fall into the deepest
melancholy which would soon deprive me of the vexations of this
life.

The same note, of love for this country and trust that his subjects would therefore stand by him, continues for almost twenty
years. But gradually other overtones begin to mix with it. He had
become the target of virulent attacks and unjust suspicions which
he deeply resented. Thus to Lord North on 7 March 1780:
'. . . however I am treated I must love this country'.[1] And to the
Prince of Wales on 14 August 1780:

> The numberless trials and constant torments I meet with in
> public life, must certainly affect any man, and more poignantly
> me, as I have no other wish but to fulfill my various duties; the
> experience of now twenty years has convinced me that however
> long it may please the Almighty to extend my days, yet I have no
> reason to expect any diminution of my public anxiety; where am
> I therefore to turn for comfort, but into the bosom of my own
> family?[2]

And he appealed to his son, the future George IV, to connect himself only with young men of respectable character, and by his
example help 'to restore this country to its former lustre'—the
old tune once more. And in another letter:

> From your childhood I have ever said that I can only try to save
> my country, but it must be by the co-operation of my children only
> that I can effect it.[3]

In the 1780s there is a more than usually heavy crop of bitter
complaints about the age by one 'righteous overmuch':' it has
been my lot to reign in the most profligate age', 'depravity of
such times as we live in', 'knavery and indolence perhaps I might
add the timidity of the times. . . .' And then:

> I thank Heaven my morals and course of life have but little
> resembled those too prevalent in the present age, and certainly of
> all objects in this life the one I have most at heart, is to form my
> children that they may be useful examples and worthy of imita-
> tion . . .[4]

With the King's disappointments in country and son another note
enters his letters. He warns the Prince—

[1] Fortescue vol. v, No. 2963.   [2] Windsor MSS.
[3] Ibid.   [4] Ibid.

in other countries national pride makes the inhabitants wish to paint their Princes in the most favourable light, and consequently be silent on any indiscretion; but here most persons if not concerned in laying ungrounded blame, are ready to trumpet any speck they can find out.[1]

And he writes of the 'unalterable attachment' which his Electoral subjects have shown to their Princes. When George III went mad in 1788, he wanted to go back to Hanover. Deep down there was a good deal of the Hanoverian in him.

His insanity was a form of manic-depression. The first recorded fit in March 1765 was of short duration, though there may have been a slight relapse in May; and a year later he wrote to Bute—

if I am to continue the life of agitation I have these three years, the next year there will be a Council [of] Regency to assist in that undertaking.

During the next twenty-three years he preserved his normal personality. The attack in 1788 lasted about half a year: the King was over fifty, and age rendered complete recovery more difficult. His self-control weakened and his irritability increased. He was conscious of a growing weakness. Yet there was something about him which more and more endeared him to the people. He was never popular with London society or the London mob; he was much beloved in the provinces—perhaps it was his deeper kindness, his real piety, and sincere wish to do good which evoked those feelings. These appear strikingly, for instance, in his own account of his journey to Portsmouth in 1788,[2] and in Fanny Burney's account of his progress through Wiltshire in 1789.[3] He was not a politician, and certainly not a statesman. But in things which he could judge without passion or preconceived ideas, there appears basic honesty and the will to do the right thing. I shall limit myself to two examples. When in 1781 a new Provost was to be appointed at Eton, George III insisted on choosing a man 'whose literary tallents might make the appointment respectable . . . for Eton should not be bestowed by favour, but merit'.[4] And when in 1787 a new Lord Lieutenant had to be chosen for Ireland, the King wrote to the younger Pitt about the necessity

of looking out for the person most likely to conduct himself with temper, judgement, and an avowed resolution to avoid partiality

[1] Ibid.   [2] Windsor MSS.
[3] Fanny Burney, *Diary* (1905), vol. iv, pp. 310–11.
[4] Fortescue vol. v, No. 3455.

and employ the favours he has to recommend to with the justice due to my service and to the public. . . . When I have stated this Mr. Pitt must understand that I do not lean to any particular person . . . when I state that a Lord Lieutenant should have no predelection but to advance the public good I should be ashamed to act in a contrary manner.[1]

I have given here a picture of George III as seen in his letters, 'warts and all'. What I have never been able to find is the man arrogating power to himself, the ambitious schemer out to dominate, the intriguer dealing in an underhand fashion with his Ministers; in short, any evidence for the stories circulated about him by very clever and eloquent contemporaries. He had a high, indeed an exaggerated, notion of royalty but in terms of mission and duties rather than of power; and trying to live up to this idealized concept, he made unreasonable demands on himself. Setting himself unattainable standards, he could never truly come to grips with reality: which condemned him to remain immature, permanency of inner conflict precluding growth. Aware of his inadequacy, he turned to others and expected them to enable him to realize his visionary program (this appears clearest in his relations with Bute); and he bitterly reproached them in his own mind, and blamed the age in which he lived, for his own inevitable failure. The tension between his notions and reality, and the resulting frustration, account to a high degree for his irritability, his deep-seated resentments, and his suppressed anger —for situations intolerable and disastrous for himself and others; and it may have been a contributory factor in his mental breakdowns. The desire to escape from that unbearable conflict repeatedly shows itself in thoughts of abdication which must not be deemed insincere because never acted upon (men of his type cannot renounce their treadmill). He himself did not understand the nature and depth of his tragedy; still less could others. There was therefore room for the growth of an injurious legend which made that heavy-burdened man a much maligned ruler; and which has long been accepted as history.

[1] Windsor MSS.

10

GEORGE III SPEAKS OUT

WHEN I once explained to a friend my idea of how biographies should be written—'Oh, I see,' he remarked, 'you would call in Scotland Yard and the Royal College of Physicians.' In the case of George III, undoubtedly some assistance from the College is required, and as for *The Diaries of Robert Fulke Greville*,[1] an expert review by a Fellow specializing in mental diseases might have been most appropriate, for the greater part of the book— and the only one which is of any importance, interest, or value— consists of day-by-day accounts of the King's acute fit of madness, October 1788–March 1789.

George III had never been sweet-tempered or well-balanced or taciturn. But in October 1788 he became 'more peevish than he used to be,' and 'now talked much more than usual, and spoke to everybody on strange varieties of subjects':

> His incessant talking became at last so remarkable, that it was thought necessary to recommend H.M. to be a little more silent; his physician, Sir George Baker, accordingly hinted to him that it was essential to his health to be less frequent and earnest in his conversations.

During the next days the 'incoherence in thought and expressions increased'. Occasionally he tried himself to check his incessant talk; thus Greville writes on 15 November 1788:

> In the evening, sensible (without prompting) that he was talking very fast, he altered and spoke in the third person—'The King did so—The King thinks so', etc. This correction he thus explained: 'I speak in the third person, as I am getting into Mr. Burke's eloquence, saying too much on little things.'

But even such insight was of little avail; Greville notes on 19 November—to quote but one example—that 'H. My. had talked for nineteen hours without scarce any intermission'.

[1] *The Diaries of Colonel the Hon. Robert Fulke Greville, Equerry to H.M. King George III,* ed. by F. McKno Bladon.

At first Greville avoids mentioning the contents of those rambling talks, and merely hints that there were subjects 'which, had he been well, he probably would have concealed' (20 November); and that 'every now and then' the King was 'talking much unlike himself, I mean indecently, which never was his practice while in possession of his reason' (23 November). But finally Greville recognized his duty as a diarist:

> It is painful to mark such details, but the real state of His Majesty's mind, from time to time, is an object of so much interest and importance, that the progressive circumstances connected with it cannot be withheld in fair narration, where continued memorandums refer to daily occurrences.

Things repressed by George III in his youth were coming up' or, to put it in Greville's words, 'his clouded judgment now was running riot against that which nature had blessed him with in his unembarrassed days'. He had renounced the women he had loved, had married one chosen from the Gotha Almanack, and had been faithful to her all these years. Now, in his ramblings, he declared that he did not love her and 'that he preferred another'. He talked continually about Lady Pembroke, calling her sometimes 'Queen Esther'; wished to go to see her; and inscribed declarations of his love for her on playing-cards formally addressed to his doctors. On one occasion he asked Greville to go to the library

> and look for Paley's Philosophy, in which he told me I should find that tho' the law said that man might have but one wife, yet, that Nature allowed more.

Even when he was well on the way to recovery, he would still refer to the subject of Lady Pembroke, though in a more restrained manner. After a visit from the Lord Chancellor Thurlow on 22 February, Greville heard

> that H. My. told the Chancellor that he had had an attachment thirty years ago, and that on this the Chancellor had advised him to drop such ideas at fifty.

George III in his youth had talked of Hanover as 'that horrid Electorate', and professed to loathe it—because it was the home of his hated grandfather; he 'gloried in the name of Britain'. During his illness he continually talked of 'retiring to Hanover', declared that 'he would leave the country, and then in great joy exclaimed "Victoria, Victoria"'; though on one occasion, when he heard of the difficulties which the French had in Martinique, he rejoiced and 'then animatedly added that he was become an Englishman again'. The idea of returning to Hanover—for George III's English attendants a most unmistakable symptom of madness— similarly persisted well into his recovery.

In short, mixed up with madness was a reversion to type. At a time when the strait waistcoat was frequently applied to the King, he declared to one of his doctors that 'the late King of Spain was mad, but yet that he had his State around him, and that no King but the King of England could be confined in a strait waiscoat'. How truly Hanoverian!

The stories of the strait waistcoat in Greville's *Diaries* are pathetic. The man who, even in his madness, declared that he was born to command, and not to obey, was constantly threatened, or restrained, with it:

> Dr. Willis . . . recommended him to be more calm, or that he would certainly talk himself into a strait waiscoat. (21 December.)
>
> During the disturbances of this morning the waiscoat was brought in and shown—but it was not put on. (18 January.)
>
> At one time he took his opportunity of complaining to Sir Lucas [Pepys] and me, of the situation of a King in a strait waiscoat (and he now not unfrequently wore a precautionary one under his coat) in a most affecting manner, and when Dr. Willis was out of the room he opened his waiscoat and shewed us the strait waiscoat taking down its long sleeves, and strings—
>
> After this melancholy display it was necessary to pull off his coat to set it to rights again—He stripped and never shall I forget the painful, and unpleasant sight—Heavens! What a spectacle to see the dear afflicted King standing in a strait waiscoat, and tucking up himself, the sleeves and strings, until they might be wanted! ! (2 January.)

Robert Fulke Greville was truly attached to his King: and that is the best that can be gleaned about him from his *Diaries*. He was Fanny Burney's 'Colonel Well-bred', and this, too, is a quality with which he can be readily credited; temperament, critical thinking, and a sense of humour tend occasionally to interfere with the results of good breeding, but his mind and character seem to have been fully innocent of any such disturbing qualities. It would be difficult to imagine anything more insipid and inane than the account which Greville gives of his own life at Court in 1781, when the American Revolution was reaching its climax. 'Ceremonies impressively attended to in all parts', rides in the country, their Majesties walking on the Terrace at Windsor, tea at the Lodge, evenings closing 'with the usual harmony of the King's band'—these things fill his time and mind. On one occasion he had 'the honour of handing the Princess Royal up one of the narrow staircases in the dark and landed her in safety, without one false step'; on another, the King at table 'took the best possible care of me, and among other things, recommended me to eat some beef steaks which he was then eating himself, and which he thought excellent'. His attendance as Equerry during that year formed 'the happiest month of my life'.

THE LETTERS OF GEORGE IV

In February 1812, after more than half a century, the reign of George III virtually reached its term. There was no hope for his recovery, and his son was sovereign in all but name. A new reign in a new age: but it started with the old expectation of a consequent change of Government. Once more the Opposition was to be disappointed: the Regent did not mean to dismiss the War Ministry. The letter announcing this decision opens with a statement of his constitutional position:

> Altho I consider myself as under no obligation to explain to any persons the reasons which may, at any time, induce me to arrange, as I think best, for the public service, the administration of the Government . . .

And it was necessarily in terms of the Regent's right freely to choose his Ministers that Whigs, who had expected office from his favour, formulated their reproaches:

> As the restrictions upon the exercise of the Royal authority by your Royal Highness have now ceased, from which you are enabled to form such an Administration as you conceive the best calculated for conducting the affairs of the Empire . . .

For the last one hundred years every group or party had 'upheld' the 'independency of the Crown', when exercised in their favour; and denounced similar expectations in others as 'attempts to storm the Closet'. 'I am convinced', wrote in 1812 the Duke of Northumberland, 'that H.R.H.'s . . . decisive character will frustrate every attempt which arrogance, ambition, or folly may make to take him prisoner and bind him in fetters.' In March 1827, Lushington, Secretary to the Treasury, when urging that Canning, rather than Wellington, should replace Liverpool at the head of the Government, wrote: 'The Crown has an unqualified choice, and the present posture of our affairs . . . illustrates

the wisdom of our forefathers, in leaving the appointment absolutely to the King'; while Canning inveighed against aristocratic
'confederacies' and declaimed about 'the real vigour of the Crown
when it chooses to put forth its own strength'.

The language and forms of politics had changed little since
1760. Only the 'extinction of parties', prayed for on every accession since parties had come to exist, no longer figures in the 1812
edition of the catalogue of cant: its place is taken by wishes for a
'union of parties.' These were now acknowledged as a basic element in British public life, and the real transition from Royal to
Parliamentary Government was preparing in the minds of men
and in the technique of politics. For it is the mechanism of coherent
and disciplined parties which has gradually deprived the Crown
of that power to choose its Ministers which in 1812 and 1760, no
less than in 1714 and 1727, was ascribed to it by theory and conceded by practice (with restrictions inherent in all practice).

An observer, revisiting England after fifty years in 1812, would
probably have been struck most by the growth of effective routine
in Government, of maturity and skill, a sureness of touch which
people still lacked in his day; and now it was needed, for there
was so much more to do. Everything had grown in size: the
population, the wars, the taxes, the Debt; Parliamentary sittings
were longer, though (Burke and Fox being dead) perhaps not
Parliamentary speeches. The Effective Cabinet had reached a
normal size of fourteen, about double that of, say, 1765. They
still wrote Minutes to the Sovereign and described themselves as
his 'confidential servants', though he called them already his
'Cabinet'. Within that body there was a growing cohesion, and
the consciousness of being the King's 'responsible advisers',
without whom he could not, and must not, act; George IV's
character added poignancy to this conviction and to the manner
in which it was occasionally expressed. The moral tone of the
Government and nation had risen since 1760, that of the King
and his family was lower in 1820.

Over a good deal of this correspondence[1] lies the stale reek of
reckless and even sordid transactions condensed into debts and
blackmail. The Regent continues overspending while Ministers
exhort him that 'most of the landed gentlemen of the country are
obliged to submit to losses and privations as well as to retrench-
ment' (March 1816). The Duke of York goes on with his 'un-
principled foolery', and George IV, when paying £50,000 of his

---

[1] *The Letters of King George IV: 1812–1830*, ed. by A. Aspinall. Three vols.

debts, writes to him on 3 December 1823: '. . . had I myself continued on the turf, etc., it might have been difficult, without great inconvenience to the country, for me to have fulfilled the high duties of my present station.' Other brothers, too, have debts, claims, or grievances. The Regent's daughter, Princess Charlotte, at the age of eighteen, owes 'no less a sum to different jewellers and dressmakers than £20,000 and upwards'; and letters and presents of hers have to be extracted from the hands of a shady (illegitimate) cousin. The Duke of Cumberland complains that in England 'every blackguard newspaper can at once ruin the character of a man'; but when he quarrels with his old mother, he swears 'by the Lord, HER letters shall be made public' (about which letters nothing was unseemly except their publication). The King is blackmailed by ex-mistresses, quondam friends, creditors, journalists, etc. And when his secretary leaves his service, ample provision is made for him in a prophylactic way, but he is pressed to accept a colonial or a diplomatic post, Ceylon or Sweden. At times George IV seems, to use his own words, 'almost distracted' by anxieties. Knighton writes to him on 12 February 1822:

> I trust that the Almighty will give you peace, and that your afflicted mind will cease to be tortured by the overwhelming inquietudes which have of late made such painful inroads on your health. . . .
> Do not let your mind, Sir, be tied down by fetters of apprehension; anticipate, I beseech you, no ill, for I will not believe that any is to happen us.

And George IV writes to Knighton about his worries on 30 December 1827 (most of it underlined):

> . . . to you, and to you alone, dear friend, it is that I can and that I do look therefore for my relief, as it is you and you alone who can and who I am sure will (from your real affection and attachment to me) entirely put an end to them, and by your powerful exertions and means, crush and put the extinguisher upon that host of vipers and hornets, which seems in particular at this moment, to have congregated itself together and purposely, to sting me personally. . . .

This is a mere fraction of a sentence, and a fair sample of his style; for sentences of 100–300 words, of the most drivelling kind, abound in his familiar, and especially in his jocular, letters.

Fortunately George IV's letters to his Ministers are mostly in a different style, having obviously been drafted by his secretaries;

how far their ideas were the King's own, it is of course impossible
to tell, though some sensible and some silly remarks clearly bear
his imprint. But the King's magnificent Memorandum written
on the formation of the Goderich Ministry, is in Knighton's hand
and is such as, in any age, a royal secretary or official would
delight to write to noble lords:

> The office [of Chancellor of the Exchequer] requires ability and
> not aristocracy . . .
> The King will have those that are proper for their business and
> if there be room after this—the Cabinet may if they please look out
> for ornaments.

Of the letters from the Ministers, those of Liverpool are precise
and formal; Canning's brilliant, incisive, at times even boisterous
—for instance, that about a peerage to be granted with remainder
to the second son, a proposal which at first had appeared 'strong'
to him:

> . . . but . . . as the eldest son is represented to be an idiot, and as it
> appears to Mr. Canning (after some recent exhibitions in the House
> of Lords) peculiarly desirable to avoid encreasing, among their
> Lordships, the number of specimens of irregular understanding,
> in another generation . . .

The relation of George IV to Canning and Canning's letters
to him suggest a curious human side in the King's nature; or
otherwise Canning would hardly have made, as he often did, an
unusual addition to the ordinary form of address: 'Mr. Canning
presents his humble and affectionate duty to your Majesty. . . .'
Good deeds performed by George IV are on record in this correspondence, which covers eighteen years; but even in these the
sincerity or depth of his feelings does not always appear in a
convincing manner. Sometimes it is compassion for fellow-sufferers
and fellow-sinners: 'I am quite aware of the trifling objection to
some of the fooleries of his past life, but who is exempt from some
nonsense or other?'

12

THE STUNTED GIANT

LORD CHESTERFIELD was the heir to a great political tradition; was a brilliant *raisonneur*, with a clear, incisive mind; had judgment and foresight; knew how to work, could speak, and could write; held two of the highest offices of State, and, when in Opposition, was one of its chief leaders; and mismanaged no task with which he was entrusted. He ought to have made a considerable figure in politics; and yet he proved, most undeniably, a failure. The letters to his son[1] are, to a high degree, the unconscious record of his unavowed disappointment, and the sequel to it; where he had failed, his son was to succeed; instead of a coronet he had the bar-sinister—yet he must succeed. What good had all the inherited advantages been to Chesterfield? Perhaps he thought he knew by now where he had failed, and why; in the person of his son he meant to try once more.

> I am going off the stage, you are coming upon it; with me, what has been, has been, and reflection now would come too late; with you everything is to come. . . . (12 October, 1748).
> His success in the world is now the only object I have in it. . . . (18 May, 1751).
> I hope, I wish, I doubt, and I fear alternately. . . . (February 16, 1748).

With an insistence which at times rises into frenzy, he presses the boy to carry out the task along the lines he has drawn—like a ghost trying to make a living man do something he himself had omitted to accomplish, and which alone, when done, can free him from his agony. Before long Chesterfield was to know that he had failed a second time.

What were the reasons of his own failure? He was too critical, too fastidious, too consciously intellectual, and, with all that,

---

[1] *The Letters of Philip Dormer Stanhope, Fourth Earl of Chesterfield,* ed. by Bonamy Dobrée.

shallow. He despised the thoughts, or 'errors', of the generality of men ('the ablest . . . are only comparatively able, with regard to the still weaker herd'), but set a high value on the human mind as such—on his own mind. He had neither creative passion nor unity of purpose, and therefore lacked single-mindedness; and while ready to pursue an interesting line of inquiry or argument, he easily tired of drudgery—'a half lazy man'. He was not a fighter, nor a master-builder, nor had he the personality of a leader; in fact, he did not even apprehend of what weight personality is in the affairs of men. To him Bolingbroke was the ideal all-round man, and the shining verbiage of his writings Chesterfield deemed worthy of being 'got by heart'; while in Pitt he singled out the graceful action and harmonious enunciation— 'his periods are well turned, and every word he makes use of is the very best'. For 'everybody knows the matter almost alike', and 'manner is all in everything'. Active contact with reality, on the few occasions when it occurred, left a singular, disproportionate imprint on Chesterfield's mind. As a young man he was Ambassador to Holland, which remained to him what Persia was to the late Lord Curzon. In 1745–6, he was Lord Lieutenant of Ireland, and ever after that country engaged his interest and sympathy. There alone had he achieved success; there he had held a viceregal position; had been unhampered by colleagues, never in competition with equals; and, which may have preserved his success, he was there less than a year. On his return to England, as Secretary of State, he failed either to prevail against colleagues whom he despised, or to co-operate with them in a practical manner; and soon gave up the Seals, with no loss to the public, and with the determination never to resume office. Chesterfield admired, and often quoted, Cardinal de Retz: 'I can truly call him a man of great parts, but I cannot call him a great man. He never was so much so as in his retirement.' Was there not a touch of self-identification in that description?

Lord Hervey has left a picture of Chesterfield which, though unpleasant, is no mere caricature. He writes:

> Lord Chesterfield was allowed by everybody to have more conversable entertaining table-wit than any man of his time; his propensity to ridicule, in which he indulged himself with infinite humour and no distinction, and with inexhaustible spirits and no discretion, made him sought and feared, liked, and not loved, by most of his acquaintance; no sex, no relation, no rank, no power, no profession, no friendship, no obligation were a shield from those pointed,

glittering weapons, that seemed to shine to a stander-by, but cut deeply in those they touched.

Compare with this Chesterfield's warning to his son in 1748:

Never yield to that temptation, which to most young men is very strong, of exposing other people's weaknesses and infirmities, for the sake either of diverting the company, or of showing your own superiority. . . . If you have wit, use it to please, and not to hurt. . . .

Seventeen years later he wrote to his godson:

If God gives you wit, which I am not sure that I wish you, unless he gives you at the same time an equal portion at least of judgment to keep it in good order, wear it like your sword in the scabbard, and do not brandish it to the terror of the whole company. . . . The more wit you have the more good nature and politeness you must show, to induce people to pardon your superiority, for that is no easy matter.

And in another letter, which was to be delivered to his godson after his death:

Yes, I have been young, and a great deal too young.

Hervey says that Chesterfield's person was

as disagreeable as it was possible for a human figure to be without being deformed. . . . He was very short, disproportioned, thick, and clumsily made; he had a broad, rough-featured, ugly face with black teeth, and a head big enough for Polyphemus. One Ben Ashurst . . . told Lord Chesterfield that he was like a stunted giant, which was . . . really apposite.

Writing to his son, Chesterfield hopes that exercise will 'lengthen you out a little'; and continually inquires about his teeth:

Do you take care to keep your teeth very clean, by washing them constantly every morning and after every meal? (30 July, 1747.)

I hope you take great care of your mouth and teeth. . . . I do insist upon your never using those sticks, or any hard substance whatsoever, which . . . destroy the varnish of the teeth. . . .

According to Lady Cowper, Chesterfield used to keep his upper lip drawn down to hide his black teeth.

To Chesterfield 'the most useful art of all', the highest, the greatest, was 'the art of pleasing.' 'To please, is almost to prevail'; 'he who pleases the most will rise the soonest and the highest'. A man should please by his manners, his appearance, his movements, his demeanour, his address, his conversation; he should insinuate, ingratiate himself, even with the multitude, because with them is the strength. He should cultivate women.

> I began the world, not with a bare desire, but with an insatiable
> thirst, a rage of popularity, applause, and admiration . . . this . . .
> made me attentive and civil to the women I disliked, and to the
> men I despised, in hopes of the applause of both. . . . To men, I
> talked whatever I thought would give them the best opinion of my
> parts and learning, and to women, what I was sure would please
> them—flattery, gallantry, and love. . . . By these means I soon
> grew in fashion . . . I gave the tone.

But was he truly successful? The advice he gives to his son suggests
different conclusions:

> Take the tone of the company that you are in, and do not pretend
> to give it . . . this is an attention due from every individual to the
> majority. (16 October, 1747.)
> . . . abstain from learned ostentation. . . . Wear your learning,
> like your watch, in a private pocket; and do not merely pull it out
> and strike it merely to show you have one. (22 February, 1748.)
> Take this rule for granted, as a never-failing one; that you must
> never seem to affect the character in which you have a mind to
> shine. (17 May, 1750.)

At one time Chesterfield's letters to his son were considered
immoral; and, in spite of their brilliancy, they are certainly
unpleasant. Almost every point in them, taken singly, may be
explained, defended, admitted, or even endorsed; yet the cumula-
tive effect is downright nauseating. Carried out to any degree,
Chesterfield's teaching would change a man into a homunculus.
He asserts 'that it is in every man's power to write what hand he
pleases'. The same misconception he applies to character and
behaviour. Are there some 'layers' missing in Philip Stanhope's
'*beau vernis*'?

> Now, pray let me ask you, coolly and seriously, *pourquoi ces couches
> manquent-elles*? For you may as easily take them as you may wear
> more or less powder in your hair, more or less lace upon your coat.

Moreover, this varnish is to be variable:

> In the course of the world the qualifications of the chameleon are
> often necessary . . . you should, to a certain degree, take the hue of
> either the man or the woman that you want, and wish to be upon
> terms with.

With 'restless attention', Chesterfield constantly examines how
he could best contribute to Philip Stanhope's improvement.

> I can tell you I shall always be correcting, and never think my
> work perfect enough. . . . (23 March, 1746.)

I believe it would do you no harm if you would always imagine
that I was present, and saw and heard everything you did and said.
(9 July, 1749.)

Remember that I shall know everything you say or do at Paris,
as exactly as if, by the force of magic, I could follow you everywhere
. . . invisible myself. (8 November, 1750.)

. . . above all things . . . remember to join *the Graces*. . . . How
cruelly should I be shocked, if, at our first meeting, you should
present yourself to me without them! (8 March 1750.)

. . . if I find you ungraceful in your address, and awkward in
your person and dress, it will be impossible for me to love you half
so well . . . let your intrinsic merit and knowledge be ever so great.
(27 April 1749.)

You must . . . expect the most critical *examen* that ever anybody
underwent. . . . (11 March 1751.)

The Graces, the Graces, remember the Graces! (10 January
1749.)

What were the reactions of the poor boy to a hundred letters in
this strain? Whatever there was in him of independence and
personality must have revolted, while the desire to please his
father (or the fear of displeasing him) must have paralysed him.
We know that he grew up awkward and shy, loud and *gauche*;
could we not learn more about him? Chesterfield undoubtedly
kept his letters; if they are still preserved, why not print them?
The birds are said to sing the praise of Heaven for the worms they
find—'do the worms sing too, daddy?' asked a child on being told
the story. We have long heard Chesterfield's song: I wish we
could for once hear Philip Stanhope.

By the time Philip Stanhope had grown up—*mal formé* beyond
repair—Chesterfield resigned himself to it; and remained a kind,
attentive, tender father. But at this time starts the new series of
educational letters to his godson. Their essential doctrines are the
same; still the letters are clearer, purer, free of over-emphasis and
of hysterical endeavour; a quiet, wise old man wishes to impart
some of his experience to his successor. And next come Chesterfield's grandsons. On the death of his son, whose closest friend and
confidant he had wished to be, he learnt that the son had been
secretly married and had left children. The daughter-in-law,
whom he would hardly have chosen and whom his son had hidden
from him, Chesterfield treats with kindness and sympathy, and he
writes to her affectionately about 'our boys'. A fine and lovable
side comes out in the letters written by Chesterfield in the last ten
or twelve years of his life. Had he, indeed, been merely 'stunted'?

13

THE MEMOIRS OF LORD HERVEY

LORD HERVEY writes about himself: 'His real business in London was pleasure, but as he always told the King, it was to pick up news, to hear what people said, to see how they looked, and to inform Their Majesties what was thought by all parties. . . .' In the *Memoirs*[1] his role is reversed, and to men and women, unseen, unknown, unchosen, he recounts things learnt at Court; and he finds visible pleasure in that, necessarily posthumous, display, which satisfies his urge for creation, his desire for intellectual survival, and the need of some compensation for his own futile existence and its insincerity. In life he had to feign deference to 'royal trifles'; now he has pinned them down, and sees them writhe and shrink; and he gives it as his excuse for recording them that

> the generality of readers have so much a greater curiosity to hear the words of Kings than of other people that they are amused with the very same things from the lips of that consequence that would lay them to sleep related from any other.

Hervey, the gigolo, ridicules his masters, and establishes his contemptuous superiority over his new public, of whose presence he seems intensely conscious. He takes them to the places of their snobbish dreams, to the seats of splendour and power, where they enter with a reverential awe, an avid curiosity, and an unconscious readiness to befoul: and there he has arranged for them a monkey-show.

But below his studied malice and literary endeavour there is intellectual curiosity and an outlook on history. He was interested in the essence of things—

> trifling circumstances often let one more into people's tempers and characters than those parts of their conduct that are of greater

---

[1] *Some Materials towards Memoirs of the Reign of King George II*, by John, Lord Hervey. Ed. by Romney Sedgwick.

importance, from which one frequently knows no more of their natural turn of mind than one does of their natural gait whilst they are dancing.

He wrote for those who

look into courts and courtiers, princes and ministers, with such curious eyes as virtuosos in microscopes examine flies and emmets, and are pleased with the dissected minute parts of animals, which in the gross herd they either do not regard or observe with indifference and contempt.

His theory is that things great and small are done in the same way by people who do not differ in essentials; that there is very little foresight or design in history, and a great deal of accident; and that wisdom comes after the event, in accounts which are as fanciful as they seem plausible.

I content myself with only relating facts just as I see them, without pretending to impute the effects of chance to design, or to account for the great actions of great people always by great causes.

The lowest of people 'have five senses, and none of the highest I know of have six'; and the doings of men, great and small,

are still the same game, and played with the same cards, the disparity in the skill of the gamesters in each equally great . . . and the only difference is their playing more or less deep, whilst the cutting and shuffling, the dealing and the playing, is still the same whether the stakes be halfpence or millions.

The great, inhuman, outlines of history Hervey did not see, but he realized that where the players are many, the game has to be simple. He writes about Lord Townshend:

He loved deep schemes and extensive projects, and affected to strike what is commonly called great strokes in politics, things which, considering the nature of our government, a wise minister would be as incapable of concerting, without the utmost necessity, as Lord Townshend would have been of executing them, if there was a necessity.

And, speaking of the behaviour of another nobleman, he says that it

would have been more extraordinary than all the rest, if it had not been for that great and common solution for the many otherwise unaccountable riddles in people's conduct, which was his being a great fool.

George II is a favourite object of Hervey's invective. The King wished to appear a hero and a lover, a man who knew his mind and kept his own counsels; here he is shown doing things 'because he had once done them', as 'incapable of being engaged by any charm but habit, or attached to any woman but his wife', looking 'upon a mistress rather as a necessary appurtenance to his grandeur as a prince than an addition to his pleasures as a man', and as possessed neither of 'mental resolution', nor of political courage. And this is how, according to Hervey, things were done at Court:

Sir Robert [Walpole] communicated this scheme secretly to the Queen, she insinuated it to the King, and the King proposed it to Sir Robert as an act of his own ingenuity and generosity.

About the Queen, Hervey writes in 1734:

Lord Hervey was this summer in greater favour with the Queen, and consequently with the King, than ever; they told him everything, and talked of everything before him. . . . She called him always her 'child, her pupil, and her charge'; used to tell him perpetually that his being so impertinent and daring to contradict her so continually, was owing to his knowing she could not live without him; and often said, 'It is well I am so old, or I should be talked of for this creature.'

Lord Hervey made prodigious court to her, and really loved and admired her.

And here is a description of her relations to the King:

. . . she looked, spake, and breathed but for him, was a weathercock to every capricious blast of his uncertain temper, and governed him (if influence so gained can bear the name of government) by being as great a slave to him, thus ruled, as any other wife could be to a man who ruled her. For all the tedious hours she spent then in watching him whilst he slept, or the heavier task of entertaining him whilst he was awake, her single consolation was in reflecting she had power, and that people in coffee-houses and ruelles were saying she governed this country, without knowing how dear the government of it cost her.

But even her Hervey did not always spare. This is his account of the departure of the Princess Royal for Holland:

Her father gave her a thousand kisses and a shower of tears, but not one guinea. Her mother never ceased crying for three days. But after three weeks (excepting post-days) Her Royal Highness seemed as much forgotten as if she had been buried three years.

His descriptions of the Prince of Wales, and of others he hated
—and these were many—make one wonder how much to accept
of his testimony; he himself wondered how much would be accepted:

> . . . no one who did not live in these times will, I dare say, believe
> but some of those I describe in these papers must have had some
> hard features and deformities exaggerated and heightened by the
> malice and ill-nature of the painter who drew them.

But take the following passage:

> This conversation was interrupted by the Duke of Newcastle, who
> made his entry with as much alacrity and noise as usual, mightily
> out of breath though mightily in words, and in his hand a bundle
> of papers as big as his head and with little more in them.

I have spent years over the Newcastle Papers, and would not have
done so were they as empty as Hervey suggests; and yet the picture
bears an unmistakable likeness.

'Some Materials towards Memoirs of the Reign of King George
II' is Hervey's own description of his book; 'I look upon these
papers rather as fragments that might be wove into a history than
a history in themselves'. But after two centuries Mr. Sedgwick
finds 'the duties of an editor of the Memoirs . . . comparatively
simple,' because 'posterity has yet to write its own history' of
Hervey's time, and it is therefore 'seldom possible to correct or
supplement him'. What a gloss on our history-writing! And yet,
this new edition is of the greatest value; certain important passages
of the *Memoirs*, removed for reasons of tact and propriety by the
first Marquess of Bristol and Mr. Croker, have now been restored
from a copy which Mr. Sedgwick has found at Windsor Castle;
and a truly admirable introduction has been provided by him,
the best essay yet written on Hervey. A very thorough and extensive knowledge of the period, and a most minute, careful, and
conscientious study of the available manuscripts and of Hervey's
correspondence, form its foundation; while the story of Hervey
is told with the fullest understanding of his personality, and is
discreetly adorned with wit which itself has a Herveian, eighteenth-
century turn. There is something very peculiar about that period
in the way it affects us who work on it; when Sedgwick and I
meet, we talk eighteenth-century gossip, and tell each other
funny stories about the Duke of Newcastle, and laugh at the old
man whom, somewhere at the bottom of our hearts, we both love.

14

JUNIUS AGAIN

THE identity of Junius has never been finally established, but after every conceivable argument had been constructed with the help of the existing material, the discussion, protracted for almost a century, flagged. Valid new evidence would now have to be produced to justify a reopening of it. Mr. Everett[1] thinks he has succeeded in identifying the famous eighteenth-century statesman, Lord Shelburne, as the author of the Junius 'Letters.' With the general character of his work and his would-be proofs I have dealt in *The Nation*. Now I am to test Mr. Everett's thesis by strictly ascertainable facts and, if my view of it is correct, to lay its ghost. This can be done by showing that Junius was in London, or in its immediate neighbourhood, at a time when Lord Shelburne was admittedly travelling on the Continent; i.e., I propose to establish Lord Shelburne's alibi.

Lord Fitzmaurice, in his *Life of Shelburne*, states that Shelburne, accompanied by Barré, left England on 11 May 1771; that 'a concise journal shows the two travellers passing through France and Italy'; that they visited Milan and Rome, and 'returning to France . . . made a prolonged stay in Paris'. The date of Shelburne's return to England is not named, but obviously such a journey in the eighteenth century, carried on in a leisurely fashion and including a 'prolonged stay' in Paris, was a matter of a good many months.

Mr. Everett thus states and dismisses the fact of Shelburne's absence at a time when 'Letters' from Junius continued to appear in London (p. 51):

> During that period the following Letters appeared: 1 May; three short letters of Philo Junius which really form but one letter —22 May, 25 May and 28 May, 22 June; 9 July; 24 July; 15 August. Assuming that Shelburne was the author, what safer way was there to throw off suspicion than to go abroad, making arrangements for

---

[1] *The Letters of Junius*, ed. by C. W. Everett.

Junius to continue his appearance in the 'Public Advertiser?' The difficulties may be granted, but they would not be impossible to overcome by a man who kept forty footmen. . . .

It does not seem to have occurred to Mr. Everett to examine either the above-mentioned 'Letters' or the private letters which Junius wrote during those months to H. S. Woodfall, the editor of the *Public Advertiser*, and see whether they could have been written from the distance at which Lord Shelburne was from London. Three such private notes from Junius, covering 'Letters' which reached Woodfall during Shelburne's absence abroad, appear on p. 310 of Mr. Everett's book. Of the first, marked merely *Thursday*, the date suggested by the contents and accepted by Mr. Everett is 20 June 1771; it is the covering note to 'Letter XLIX,' announced in the *Public Advertiser* on 21 June, and published on Saturday, 22 June:

> I am strangely partial to the enclosed. It is finished with the utmost care. If I find myself mistaken in my judgment of this paper I positively will never write again.
> Let it be announced to-morrow, J[unius] to the D[uke] of G[rafton] for Saturday.
> I think Wilkes has closed well. I hope he will keep his resolution not to write any more.

But if Shelburne was Junius, how could a note written by him on 20 June reach Woodfall from abroad the same day? In defence of Mr. Everett's thesis, it might possibly be suggested that the note was sent off at an earlier date, but the dates in the note were elaborately concocted so as to disguise Shelburne's absence and strengthen his alibi. This argument founders, however, against the concluding paragraph of the note, which unmistakably refers to the letter to Horne, which Wilkes published in the *Public Advertiser* on the same day, 20 June 1771, and of which these are the opening sentences:

> I now proceed to examine your *twelfth* Letter, and, according to the notice I gave you, to close a correspondence which the Public have long ago called upon me to conclude. I shall therefore necessarily in taking leave of you consider . . .

While travelling abroad Shelburne obviously could not have read this in the *Public Advertiser* on 20 June any more than a note from him could have reached London on the day it was written. Junius was in or near London on 20 June 1771.

In the next note to Woodfall Junius writes:

> To prevent any unfair use being made of the enclosed, I entreat you to keep a copy of it. Then seal and deliver it to Mr. Horne. . . .

For this note Mr. Everett suggests the date of 16 July 1771. It is certainly the note which accompanied Junius's reply to the letter from Horne, published in the *Public Advertiser* on 13 July. Junius's reply appeared on 24 July, bearing the date of the 17th, after the following notice had been inserted on the 23rd:

> The Letter from Junius having been transmitted by the Printer privately to Mr. Horne, according to Junius's orders, Mr. Horne has directed the Printer to publish it; and it will appear to-morrow.

Now whether it was received by Woodfall on the 16th or 17th, again Junius could not have been far away to reply so soon to Horne's letter published on the 13th.

For the following, third, note the date of 13 August 1771 is rightly suggested in the British Museum MS., and accepted by Mr. Everett:

> Pray make an erratum for *ultimate* in the paragraph about the D[uke] of G[rafton], it should be *intimate*. The rest is very correct. . . .

This undoubtedly refers to 'Letter LIV' (pp. 233–40), and Mr. Everett in a footnote acknowledges the connexion. But he dates that 'Letter' 15 August 1771 (reproducing it evidently from the reprint of the 'Letters' published by Woodfall in 1772, where the same mistake occurs). In reality the letter appeared in the *Public Advertiser* on 13 August followed the next day by the desired correction:

> Errat. In the 8th line of the 12th paragraph of Junius's Letter in yesterday's paper relating to the Duke of Grafton, for 'ultimate knowledge of his character' read 'an intimate knowledge of his character'.

Thus Junius must have been in London on 13 August 1771, to read his own 'Letter' in the *Public Advertiser* of that day, and send Woodfall the correction inserted the next day.

In short, the author of the Junius 'Letters' was in or near London in June, July, and August 1771, when Lord Shelburne was travelling in France and Italy. The bottom falls out of Mr. Everett's theory.

15

THE EAST INDIA COMPANY

THE East India Company, or, to give it its full name, the United Company of Merchants of England trading to the East Indies, was formed in 1709 through a union of the 'Old' and the 'New' Companies. From the outset it had to encounter European rivals supported by their own Governments, and to carry on commerce sword in hand in an India where the power of the Moguls was crumbling. This need of armed support increased its dependence on the Crown, from whom it anyhow held its charter and trading monopolies: thus a close association with the Government was inevitable, which exposed the Company to difficulties and perils in times of political crisis. Happiest for it were therefore the days of Walpole and Henry Pelham: it was then that it became

> the prosperous, respectable, and sound commercial and financial corporation which was not only far and away the biggest and most complicated trading organization of the country, but was (together with the Bank of England and the South Sea Company) the centre of the financial market rising in London and of the Government's political and financial interest there.[1]

Its management was in a chairman, deputy chairman, and in twenty-four directors elected annually by the Court of Proprietors, in which every holder of at least £500 stock had a vote, and one vote only, however great his holdings. The membership of the Court of Directors was remarkably permanent in the reign of the first two Georges; the 'House list' submitted by the outgoing executive was carried without much difficulty by the prestige of its leaders, and by a voting strength built up on patronage, on merchant shareholders dealing with the Company, the shipping interest, etc. The business organization of the Company was efficient; the produce of its sales about the middle of the century was roughly £2m. a year; its shares were widely held; and

---

[1] Lucy S. Sutherland, *The East India Company in Eighteenth-Century Politics.*

a good many of its directors sat in Parliament, without the Company as such engaging in political controversy. But about 1746 conditions began to deteriorate: there were war with France, conflicts with rival Indian rulers, and growing difficulty in controlling the Company's own servants; and ten or twelve years later, a permanent crisis supervened in its affairs.

> The new period was to see . . . English control spread over the neighbouring Indian territories and an expansion of territorial power which [was] . . . inevitable but which, thanks to . . . the spectacular exploits of Clive . . . came more suddenly than anyone could have expected. The Company had long experience of the problems of government as well as those of the administration of commerce; but now . . . those of government . . . began to prevail. In addition . . . the new period brought . . . a desperate struggle in England for the control of the Company's political machine . . . between Robert Clive, the Company's greatest soldier, and Laurence Sulivan, its ablest ruler since Sir Josia Child . . . a struggle involving issues vital for the Company and the State, but one in which personal hatreds and personal interests played the greatest part. . . . The period was also to see the re-entry of East Indian affairs into the sphere of party politics and the intervention of the State in the affairs of a Company become at once so rich and so disordered. There was Chatham's first intervention in 1766-7, Lord North's Regulating Act . . ., Fox's India Bill, Pitt's India Act, and, as a sequel, the long-drawn-out agony of Warren Hastings' impeachment.

It was the story of 'a company struggling to adapt itself to totally new responsibilities oversea, hampered at every turn by disorganization arising from too-sudden wealth and the speculation born of it'; and of shifting Governments and violent Oppositions, whose component groups found advantage in forming connexions with interests and groups within the distracted Company.

A rich historical literature on East Indian questions during this period has hitherto been focused on a few great figures and their exploits in the field, in administration, or in Parliament. But of the history of the Company itself, its management, negotiations, and internal struggles, and its relations with Government and Parliament, that 'intricate and often unedifying background' to more spectacular activities and scenes, no proper analysis had so far been attempted: hence a fragmentation of that history which rendered it wellnigh impossible to see its disjointed sequence in perspective. And yet Indian affairs impinge all along on British domestic history during the first twenty-five years of the reign of George III, and deeply affect its course. It was high time that they were elucidated and worked into the pattern of which they are an essential part. This has now been achieved by Miss L. S. Sutherland in her book on *The East India Company in Eighteenth-Century Politics*, a piece of historical research so thorough and comprehensive in its groundwork, and so masterly and lucid in its presentation, that it must rank among the foremost works on the period, a standby and directive for students in cognate fields, and a secure foundation for further research in its own. Miss Sutherland's knowledge of City finance and politics in the eighteenth century, and also the practical experience of administration which she acquired during the last war, have served her well in her study of the East India Company; she has been able fully to appreciate the problems of its day-to-day management, to value the work of a Laurence Sulivan, and to pay well-deserved tribute to the honest and intelligent labours of John Robinson and Charles Jenkinson, forerunners of the modern Civil Service: administrators who laid the foundations for constructive reform in India but, despised by men of fashion in their day and maligned by orators and pamphleteers, continue to appear as sinister or suspect figures in books of a well-known type. Still, while doing justice to these men, and also to Warren Hastings, 'the greatest Company servant of his day', Miss Sutherland takes a lenient, and even generous, view of his persecutor, Burke.

> He may have adopted the East Indian question for party and personal reasons; he may have placed his trust in most unworthy witnesses, in his contemptible cousin William . . . and the virulent and disappointed Francis . . . ; and he showed far more interest in exposing abuses and attacking individuals than in working out a constructive policy of reform. But he was sincere in his savage anger, had mastered a mass of complicated information and . . . was undoubtedly one of the formative influences on the development of a government policy for India.

Laurence Sulivan spent more than twenty years in India; owed his advance in the Company's service solely to his competence; returned to England in 1752 a wealthy but not a rich man, and further improved his fortune in the City; was elected a director in 1755, and deputy chairman in 1757, when developments in India called for men with Indian experience; and entered Parliament in 1762. Meantime Clive by his Arcot campaign, the recapture of Calcutta, and the battle of Plassey laid the foundations of

British rule in India; but there was a price to pay: his example and victories did a great deal to upset the precarious balance between public and private interest hitherto observed by the Company's servants. Convention allowed senior officials to make fortunes 'through the recognized channels of perquisite, private trade, and money-lending'; but Clive, having replaced Siraj-ud-daula by Mir Jafar, accepted from him more than £200,000 in presents and an annual *jagir* of £27,000: the first of the gainful interventions in conflicts between native rulers. Moreover, as conquerors the Company's servants now freely extended their private trade in the hinterland, making profits and committing abuses; thus enriched they became unmanageable, or if recalled came back acutely hostile to the directors, spreading disorganization to the headquarters in London; lastly, servants of the Company in India would remit their gains to England by bills on it, after having laid out the money on occasions and terms largely of their own making: all this at a time when the administrative responsibilities of the Company were rapidly increasing.

A split among the directors produced a contested election in 1758; Sulivan's side was victorious; he was elected chairman, and retained control for the next six years. In that election he had Clive's support. But a General Letter which Sulivan sent to Bengal in March 1759, with bitter reproaches for remittances, etc., gave umbrage to Clive, although Sulivan had taken care to dissociate him from the criticism. 'The seeds of the great feud had been thrown.'

Clive returned home in 1760, determined to cut a great figure in the country. The *jagir*, the fee of a purely nominal office under the Mogul, became his dominant concern, overriding every other consideration. 'My future power, my future grandeur,' he wrote to a friend, 'all depend on the receipt of the jaghire money'; and again: 'Believe me there is no other interest in this kingdom but what arises from great possessions'—had he stayed in India and acquired a yet greater fortune, he might have been 'an English Earl with a Blue Ribbon'. But the Company hesitated to recognize his *jagir* by transferring to him a yearly rent for lands near Calcutta payable by the Company to the Nawab, who still owed them reparation for damage suffered from his predecessor. The peace negotiations of 1762–3 increased ill-feeling between Sulivan and Clive—there was no conflict of principle, but Clive, excluded from a share in the intricate discussions, attacked the terms which Sulivan had accepted; and when a formed opposition

arose over them in the Company, he announced his adherence to it. 'The great Civil War of the Company had broken
out.'

The election of directors in April 1763 was marked by new
and ominous features: large-scale organizations were set up for
the production of faggot-votes—East India stock was bought
and holdings were 'split' to create voting qualifications; the
Government, whose Peace Treaty was impugned, intervened
in favour of Sulivan (Fox using the resources of the Pay Office);
consequently the Parliamentary Opposition aided Clive; and
both sides rounded up supporters. Sulivan won; and payment
of Clive's *jagir* was stopped by order from India House. He appealed for help to the Opposition, but was told that it was hope-
less to raise the matter in Parliament. To save his *jagir* he now
swore fealty to the Grenville Administration; still, the compromise which they tried to patch up for him was rejected by the
directors. But his chance came when news reached London of
administration chaos and renewed fighting in Bengal; his return
to India was urged by anxious stockholders; he, however, refused
while Sulivan headed the Direction; and at the ensuing, bitterly
contested, election in April 1764, Clive had the support of the
Government. The result was a dead-heat; but soon Sulivan's
following began to crumble; Clive's demand for recognition of
his *jagir* for ten years was accepted; and he sailed for Bengal,
armed with wide discretionary power. The election of 1765 completed his victory over Sulivan—he had won a decisive round.
Still, as early as May 1764, Charles Jenkinson wrote:

> The affairs of this Company seem to be become much too big for
> the management of a body of merchants . . . these disputes will
> probably end in a Parliamentary enquiry.

In April 1766 news reached London of Clive having assumed,
on behalf of the Company, control of Bengal's finances; he himself estimated the net gain at more than £2m. a year, a view
widely accepted in spite of scepticism among the directors. A
wild boom in East India stock ensued in London, Amsterdam,
and Paris. Rich men, including Clive himself, invested in it,
while speculators started large-scale dealings in 'differences'.
One such group of prominent men was headed by Lord Verney,
M.P., Edmund Burke's patron, and included several other
M.P.s; and its affairs were managed by two adventurers, William
Burke and Lauchlin Macleane, who now began their long and

discreditable connexion with Indian affairs. When the directors would not raise the dividend, the 'bulls' set out to obtain a majority in the General Court; split stock and organized an unprecedented publicity campaign; obtained support from deluded proprietors and from the Clive group (which, besides being engaged on the 'bull' side, hoped in the glow of Company affluence to secure an extension of the *jagir* for a further ten years). The speculators succeeded: in September 1766, the dividend was raised from 6 to 10 per cent; and they emerged as a new element in Company politics.

Stock-jobbing was at all times in ill-repute with the nation, and the rich, monopolistic Company with the 'popular' party in the City; dislike of Nabobs forcing their way into Parliament and society was growing among the country gentry; and uneasiness was spreading at the 'rapine and oppression' practised in India. The State was grappling with problems of post-war finance, and the question naturally arose what right a trading company had to the territorial revenues of a province subdued with the help of the King's forces. Chatham, in office since July 1766, denied it, and desired a parliamentary inquiry into the Company's affairs as a prelude to State intervention. But his illness, and divisions in his Government, prevented the attack from being pressed home, and, after long debates, manœuvres, and negotiations (for the first time properly elucidated in Miss Sutherland's book), an agreement was reached for two years: the Company undertook to pay the Treasury £400,000 a year. In the meantime the speculators rashly used their majority in the General Court further to raise the dividend from 10 to $12\frac{1}{2}$ per cent. The Government replied with the first Parliamentary intervention of the century in the internal affairs of the Company: by an Act limiting the dividend to 10 per cent, and another against gerrymandering elections—no one was to vote who had not held his qualification for at least six months. And such intervention had to be continued in order to safeguard the financial interests of the Treasury and of the nation, and to replace the short-term agreement of 1767 by a new settlement. Still, this again was for five years only; the contribution of £400,000 per annum was maintained, but if the Company at any time had to reduce its dividend to 6 per cent the claim would lapse; the maximum dividend was set at $12\frac{1}{2}$ per cent.

The Act against faggot-votes proved ineffective: operations had merely to start half a year earlier. The opposition in India

House, led by Sulivan, was gaining strength, and the election of directors in 1769 was most fiercely contested; the Government intervened, while groups of rich men recklessly bought up stock at inflated prices. The result was a draw which brought Sulivan back into office. A month later election-mongers and speculators were caught by a sharp break in price caused by news of fighting in India and rumours of an impending French attack: Verney and the Burkes, Sulivan, Macleane, and a great many others were brought to the verge of ruin. But the storm blew over; an attempt of the Government to interfere in the Company's territorial affairs by agents sent out to India ended in failure; and by 1770 a lull supervened in the faction fights at India House, as also in Parliament; during the next two years relations between the Company and the Government were remarkably free of political implications. Meantime information reaching England about Company misrule was producing genuine dismay both in Parliament and in the country, and Sulivan made serious attempts at reform from within. But for this the Company's control over its servants in India had to be strengthened; and moves in that direction were defeated by powerful ex-servants with more than doubtful records. Sulivan's only success was in the re-modelling of the Bengal administration, where the man he had chosen, Warren Hastings, laid the basis for Bengal's prosperity under British rule.

But a new crisis in the Company's affairs was impending, High dividends and payments to the Government were based on an illusory surplus from the Bengal territorial revenues. The truth was masked for some time even from the directors, who in March 1771 raised the dividend to 12½ per cent. But even when the situation became clear to them they did not reduce the dividend (which would have stopped also payments to the Government) for fear of a catastrophic break in East India stock, which some of them were heavily 'bulling'. The maximum dividend was continued in August 1771 and March 1772. Then in June a severe financial crisis set in, causing widespread bankruptcies in this country and on the Continent; and now the financial problem of the Company had to be tackled. At first it was hoped that an unspectacular way might be found for the Treasury to help the Company out of its difficulties; but its commitments proved excessive; on 24 September 1772, the half-yearly dividend was passed; and the consequent panic 'raised a frenzy of indignation among shareholders, speculators, and the public at large.'

This, on top of the mounting anger of humanitarian opinion, produced a demand for Parliamentary action. The North Administration were forced to evolve an Indian policy.

The view universally held that if the Company were to be helped this must be in return for radical improvements in its organization and rule was grounded 'not only in the desire to obviate financial loss or military danger to the nation but in a wider sense of obligation for law and order in India'. Some favoured the assumption by the Government of full responsibility for the administration of India; but the machinery of government was as yet entirely inadequate for intervention in that distant and unfamiliar field, and the purpose of the temporary settlement embodied in Lord North's Regulating Act of 1773 was 'to leave the Company in control both of trade and day-to-day administration, while checking its worst excesses at home and abroad', and 'to prepare the ground for a more permanent and sweeping reorganization when the Company's charter came up for renewal in 1780'. A small Parliamentary committee was set up of Government supporters, with Jenkinson for *rapporteur*, to examine the Company's books and report on reform. Although its proposals met with considerable opposition, especially in the General Court, the difficulties did not prove insuperable. The Parliamentary Opposition was disunited over India and ineffective; while in India House the Government secured in 1773 a compliant directorate. The Government was ready to help the Company with a loan, and concessions regarding the export of tea; but in three ways established its control over the Company: through the right to receive copies of the Company's accounts and correspondence (henceforth carefully scrutinized by the Secretary of the Treasury, John Robinson); through the nomination of the Governor-General of Bengal and his Council; and through a Government-controlled majority in a reorganized Court of Directors.

. . . there began . . . the first period of indirect control by the Government over the East India Company. During this period the 'management' of the Company became one of the regular activities of the Treasury; the King was kept as regularly informed of East Indian elections and of important votes at East India House as he was of the proceedings of Parliament, and there arose to prominence those official experts in Indian affairs of whom Robinson and Jenkinson were the pioneers, and Henry Dundas the most famous.

Here too began the participation of government in the administration of India . . . none the worse for basing itself on no particular doctrine of relations of government and Company. . . .

. . . A step had to be taken that could not be reversed and some of the worst abuses of the Company's rule both in India and at home disappeared for ever. . . .

The Government, 'looking for capacity rather than connexions', appointed Warren Hastings Governor-General, but joined to him three councillors (including the notorious Philip Francis) who within seven days of their arrival launched an attack against him; and from Miss Sutherland's lucid and impartial account of the conflict Hastings comes out much better than his opponents. He was an excellent administrator, absorbed in his work and devoted to duty, and 'widely known among Company servants for his indifference and carelessness about his private fortune'; and though his financial principles hardly 'transcended the conventions of the day, his hands were a good deal cleaner than those of most of his contemporaries': the fortune he amassed was not great by the standards of the time. But the services which he rendered were incalculable; in the circumstances of his last years of office 'it is difficult to think of any other man then concerned in Indian affairs who would have averted disaster'. As for the Parliamentary Opposition, their attitude over those affairs was dictated by personal considerations and the desire to harass the Government. Francis long endeavoured in vain to rouse Burke's concern at the alleged misdeeds of Warren Hastings, and when the Government and the directors decided to recall Hastings, the Rockinghams came out on his side; when Hastings's (ill-chosen) representatives concluded a compromise with the Government, the Rockinghams swung over to the other side; but when Hastings incurred the wrath of the King and the Ministers by refusing to accept that agreement, the Opposition attacks against him stopped abruptly, only to be resumed with increased virulence when he made his peace with the Government.

In the summer of 1778 Robinson started to draft a plan to be followed when in 1780 the renewal of the Company's charter would come up for settlement. While he thought that the Company should resume its contributions to the Exchequer, his experience of the last five years did not make him favour the transfer of the Company's territorial acquisitions to the Government: the change would be dangerous in war-time; the administration

of those territories, their commerce, and the remitting of revenue
from India were 'greatly connected'; lastly, 'the errors which
must be committed in the management of such acquisitions at
so great a distance . . . had better fall upon the directors of the
Company than . . . upon the Ministers of the King'. But while
the Cabinet was preoccupied with America and the war, and the
Government in a weak position, little progress was made with
regard to Indian affairs; the Act of 1773 was renewed for one
year, and in May 1780 for another year. It was not till January
1781, after the Gordon Riots and the General Election, that
Indian matters came again to the fore; but even then the strength
for decisive measures was lacking. The agreement renewing the
charter for ten years was, in Sulivan's words, 'a paltry performance'; further legislation was vaguely promised. News from India,
first of serious conflict in the administration, and next, of military
danger in the Carnatic, led to the appointment of two important
Parliamentary committees. When in February 1781 the Opposition demanded a committee of investigation,

> it did not seem necessary for the Government to oppose it. Care-
> lessness and indifference on North's part, however, permitted . . .
> the election of a Committee in which members of the Opposition
> preponderated both in numbers and quality. . . . Thus came into
> existence the famous Select Committee . . . the field of Edmund
> Burke's Indian activities.

And in April a secret committee was set up to investigate the
causes of the war in the Carnatic; but this time Robinson took
care that it should be controlled by the Government side: Dundas
was its chairman, with Jenkinson as his right-hand man.

In the two years between the fall of the North Administration
and the rise of Pitt, the Indian question became 'one of the major
controversies and problems which claimed the attention of
Parliament'. Nothing in the terms of reference of either committee suggested that they were intended to formulate general
policies of East Indian reform; but under the short-lived Administrations of 1782–4, the two committees became increasingly
important, changing their political status several times: the secret
committee was connected with the North, Shelburne, and Pitt
Administrations, and the select committee with the Rockinghams
and the Rockingham Coalition. The Rockingham Administration took no initiative in Indian affairs, and its record was 'somewhat ignominious'. Shelburne inserted in the King's speech of

5 December 1782, a reference to 'fundamental laws' to be framed for India, and Dundas was preparing a Bill (based on the work of Robinson and Jenkinson) which is 'a landmark in the history of Indian legislation', 'the blue-print of Pitt's East India Act of the next year'. Ignoring 'the dislike of the executive characteristic of eighteenth-century political opinion', it proposed to increase the powers of the Governor-General and the Governors; to settle the claims of the rulers of Tanjore and Arcot, and investigate their notorious debts to Company servants; to prevent the General Court from overriding the directors on political matters; and to strengthen the Government in its dealings with the Company. But brought in after the Shelburne Government had fallen, it seemed still-born.

Now the Rockinghams and Burke had their innings. They had long opposed an increase of the authority of ministers over the Company because of the patronage this would give them, and of that of governors as leading to tyranny. Their Bill, which adhered to those tenets, was 'a product of Burke's intelligence', ingenious and unpractical. It was a most sweeping attack on the independence of the Company; the powers, however, and the patronage taken from it were not to be vested in the Crown but in seven commissioners, nominated in the Act for at least four years: that is, in Fox's party whether or not they were in power. Misrule in India was to be checked by a complete subordination of the Indian administrators to commissioners sitting in England —which shows how little Burke understood of the problems of administration. It was a poor Bill, and although its defeat was due to the action of a few resolute men, these were helped by the 'widespread hostility and dislike' which it aroused 'not only among the threatened Indian interests but among a wide body of opinion throughout the country'.

When Pitt in turn introduced his India Bill it was in an understanding with the Company; after what had threatened them they accepted a measure which under normal conditions would have created an uproar. It was Dundas's Bill, modified to meet objections: some of the powers of the Governor-General were dropped, and the extent of the Government's declared patronage was limited. A board, the future Board of Control, was established for India, and measures were enacted against oppression and abuses by the Company's servants.

What Pitt and Dundas had set out to do was to give themselves both the sanctions and the machinery for carrying out the methods of government supervision and infiltration which North and Robinson had been seeking to employ ever since the Regulating Act of 1773.

And although much remained which called for improvement in Indian administration,

the confusion of the past twenty-five years had come to an end and a new era had begun in the Government of India and in the relations of State and Company.

16

THE TREASURE ISLANDS

In the Caribbean Islands the wealth of the Indies, fabulous, real, and multiform, came within the grasp of Restoration England. The introduction of the sugar cane made them into the Rand of the century that followed. To North America Englishmen went in search of new homes, to the West Indies they went in search of treasure. Fortunes, big and blatant, were acquired, to be spent in England. The Sugar Islands loomed large in the public eye, and the West Indian cut a figure in eighteenth-century English society. When in 1757 the creation was mooted of a Secretary for the Colonies, the Duke of Newcastle referred to him as 'Secretary for the Indies', or for 'both Indies'; and when the Seven Years War was drawing to a close the question which conquest it was preferable to retain, Canada or Guadeloupe, was seriously argued in Government circles and widely canvassed in print. The repatriation of men and money was a dominant concern in the colonial policy of the age. In 1698 Charles Davenant estimated the yearly emigration from England to the West Indies at about 1,800—but then

> for these last 20 years the West Indies have sent us back annually about 300 persons of their offspring, with this advantage that their fathers went out poor and the children come home rich.

In 1778 an anonymous West Indian wrote about the Sugar Islands: 'Few proprietors continue to live in them who think themselves able to remove to Britain.' And Charles Townshend, when pleading in 1760 for the retention of Guadeloupe, favourably contrasted the West Indians with the Continental settlers, firmly rooted in their American lands:

> The inhabitants of the West Indian islands never consider themselves at home there; they send their children to the Mother Country for education; they themselves make many trips to the Mother Country to recover their health or enjoy their fortunes; if they have

ambition, 'tis hither they come to gratify it. I need not, I suppose, observe to you, how many gentlemen of the West Indies have seats in the British House of Commons.

They have 'a very formidable number of votes in the House of Commons', wrote Israel Mauduit, agent for Massachusetts, in 1764, when over the Sugar Act their economic interests clashed with those of New England.

Important, prominent, and exotic, the West Indians flash across the eighteenth-century scene leaving an impression which survives in vague statistical exaggerations, reproduced even by some of the best modern historians. Among recent books on the West Indies that are of outstanding merit are the works of two American scholars, Professor F. W. Pitman and Professor L. J. Ragatz, which, complementing each other, supply a comprehensive picture and a thorough analysis of the history of the British Caribbean in its growth and decline. Yet even they, observing the network of the West Indian interest, and seeing eighteenth-century England along its lines, tend to over-emphasize its importance. Thus Ragatz writes in the preface to his book on *The Fall of the Planter Class in the British Caribbean, 1763–83*:

> The sugar planters were the conspicuously rich men of Great Britain in the middle of the seventeen hundreds. . . . Firmly entrenched in Parliament, they exercised a preponderant influence on the course of events. Sugar was king, they who produced it constituted the power behind the throne, and the islands, on which their opulence and commanding position had been reared, were regarded by all as the most valued of oversea possessions.

'Conspicuously rich' some of the sugar planters undoubtedly were, but 'the conspicuously rich men of Great Britain' is saying far too much. Home agriculture was the massive mountain-range against which any single interest stood out as a minor peak: and cloth, coal, and iron, shipping, brewing, and banking, each produced its conspicuously rich men and its interest in Parliament, although this, as a rule, did not become apparent till a disturbance brought it into the open. Thus, an ill-considered tax in 1763 proved how 'firmly entrenched' even cider was in Parliament — expressions such as 'the cyder-counties', 'cyder-members', and even 'the cyder Lords', are current in contemporary correspondence.

Pitman, in his book on *The Development of the British West Indies, 1700–1763*, seeks to illustrate the power of the West Indians in

Parliament by a debate on sugar in 1744, opened by Colonel Martin Bladen, whose wife owned a great West Indian estate; the speakers mentioned on the planters' side were: Sir Henry Liddell, S. Jenyns, William Pitt, G. Heathcote, Sir J. H. Cotton, W. Calvert, and Sir John Barnard: every name in this list signifies a great deal to the parliamentary historian, but none of them except Heathcote had any marked personal interest in the West Indies, and the debate demonstrates the attention paid to an important economic interest, but hardly its own 'power' in Parliament. In fact, the number of Members whose 'opulence and position' was based on West Indian plantations, and who, strictly speaking, can be classified as West Indians, did not as a rule exceed fifteen in a House of 558; with an outer ring of some fifteen to twenty who had an important, though not preponderant, interest in sugar plantations or the sugar trade. Far more numerous became, towards the turn of the century, the East India 'lobby'; yet even they can hardly be said to have had 'a preponderant influence on the course of events'.

From wider surveys, however excellent, it is necessary to pass back to case-history and explore the general in its individual setting, of a man or a family, combined with estate or business; and thus to perceive it in its complex, concrete incidence. Only a rich literature of that type, exploring the various interlocking 'interests', will yield a well-balanced, three-dimensional presentation, in which every element is embodied in plastic, human figures—not a biographical approach in the old sense, but through the numbers involved and the features observed much rather a demographic approach to history. The idea of such a technique has occupied Professor Pares for some time past, and in his new book, *A West-India Fortune*,[1] he has carried it through with regard to the Dorset family of Pinney and its West India interests: he was enabled to do so by the truly wonderful collection of business records and family correspondence preserved by them, and willingly placed at his disposal. Collections of this kind are rare, especially for the West Indies. Very few have survived in the islands: estates have changed hands, families have left, the European community has shrunk to a mere remnant, and papers exposed to hurricanes, fires, and the extremely rich insect life of the islands, have perished at a rate exceeding the normal. It is therefore mainly in this country that material for the family and business history of the West Indies has to be sought; and even here one

[1] Richard Pares, *A West-India Fortune* (Longmans).

of the richest known collections, that relating to the West Indian interest and estates of the Lascelles family, went up in smoke during the blitz in a City office, in which it had been carefully preserved for generations. Moreover, the Pinney records present one peculiar feature; the Pinneys, half-way through their West Indian career, after having for a century been Nevis planters, turned into Bristol sugar-factors, plantation financiers, and shippers, thus continuing the game from the opposite end; and so far this side of the game had not been given the full and expert treatment which, on the basis of the Pinney records, it now receives in Pares's book.

The West Indian story of the family opens with Azariah Pinney, son of a Nonconformist minister in Dorset, ejected from his living at the Restoration, and turned lace-dealer. In 1685, Azariah, aged 23, having become involved in Monmouth's Rebellion, had to clear out to the West Indies; landed in Nevis, the smallest of the Leeward Islands, with £15 in his pocket; started as a commission agent; prospered, and in 1696 was returned to the House of Assembly, 'an august body of ten men'; became treasurer of the island, receiving 8 per cent of the taxes collected; and died in 1720, owner of several plantations: 'the founder of a great colonial fortune'. His son, John, born in England and educated at Oxford and the Middle Temple, 'a harmless if ostentatious youth' who, to his father's annoyance, lorded it in London, and took 'his fortune a little too much for granted', finally settled in Nevis, was returned to the Assembly, and next became Chief Justice of the island: 'a post of honour and not of emolument', stated a report of the Board of Trade in 1782, 'seldom if ever . . . held by a person versed in the knowledge or practice of the law'. He survived his father by only a few months, and his son John Frederick, born in 1718 and educated in England, hardly regarded himself as a West Indian; still, when in 1739 he made his appearance on the island, to put his plantations in order so that he could resume the life of an absentee in England, he, too, was 'elected, as of right, a member of the Assembly'; but left in 1742, returning only once more in 1749. He sat in the British Parliament for Bridport, 1747–61, and died, unmarried, in 1762. At his death the Pinney plantations were worth about £23,000, but were heavily burdened with debt, and the story might have closed with that proverbial 'third generation' but for a young man, John Pretor, second cousin once removed, to whom both John Frederick and another cousin, a

Dorset squire, left their estates on condition that he assumed the name and arms of Pinney.

This John Pinney, 'one of the most successful planters and West Indian merchants of his time', became the second founder of the fortune, which at his death in 1818 amounted to some £340,000. But irretrievable decline had now set in for the plantation economy of the West Indies: 'the price of sugar plunged downwards after 1815', and the days of slave labour were numbered. The problem which faced John Pinney's sons, settled in England, was how to 'repatriate their capital, more or less intact, from the doomed islands'. The ablest and most active of them, Charles, in 1831 Mayor of Bristol, wrote from Nevis in 1828: 'The expense and vexation in this detestable country is tremendous. I wish we were well quit of it.' This they managed to achieve in the next twenty years, though not without heavy losses; by 1850 the story of their West Indian fortune had run its course and reached its term. To Charles's nephew, William Pinney, M.P. for Lyme Regis in 1832–41 and 1852–65 (when the borough was disfranchised), and for Somerset in 1847–52, 'the West Indies were at most a troublesome source of income, and long before the end of his career they were nothing more than a memory'.

John (Pretor) Pinney is the central figure of Pares's story. He arrived in Nevis in 1764 with no intention to stay there very long: like his cousin, he thought of the plantations merely 'as a convenient source of income for a Dorset country gentleman'. But it was July 1783 before he at last left the West Indies, having by almost twenty years of hard work greatly enlarged and improved his plantations, without himself striking roots in the island: his greatest pride, he told a friend in 1778, was 'to be considered a private country gentleman', and he was resolved to 'avoid even the name of a West Indian'. When returning home he wished to transfer most of his fortune to England; wherein he did not succeed. For he now settled as sugar-factor at Bristol, sending out the planters' stores and selling their sugars, providing ships for the trade between Bristol and Nevis, and—which was to prove the most troublesome but also the most profitable part of his business —financing his West Indian correspondents by money advanced on their produce. But balances on chronically overdrawn current accounts tended to change into loans and mortgages, and mounting mortgages to finish in foreclosures, resulting in, not always welcome, additions to the West Indian estate. Thus John Pinney's transactions as planter, merchant, shipowner, and financier cover almost every aspect of West Indian business, and that with a wealth of documentation illustrative of the mind and style of the man: the trader or early capitalist glorified by writers from Defoe to Samuel Smiles. John Pinney's letters to his sons, relatives, or employees, which enjoin 'a strict application to business united to an unexceptional conduct', warn against idleness and dissipation, and speak with a 'shudder' about debts ('interest money is like a moth in a man's garment, never asleep'), are but the frigid commonplaces of his class and time. But what distinguished John Pinney was, in Pares's words, 'the emotional intensity with which he felt and lived them.' Precise rather than mean, 'he made a religion of his accounts; in them he expressed his most passionate feelings . . . in long vehement comments on particular items, or in marginal rubrics.' He was cautious and timorous; and it is the fears of men, at least as much as their vanity, which supply the historian with rich materials: the men who anxiously fix things in writing, and preserve every receipted bill or scrap of paper for their own reassurance or 'justification'. Indeed, some of John Pinney's book-keeping bordered on the pathological; or, as Pares considerately expresses it, must have given him 'purely intellectual or emotional' satisfaction—for instance, 'he opened an account with each of his children from the moment of its birth', charging it with its midwife, christening fee, its share of the nurse, etc. But what a treasure such a man's papers, carefully preserved by his descendants, are for the economic historian!

> John Pinney's success as a planter [writes Pares] is best judged from a summary of his accounts—that, indeed, is how he would have wished to be judged. . . . The result of his twenty years in Nevis can be summed up by saying that his fortune in money was at least £35,000 better than he found it.

He had settled one estate, improved his most important (the Lowland) plantation, and bought some more land. In his own words, 'the completest and best single estate in Nevis' had come into being. The Lowland Plantation comprised only about 400 acres, but half of it was caneland—the crop that counted; Pinney's other land, less than 300 acres in all, was largely mountain and pasture. (Comparison between different estates is difficult, especially if on different islands: on some of the large Jamaica estates of 10,000 and 20,000 acres, one-fifth or less was caneland, whereas in Barbados the best part of the acreage.) The average yearly production, 1768–83, of the Lowland Plantation exceeded 100 hogsheads of sugar, of a value of £2,000 to £4,000. The fascination which the story—of how the crop was grown, cut, ground, and boiled—had for Pares he has succeeded in communicating to the reader, who shares the life and concerns of the planter, to the last stage of production and shipment, and to this, by no means surprising, conclusion:

> With all their experience, there was something in the manufacture of sugar which neither planters nor merchants could explain or predict. . . . Some sugars would look well in the curing-house and arrive in England much drained and the worse for wear. . . . All that John Pinney could say about these mysteries was that 'Gentlemen in the West Indies are often deceived in the quality of their sugars, as some will mend on the voyage and others will turn out much worse.'

A husbandry so elaborate, a crop so delicate, variable, and costly, and a manufacture so full of surprises, naturally gave rise to a variety of theories and views; and John Pinney, after having left the island, would expound his own to his managers in letters and instructions which, in their entirety, form a remarkable treatise on plantation management. 'It is not the quantity of land that makes the sugar,' he wrote, 'but the number of acres under proper cultivation. . . . Half the quantity of land well dunged and properly worked will make more sugar than the whole planted in a slovenly manner and suffered to be overrun by weeds.' 'A sugar estate must be cultivated more like a *garden*, than like a *farm*.' But what he had still to learn to his cost was, in Pares's words, that

> not every manager could figure, in return for a salary of £200 and his keep, as the perfect agriculturist, manufacturer, disciplinarian, accountant, and business man.

John Pinney had to undergo the usual 'torments of the absentee', who in the long run was left with 'the choice between eternal friction . . . and a gentle decline into bankruptcy'. Here is his rubric on the plantation accounts for 1792:

> Thank God! This is the last crop put in by my late miserable manager . . . or rather, by my late mismanager.

And here is the epitaph of the successor, written in the account-book in red ink:

> The enormous expenses and injudicious conduct of my present manager . . . cannot be submitted to any longer. He is too bad! My losses under him has been very great, one crop in four! . . .

Inefficiency and injustice were the common lot of absentees.

> Whatever vows of fidelity managers, attorneys, friends, even
> brothers might make [writes Pares], it was almost a law of nature
> that every month a planter stayed away from the islands, he was
> treated more and more as a stranger whose interests went to the wall.

And local public opinion was always against the absentee—
'nobody helped him and many protected the culprit'. It became
obvious that the changing of managers would lead nowhere;
Pinney decided to sell his plantations; and at last succeeded in
doing so in 1808. But even this did not end the Pinneys' connexion
with West Indian land: new estates came to them as Bristol
merchants.

Part II of Pares's book includes chapters on the Bristol sugar-
market and on West India shipping and finance; once more,
things of general import and occurrence appear in the concrete
form of individual experience. Those acquainted with commodity
markets will find in the story familiar features of the extension to
which a factor's or broker's business is liable, and of risks taken
for the sake of retaining or acquiring customers.

The sugar-factor's 'main business in life was to sell sugar, and
his main revenue—or so he thought—was the commission upon
these sales', a $2\frac{1}{2}$ per cent for work which required judgment,
experience, and constant attention. In the sugar-market he had to
face the grocers, refiners, re-exporters, distillers, and speculators,
and know their requirements or habits. There was a seasonal
rhythm in prices, 'as well as irregular fluctuations brought on by
the weather, politics, war, economic development and fiscal
policy'. Hurricanes and slave troubles were endemic to the West
Indies, and war was very nearly so—considerably more than half
of the period 1739–1815 consists of war years; and in the nineteenth century abolitionist agitation, free-trade propaganda, and
the general economic and financial rhythm of business added to
the troubles of a highly sensitive market. But this is a bird's-eye
view of the sugar trade.

In everyday practice,

> the sugar-factor . . . was the |planters' factotum in England, and
> executed all their commissions, of whatever kind. He made what
> sense he could of their (often tardy or inaccurate) orders for planta-
> tion stores or personal luxuries; bought, packed, and shipped these
> supplies, and listened to complaints about quality, the price, and the
> terms of payment.

His reward again consisted of a 2½ per cent commission, and interest on the debit balance of the current account. Besides, he attended to the personal affairs of his correspondents: would procure for them white employees, manage their law business, help them to obtain seats on the council, or executive office, etc. —'for the sake of the commission on the homeward cargoes of sugar'.

And even this was not all. The sugar-factor could only hope to get business if he could help the planter to ship his sugars to England; and so he had to own or control shipping—a new chapter in his transactions and in Pares's book. And last but not least the factor had to finance his West Indian correspondents—lend them money for the sake of consignments, advancing sums even in excess of their probable value.

> Planters slid inexplicably but surely into debt to their factors. . . . Debts on account current continued to increase even in the years of high prices.

> It might have been hoped that the debit balances of some planters would be offset by the credit balances of others. But there were four or five planters with debit balances for every one with a credit balance. . . .

In the last year of John Pinney's life (1818), his loans converted into mortgages on West India property exceeded £127,000, besides one small estate taken into possession, and some £45,000 in mortgages owing to the firm as distinct from Pinney himself.

Pares seems puzzled by 'the natural history of that malignant organism, a West-India debt'; and having adduced various reasons for its growth, concludes:

> All these encumbrances which the planters and merchants themselves created—personal extravagances, excessive endowments of families and high interest—do not explain the whole increase of West-Indian indebtedness. Much of that increase could not be explained and never was explained at all.

He quotes a case where neither extravagance nor persistent mismanagement, nor absenteeism, could be alleged and yet a good plantation sank deeper and deeper into debt. And he comes near to one basic reason of this wellnigh universal tendency in rural economy:

> The truth was that one could not put much trust in the planters' estimates of their financial position and prospects. They were always over-sanguine. Next crop was always to be a bumper crop and the sugars were sure to arrive at an improved market.

Whoever has grown up in a community of 'green squires'—so-called because they invariably had to sell their crops when they were still green—will feel at home in that financially embarrassed West Indian milieu. Behind the chronic miscalculations loom unconscious moral postulates: that he who sows should reap, and that the worker is worthy of his hire. Hence a good year is accepted as normal, while a bad one is an 'act of God' within the meaning of English Common Law: 'what no reasonable person can foresee'; and the standard of life is based on what is considered normal. Further even a surplus will not, as a rule, render the position of the farmer more liquid: farmers who will keep it in cash are far fewer than those who will sink it into improvements or new land. Indeed, in that way good years, by encouraging investments, are apt to add to the farmers' indebtedness. But when luck turns, they have to contract debts. And interest money, in John Pinney's words, is like 'a moth in a man's garment', or in Pares's more modern simile, 'ticks up like a taxi'.

On the other hand, here is the question put from the creditor's point of view:

> It is easy . . . to see many reasons why the planters borrowed so much and repaid so little; but why had the Pinneys ever lent them the money?
> . . . [they] did not always know what they were doing, nor proceed upon any plan. Still less had they any conception of the lengths to which they were fated to go, nor could they always explain afterwards how they had been brought to advance so far. . . .

On one occasion John Pinney was accused of deliberately lending money in order to get his debtor's estate; this he sincerely and indignantly disclaimed; but he did get the estate, against his own wish.

> Why then did he lend so much? There were three reasons: . . . out of personal friendship, for the sake of consignments in his business as a sugar-factor, and finally for the sake of the interest upon these investments, which he recognized, more and more clearly, as the chief source of his income.

And this is perhaps the most surprising conclusion from Pares's close study of the Pinney accounts: that in spite of endless trouble, sometimes severe losses, and the final liquidation of the West Indian business under the highly adverse conditions of 1830–50, the interest upon the Pinneys' loans was the greatest source of their West India fortune, whose main growth falls into the

Bristol period; commissions, profits from shipping (if any), and plantation income contribute far less to it. Interest in Nevis in John Pinney's time was up to 8 per cent, at which rate even, with minor setbacks, capital might double in ten years; and a five-fold increase in fifty years would allow for considerable losses.

When in 1833 Parliament voted twenty million pounds for compensating the West Indian owners of slaves, little of that money went into the pockets of the planters: most of it went to their creditors. Sugar production in the old islands had ceased to pay: its vast extension to other countries and climates had resulted in a catastrophic drop in the price of sugar, while exhaustion of soil had set in on the long-overcropped islands. 'The old plantation economy of Nevis was decaying fast', writes Pares. 'Some planters could not raise the cash to pay wages to their former slaves; others could no longer keep the negroes on the plantation at all, or even in the island.' And by 1830 'nearly every educated white man had abandoned the colony'. One of the few remaining big planters wrote from Nevis to a son of John Pinney in 1852: 'I am sorry to say our crop will not bear the expense of labour and contingent expenses, and if the Government of Her Majesty do not take our deplorable condition into consideration, I see nothing but ruin. One third of the island is now out of cultivation. . . .'

By that time the Pinneys had completely cleared out of the doomed islands, cutting their losses where necessary, but still repatriating a good fortune to their old home. 'They had never lost touch with England, and even kept most of their original lands', writes Pares. 'An excursion of a century or two is not very long in the history of a family. Once more there are Pinneys in Dorset, in the old houses, the old fields, and the old churchyards. It is as if they had never been out of the county.'

17

CHURCH AND STATE IN EIGHTEENTH-CENTURY ENGLAND

THE history of the National Church in the eighteenth century is not the exclusive concern of ecclesiastical historians or of students of religious thought, for the Church was an essential branch of England's national organization, and men in Orders formed a high proportion of the intelligentsia; and it is the distinguished merit of Professor Sykes's work[1] that to a minute knowledge of every aspect of the Church's inner life, he joins a proper appreciation of her political tasks and social affiliations. After the spiritual and political upheavals of the preceding age, this was the time of England's inner consolidation, when common sense and ready toleration—in other words, insistence on a conformity of a singularly unexacting type—effected a reconciliation in this country such as France was never to reach after her great Revolution. To some, non-jurors or 'tender consciences' on the Dissenting side may be more attractive, and they probably were intellectually more consistent, than the ecclesiastic statesmen of the Hanoverian period; but they might easily have plunged England into further civil wars, while the Church, such as it was, helped to heal the divisions and to reunify the nation.

Pluralism, favouritism in appointments, and laxity in the discharge of ecclesiastical duties, are the overt reproaches most frequently levelled at the eighteenth-century Church, almost as if such things had been unknown in preceding ages, or in the eighteenth century had been peculiar to the Church. (But when pluralism occurs in a man like Archbishop Sancroft, a non-juror, the glowing devotion of an admiring biographer makes it into a ground for praise—'a stronger proof can scarcely be afforded of the general estimation in which his character was held than by the fact of so many preferments flowing upon him, in this short

[1] *Church and State in England in the Eighteenth Century*, by the Rev. Norman Sykes.

space of time, from so many various quarters'.) Pluralism was, to a large extent, the ecclesiastical equivalent of sinecures in the State—the Church could not but reproduce the dominant features of the national structure.

As to oligarchy, its extent in the eighteenth century has been greatly exaggerated, both in State and Church. For while a Duke of Grafton or a Lord Rockingham could attain high office without much work or merit, men like Walpole or Pitt towered far above them. Similarly, in between the prelates of noble family and extraction,

> there sat bishops such as Secker, educated first at a dissenting academy. . . . Warburton, who was a graduate of no University . . . and Maddox, whom Gibson fostered as an orphan in a London charity school. . . .

Dr. Thomas Newton, subsequently Bishop of Bristol, thus explained the theory of ecclesiastic preferments in a sermon preached at the consecration to the episcopate of William Warburton:

> Though the apostles, for wise reasons, were chosen from among men of low birth and parentage, yet times and circumstances are so changed that persons of noble extraction by coming into the Church may add strength and ornament to it; especially as long as we can boast of *some* who are honourable in themselves as well as in their families. . . .

And George Grenville distinguished two kinds of bishoprics—'bishoprics of business for men of abilities and learning, and bishoprics of ease for men of family and fashion'.

Again with regard to nepotism (a form of favouritism objectionable so long as it remains merely an inept approach to heredity), a similar parallelism can be traced between Church and State. Lord Sandwich wrote, in August 1764, to a naval officer about to quit in disgust at having been passed over:

> . . . as to Sir William Burnaby's making his son a Captain, it was very natural for him to do it. . . . I am satisfied in my opinion that no one has a right to complain that he has given his son the preference over every recommendation.

And a poor curate, displaying the virtue of humility, wrote to Archbishop Wake in 1724:

> I don't presume to find fault with the Bishop of Worcester for preferring his nephew. I only wish it were my good fortune to be a Bishop's nephew too.

As for laxity in the discharge of ecclesiastical duties, Professor Sykes's very extensive study of the life of a great many eighteenth-century prelates goes far to rebut that reproach and presents a picture of a good deal of honest, hard work done under difficult conditions. But

> at the heart of the problem of episcopal administration lay the distraction from the proper business of diocesan oversight involved in the residence of bishops in London during the greater part of each year.

Between 1715 and 1780 the House of Lords had a membership of about 220, and an average attendance of 120–145; and the twenty-six bishops 'represented a not inconsiderable proportion even of the numerical strength of the House'. Attendance in Parliament on their part was a duty to the State, no less than to the Church, 'in an age which saw so great an advance in the prestige and authority of both Houses, and in which the House of Peers played no insignificant part in debate and legislation'.

The saddest aspect of the eighteenth-century Church (as also of the Army and Civil Service) was the condition of the depressed subalterns—curates and the unbeneficed clergy—who, even after having overcome numerous initial obstacles, still found the greatest difficulty in eking out a subsistence. Here was an intellectual proletariat such as we sometimes incline to think peculiar to our own age. How modern sound some of the contemporary remarks on the problem! Even in the Caroline age, Bishop Stillingfleet

> wished to discover some means by which 'the multitude of ordinations could be prevented, which had long been a great injury to the Church', since 'there were at least double the number of clergymen to the benefices and preferments in the kingdom'.

And in 1711, Addison wrote:

> I am sometimes very much troubled when I reflect upon the three great professions of divinity, law, and physic; how they are each of them overburdened with practitioners and filled with multitudes of gentlemen who starve one another.

There is, unfortunately, no statistical estimate of the proportion which men in Orders formed of the eighteenth-century intelligentsia, though this could be obtained with the help of university and school registers.

18

AN EIGHTEENTH-CENTURY
TRAVELLER

———————————

I

JOHN BYNG often wondered what it was that made him travel—
why people should leave comfortable homes and

> lavish their money abroad, hunting after idle pleasures, in which
> pursuit they are sure to encounter real miseries . . . and yet neither
> deters me nor others, from running wild about the world. . . .[1]

He loathed uncomfortable beds, noisy inns, and late suppers
('but being obliged to order, I think myself obliged to eat'), stony
roads and muddy lanes, the hardships of pleasure parties and the
gloom of the unsettled life in watering-places. At the end of his
Tour, on 6 July 1781, he wrote:

> The imposition in travelling is abominable; the innkeepers are
> insolent, the hostlers are sulky, the chambermaids are pert, and
> the waiters are impertinent; the meat is tough, the wine is foul, the
> beer is hard, the sheets are wet, the linnen is dirty, and the knives
> are never clean'd!!

And this at the end of the third of the fourteen tours of which
the record has been preserved:

> This will probably be my last expedition of the kind. . . . I feel
> myself unequal to a daily worry, and a nightly change of beds; in
> consequence my nerves shatter, and my spirits tire. . . . Valetudi-
> narians must live where they can command, and scold.

Formal parks, with 'staring temples and obelisks', so dear to
the generation which had immediately preceded his own, were
not to his liking; nor did he enjoy wild scenery and extensive

———

[1] *The Torrington Diaries*. Containing the tours through England and Wales of the
Hon. John Byng (later fifth Viscount Torrington). Vols. i and ii. Ed. by C. Bruyn
Andrews.

views which his contemporaries were beginning to appreciate. He would not climb Cader Idris: 'I hate distant views; am giddy on heights; and very hot and nervous.' Even the Malvern Hills were too much for him—his nerves felt 'much harrass'd, from being unused to such heights and declivities'. And about Leck-hampton Hill he writes: 'This is a truly fine prospect; yet prospects please me but for an instant, for they fatigue my eyes, and flurry my nerves, and I allways wish to find myself in the tranquil vale beneath.'

Again and again the reader will ask himself—what is the curious attraction of this seemingly unattractive book? His descriptions of the things he saw are seldom vivid; while their enumeration is hardly illuminating where the ground he covers is unknown to the reader, and is meagre where it is familiar (though occasionally he will find interesting details about some particular place or building). Perhaps largest of all loom the problems of Byng's everyday existence—lodgings, food, and drink. They engrossed his mind and fill the pages of his diary, and their discussion is raised to the heights of a theory; for he objects to tours being written

> too much in the stile of pompous history; not dwelling sufficiently upon the prices of provisions, recommendation of inns, statement of roads, &c. so that the following travellers reap little benefit from them.

Byng supplies such information though he was writing for posterity only. He was determined that his diaries should not be published in his lifetime, but hoped that they would be read with avidity a hundred years hence,

> as descriptive of the manners of our travelling, the rates of our provisions; and of castles, churches, and houses, that may then be levell'd with the ground.

He speaks with contempt about 'those dirty, idle, memorials of Lilly, and Ashmole, who tells us of every shocking ailment that assailed him and how often he sweated, and purged'; from which his own account of the beds he lay in without sleep, and of the meals he consumed with oppressive results, are only one stage removed. Still,

> all diaries are greedily sought for, let them be ever so ill and foolish written, as coming warm from the heart.

His own diaries certainly come from the heart, a tortured, suffering heart. 'I find every one more retired, perhaps wiser than myself; and not so leaky of secrets, and hasty of determination.' Sociable by nature, he could not even entertain his friends with real pleasure; and describing a young host 'of modest manners and easy deportment', he adds:

> I remark this, more particularly, as I suffer so much, and am allways (in spite of inward remonstrances) constrain'd, unhappy, and fluster'd at my own table.

How he wished for the 'tranquil vale' and a real ease of mind! Here is happiness as he imagines it:

> . . . how I should like to pass a November in such a place and country with a sociable, hunting, whist party, and our own wine! To hold a good horse in my hand every morning; then a good glass of wine; and then a good quantity of trumps.

But on he went travelling; and much of the charm of his diaries lies in the contrast between the wish for peace and that restless curiosity which drove him on; between the shyness which determined him not to publish his diaries, and the desire that some day they should be read; in their simplicity and sincerity—'I am resolv'd to judge for myself and not follow the opinion of every gazer, and flatterer'; and in the discreet tolerance and practical wisdom of that inveterate grumbler. When he finds himself in the uncongenial atmosphere of his wife's family, he remarks: 'As I was only to make a short stay (for I never sacrifice but one day of the year here) I behaved with acquiescence of temper.' He praises music and card games because, though sociable, they save 'the trouble of conversation'. Even his diaries were an escape from controversial talks:

> My nerves have lately encouraged me to much writing, being not equal to violent argument, and contradiction, which ever flutter away my little capacity; and render such opinions as may be reasonable, and wou'd sound decently upon paper, of hasty, and weak effect.

And thus in the worries and misery of his journeys, he tells, half-unconsciously, about those of the much greater journey to which he himself sometimes compares them, wishing for the end of both, and yet clinging with infinite curiosity to what the world offered him.

2

Between 1789 and 1791, John Byng, in continuance of his travels, made two tours in the Midlands, one in Bedfordshire, and one in Lincolnshire. He had by now worked out a certain technique and his writing shows a growing self-consciousness—his memoirs, if they survive, will be read:

> I will now indulge in a little hasty vanity, and satisfaction, in thinking how pleasant my tours will be to readers, an hundred years hence. . . . Of all the tours I read I like my own the best (Well said, master!) because all others are so cramm'd with learned investigation, and new fangled drawings; perpersely to forward a sale, whilst all pleasure minutiae are left out, as unworthy of the public eye.

> My pleasure in touring is not confin'd to time; (tho' that I enjoy as much as any man) but the completion of my journal furnishes me employ for the following winter, as I then dilate my former notes; besides the expectant pleasure of an old age perusal.

But the reader naturally wonders what are those minutiae of pleasure, or the enjoyment of touring, to a man so regularly displeased as John Byng appears in his diaries. The tale of bad inns continues.

> Several fat, stupid, female servants attended us . . . at our bad, ill-serv'd, supper.

> . . . a most blackguard stop . . . some fat, greasy maids. . . .

> My sheets were so damp, and the blankets so dirty and stinking, and the room so smelling of putridity, that I slept very little. . . .

> My landlord, fat, stupid, and splay-footed. . . .

And so it goes on in endless succession. Once, and only once did Byng find an inn deserving of the highest praise; it was the Ram's Head, at Disley, a—

> snug little, comfortable inn . . . a neater and more chearfully situated inn I never saw. . . . The stables are excellent; the brown bread, and cheese, so good; the water so cold; the decanters so clean; and the bed rooms so nice; that I wish'd to make a return, and pass more time here.

But, as if to make amends for such high praise, a few pages further, having entered a supremely nasty inn, he adds—'these petty miseries exalt something better into superlatives'.

Nor is it clear where Byng finds any compensation for these 'petty miseries'. The country houses which he visits do not please him much more than the inns at which he stops; he dislikes Chatsworth; speaks of 'the nasty stare-about Castle of Belvoir'; of the 'mean entrance into Coombe-Abbey Park'; the 'modern, red-brick, tasteless house' of Lord Stamford, at Dunham-Massey; and the 'ugly, modern house' of Lord Hardwicke at Wimple. Mr. Okeover's place at Mapleton 'tho' in a lovely vale . . . is kept in wretched taste'; Dunnington Park, of Lord Huntingdon, Byng mistook for a gardener's lodge; the seat of Lord Pomfret at Easton-Neston is 'a great, staring, unpleasant dwelling, of neither comfort or content'; Sir Robert Burdett's 'is of vile architecture, and in a bad situation'; Sir Richard Arkwright's new house is 'an effort of inconvenient ill taste'; and Mr. Leigh's of Lime 'is in the horrid taste, and manner of Chatsworth, all windows', while his park 'is a dreary waste, abandon'd to rabbets'. And so goes on the rondeau of delights for the sightseer.

As for company in travelling, there are some discreet hints of differences and mutual disgust:

> touring cannot be taken alone; and for company to go together becomes almost impossible.

> . . . cou'd touring in company be well understood, what satisfaction it wou'd afford! But people will pull different ways, and disdain a director; so schisms and wrangles quickly arise to disever acquaintance, and friendships, that might, otherwise, last long.

> To me, who feel every wish to move at my own taste, at my own hours. . . .

It seems obvious that on such companionable tours Byng meant to be the 'director'. Was he happier when alone? Here is a significant passage:

> I had no one to speak to, my writing was quickly exhausted, and so I strove to think; but I (now) hate thinking;—I left London to avoid thinking; in youth, people won't think, and when they grow into years it is of no use!

Perhaps the chief purpose of his tours, except to give him 'employ' afterwards, was to escape London and society—for he had not become more sociable as the years went by. And this is a typical *cri de cœur*:

> I seek not company, and noise; I turn not my head to look at a woman; for I leave London that I might see Nature in her wild, and most becoming attire. . . .

Indeed, 'romantic' nature and romantic ruins are what Byng now seemed to enjoy.

> The appearance of this castle (Maxstoke Castle), so correspondent of romantic history, and legendary tale, highly engross'd my thoughts and attentions.
> A clear, surrounding, moat, an inhabited fortress of 60 yards square, turreted, and preserv'd with battlements; all this serv'd much to my inspiration!

And on another occasion:

> to me castles and monasteries in decay are the daintiest speculation.

Unfortunately even inspired speculation seemed never to call forth from Byng descriptions which could convey a vivid or pleasurable impression to the reader and therefore the book continues in its unrelieved gloom.

A new industrial England was growing up in the Midlands, nasty perhaps, but interesting; of which a contemporary account would be welcome. There is one, of a kind, but merely to complete the picture of displeasure:

> I abominate the sight of mines, and miners, as unproductive of pleasure; and the wretches who work in, and about them, seem devoted to darkness, dirt, and misery. . . .

> The silk mills [at Derby] quite bewildered me; such rattlings and twistings! Such heat, and stinks!

> Salford . . . where the noise, and drunkenness of the artisans quite overcame me, added to a long crawl over the stones.

> Manchester: this great, nasty, manufactoring town. . . .

Having visited Sunday schools at Stockport he writes:

> I am point blank against these institutions; the poor should not read, and of writing, I never heard, for them, the use.

And again at Manchester:

> . . . here let me (ignorantly perhaps) impetuously state my wishes, 'That trade was unknown'; (or that I had lived when it was but little known).

He had some foreboding of terrible upheavals:

> . . . a fear strikes me that this (our over stretch'd) commerce may meet a shock; and then what becomes of your rabble of artisans!

Lastly, here is a generalizing description of England in 1789:

. . . from my . . . observations . . . noblemen, and gentlemen have almost abandon'd the country . . . yeomanry is annull'd. . . . So, amongst the first great people, now residing there, may be reckon'd the inn keepers, the tax gatherers, and the stewards of great estates who with the lawyers rule the country. Justices . . . are afraid of the felons; constables are not to be found; the poor must plunder because not provided for; ladies dare not live in the country; taxes are evaded; enclosures of common field land, and commons, are general; corporations are venal; trade and manufactories are over strained; banks and bankruptcies in and over every town; laws, from being multiplied beyond comprehension, cannot be enforced; London markets and London prices govern the whole kingdom; and as that encreasing Wen, the metropolis, must be fed the body will gradually decay . . . there will come a distress, a famine; and an insurrection; which the praetorian guards, or the whole army cannot quell; or even the Parliament pacify. . . .

Had this been written about France in June 1789, how much would it have been quoted as a most remarkable prophecy, and an explanation of what followed.

H

19

CHARLES TOWNSHEND: HIS CHARACTER AND CAREER

For some time past I have been collecting material for a biography of Charles Townshend, and when invited to deliver this year's Leslie Stephen Lecture,[1] I decided to draw on that material for a preliminary sketch dealing with his character and certain aspects of his career.

For access to the manuscripts from which I quote my grateful thanks are due to their owners and custodians, and more especially to the Duke of Buccleuch and the Marquess Townshend; theirs are the two most important collections of Charles Townshend papers.

In the summer of 1765, Rockingham, taking stock of his Government's position in the House of Commons, marked a list of its Members with 'Pro', 'Con', or 'Doubtful' against their names.[2] Two only eluded classification: William Pitt and Charles Townshend. Not made for team work, they could not be fitted into any political system. Yet so transcendent were their gifts as House of Commons men that neither could be neglected for long. Townshend, while lacking Pitt's grandeur and undaunted courage, was unsurpassed for brilliancy: 'if there was something more awful and compulsive in Pitt's oratory, there was more acuteness and more wit in Charles Townshend's', wrote Lord Waldegrave about 1758. And he thus explained the omission of Townshend in November 1756 from 'more active employment': 'Pitt did not chuse to advance a young man to ministerial office, whose abilities

---

[1] 1959. [2] Fitzwilliam MSS. at Northants R.O.

were of the same kind, and so nearly equal to his own.'[1] This, though written before Pitt's greatness as war minister was fully revealed, is significant.

By the time Townshend reached his thirties, his character, private and public, had impressed itself on contemporaries: its various facets were described and discussed; and there is enormous material to cover the last decade of his short life; but so far no serious biography of this seemingly protean personality has been attempted. Yet there are scores of dicta about him which could serve as texts for such a biography.

Horace Walpole wrote to H. S. Conway on 4 March 1756: '. . . nothing is luminous compared with Charles Townshend: he drops down dead in a fit, has a resurrection, thunders in the Capitol, confounds the Treasury bench, laughs at his own party, is laid up the next day, and overwhelms the Duchess [of Argyll, his mother-in-law] and the good women that go to nurse him!' And David Hume, in a letter to Adam Smith on 12 April 1759, speaks of 'Charles Townshend, who passes for the cleverest fellow in England'.[2]

In August 1759, when a vacancy was expected at the Exchequer, Newcastle wrote to Hardwicke: 'If Charles Townshend had not such a character, I would make him Chancellor of the Exchequer at once, but there is no depending on him.'[3] And on 5 October: 'Will Charles Townshend do less harm in the War Office or in the Treasury?'[4] Yet on 9 December 1761, noticing at Court 'a settled inveteracy against Charles Townshend', Newcastle remarked to Devonshire: 'I should be sorry we should part with him, considering his abilities.'[5] On 11 December 1762, three days after Townshend had resigned office, Fox wrote to Bute about him—'whom I can have no personal reason to wish well to, many to do otherwise. It seems to me that he may be had. Get him with all his faults (I don't say trust him) and they [the Opposition] won't be able even to make our attendance [in the House] necessary.'[6] And on 11 March 1763, in his scheme for a new Government: 'Charles Townshend . . . must be left to that worst enemy, himself: care only being taken that no agreeableness, no wit, no zealous and clever behaviour . . . ever betray you into trusting him for half an hour.'[7] And Edmund Burke, on 9 July 1765: 'His

[1] *Memoirs*, p. 87.
[2] *New Letters of David Hume*, ed. R. Klibansky and E. C. Mosser, p. 54.
[3] 32895, f. 76.   [4] 32896, f. 300.   [5] 32932, ff. 78-91.
[6] Bute MSS.
[7] Fitzmaurice, *Shelburne*, vol. i, p. 146.

actions . . . seem never to have been influenced by his most wonderful abilities.'[1] Most penetrating of all is a remark about Townshend by his friend Chase Price, in a letter to the Duke of Portland on 18 July 1765: 'The powers of his mind and imagination so superior to the powers of his heart! The one shewing him many precipices and the other not affording a spark of constancy to support him entirely unhinged. . . .'[2] Wonderful abilities, inordinate vanity, and poverty of heart explain a great deal in the pattern of this life.

The incessant warnings and reminders that Townshend must not be depended upon or trusted are significant: so convincing and alluring was his approach, and seemingly so sincere at the moment, that men were apt to gloss over his notorious instability, however much they tried to remember it. His co-operation was sought and solicited—'we could neither do with him, nor without him', wrote Horace Walpole[3]—and at almost every change of Government between 1756 and 1766 Townshend delayed its formation by leading a giddy dance. There is something incomprehensible and almost uncanny in these performances: why did he behave, or why had he to behave, in that way, and why did others put up with so much of it? George III, Pitt, and Grenville, each of them unimpressionable in his own way, alone seem never to have fallen under the spell of his 'magic quality'. Nor did his family, which had done much to shape the pattern of his thoughts and emotions. On 18 August 1755, his father, Charles 3rd Viscount Townshend, wrote to him in one of his long, reproachful letters: 'I have done every thing in my power to deserve your affection, esteem and regard, but . . . I have not ever received any gratefull return from you. The compliances I have at any time made to your requests have not in your opinion . . . arose from a generous and good natured disposition in my temper but from the magick quality of your great abilities. . . . All the return I have had has been that of finding that my thoughts and actions have been made the subject of your ridicule and supposed wit. . . .'[4] In an earlier letter, of 31 October 1747, Lord Townshend ironically referred to Charles as a 'genius', and to himself as 'the turnip merchant at Rainham'.

Before I deal with Charles Townshend's family background,

---

[1] *Correspondence*, ed. T. W. Copeland, vol. i, p. 209.

[2] Portland MSS. at Nottingham University.

[3] Horace Walpole, *Memoirs*, vol. i, p. 327. Remark refers to spring of 1764.

[4] Charles Townshend's correspondence with his father is quoted from the MSS. of the Marquess Townshend at Raynham.

I must revert to a remark which may have puzzled you in my first quotation from Horace Walpole: 'he drops down dead in a fit'. Townshend suffered from convulsive disorders which at times incapacitated him for weeks. There are detailed accounts of them and of their after-effects in Charles's letters to his father, and a good many references in letters from relatives and friends. The fits seem to have started in adolescence: in June 1745, when Charles was twenty, his father refers to 'those disorders you have labor'd under for some time past'. The latest, discreet yet unmistakable, references to fits which I have so far found occur in 1761: on 5 July Horace Walpole wrote to Lord Strafford that Townshend has had 'a bad return of his old complaint'; and on 4 December a debate which he was to have opened and which attracted much attention, had to be postponed because of 'a severe fit of ill health' which, he said on the 9th, had left him 'in a very weak condition'.[1] Sir Charles Symonds, a foremost authority on epilepsy, has very kindly examined my material on Townshend's fits, and thinks there can be little doubt that they were epileptic; that the seizures had probably a focal origin in the left hemisphere, and were due to injury at birth; that Townshend had also inhibitory motor seizures of the minor kind; and that a succession of such minor attacks accounted for periods of malaise and misery of which Townshend complained. Sir Charles further writes: 'The presumed organic basis for the attacks makes it quite possible that some psychological abnormality may have existed in association with the epileptic liability, i.e. due to the same organic cause.' Lastly, Townshend's 'crazy constitution' (to quote his own words) may very well have been associated with his epileptic liability. One is struck, following him month by month and year by year, by the frequency and diversity of ills from which he suffered. Still, with incredible pertinacity and drive he struggled on, giving his life a brilliant and amusing appearance. The tragic side was usually overlooked.

Charles's family background was unhappy. He was the son of a formidable father, intelligent yet primitive, suspicious, vehement, and oppressive, and of a mother, fastidious and intellectual, famed for her wit and promiscuity. They separated when Charles was fifteen, and he remained with his father, professing the greatest attachment to him and indifference or even contempt for his mother. But for his father Charles felt no love either: much rather fear seeking relief in mockery, a weapon of the intelligent under

[1] 38334, ff. 19–20.

oppression. At times Charles's letters make his father appear a
petty tyrant. He wrote from Cambridge on 30 December 1744: 'I
have never felt any return of my passion for cricket since you objected to it, nor has my attendance on the tennis court been either
prejudicial to my time or my purse . . . following it under such
restrictions . . . I have never spent four shillings or four days on
this article. I shall obey your orders in discontinuing this exercise.'
But as the letter to which this is the reply is not extant, judgment
must be withheld: for in some other cases Charles is seen outdoing
behests to his own discomfort if thereby he could place his father
in the wrong.

Their correspondence is a constant struggle: in letters of por-
tentous length, rising to 2,000 words, they dissect as under a
microscope what has been said, manœuvre for position, and find
fault by putting forced constructions on what the other has said (a
technique which Charles was to use all his life). There was self-
damaging torment on both sides. This alternates with feigned
submission on Charles's part and flattery so extreme as to render
both unconvincing—thus in a letter on 1 September 1745: '. . .
your inclination is my rule, as your judgment must be best able to
promote my interest in the best manner . . . it is my interest to
acquiesce in the directions you give for my conduct, and as I
willingly acknowledge this truth in discourse, so I shall constantly
observe it in practise; . . . your choice will always be productive
of my happiness . . . an opinion which I shall practise, as well as
profess.' How this sets the tone in fervency as in non-performance
for later professions of devotion to political chiefs!

Lord Townshend seems to have placed little trust in such
declarations, especially when linked with requests for additional
financial help, which he greatly resented; and while irate reactions
of a parent on such occasions cannot be taken at face value, Lord
Townshend's reproaches, seen in the setting of their correspondence, carry a measure of conviction. He wrote in October 1747:
'I find by experience that whenever there is an imaginary want of
money my advice is call'd for and a great shew of submission and
resignation to my opinion is made.' And in January 1753, when
Charles, planning marriage, turned to him 'to make up the
fortune of this match': 'I am thoroughly sensible from what
I have experienced from your constant and uniform conduct
towards me that nothing I can offer on this occasion to dissuade
you from your present scheme will or can have any effect. . . .
Advice from me is never agreeable to you nor would you ever

throughout the whole course of your life hitherto attend to it. . . .'
And on Charles again turning to him in August 1755 about his
marriage settlement with Lady Dalkeith, Lord Townshend
affirmed that since November 1754, when he cleared the whole
charge of Charles's last parliamentary election, Charles had
never come near him, nor inquired after his health, but had with
success avoided seeing him: assertions hardly made without a
factual basis. Indeed, after marriage had freed Charles of financial
dependence on his father, relations between them became distant,
and Charles drew closer to his mother.

Nor was his marriage without effect on relations with his
political chiefs, which followed the pattern of those with his
father, and from now on assumed a seemingly incalculable character. Horace Walpole wrote to Richard Bentley on 17 July 1755:
'Charles Townshend marries the great Dowager Dalkeith: his
parts and presumption are prodigious. He wanted nothing but
independence to let him loose: I propose great entertainment
from him.' And when in April 1767 Lady Dalkeith inherited a
considerable fortune from her mother, Charles Townshend,
Chancellor of the Exchequer under Grafton, sweetly wrote to him
with resentments set free: 'Your Grace's regard for me will
incline you to be pleased with hearing that my late accession of
fortune has placed me and, what I love more than myself, my
children, in great affluence and ample station. The relish for this
is heightened in me by the recollection of former incertainties . . .
and the delay of every favour I have ever had reason to expect
from the Crown. I am now out of the reach of fortune, and can act
without anxiety.'[1]

This was written four months before his death. But illustrations
of Charles Townshend's character can be picked out anywhere
during his adult life. He did not change or mellow; nor did he
learn by experience; there was something ageless about him;
never young, he remained immature to the end. At thirty-three,
after eleven years in Parliament, during which he had alternately
sworn allegiance to Newcastle and gone out of his way to attack
him, sometimes with more outrage than wit, Townshend wrote
to him in 1758 a recantation, reminiscent of some letters to his
father: '. . . in every passage of my life, I shall wish and endeavour
to deserve your Grace's favourable opinion and the honor of your
friendship; from which if I have sometimes been too much diverted
by errors and indiscretions; they are errors which I ever remember

---

[1] Grafton MS. 452, at W. Suffolk R.O.

with regret, and indiscretions I flatter myself I have had the
sense to discover and correct.'[1] Which did not prevent him from
repeating them when occasion offered.

Or consider his performance on 8 May 1767, so near the end
of his life, when, writes Horace Walpole,[2] he displayed 'the
amazing powers of his capacity, and the no less amazing incon-
gruities of his character'. Having, early in the day, dealt very
sensibly with the affairs of the East India Company, he 'told the
House that he hoped he had atoned for the inconsideration of his
past life by the care he had taken of that business'—an odd
declaration for a leading statesman aged forty-two. But at night,
intoxicated more with high spirits than drink, he delivered his
famous 'champagne speech', a torrent of wit, knowledge, absurdity, and fiction, heightened by buffoonery; an encomium
and a satire on himself; an arraignment of Chatham's 'wild
incapacity'; and he concluded his mockery of the Government of
which he was a foremost member by saying that 'it was become
what he himself had often been called, a weathercock'. A singularly immature and self-damaging performance.

A remarkable feature in the character of this most fickle of
men was that his fickleness followed a predictable pattern, constantly reproduced. Conscious superiority over other men freely
flaunted, a capacity for seeing things from every angle displayed
with vanity, and the absence of any deeper feelings of attachment,
left Townshend, as Chase Price put it, 'entirely unhinged'. Perhaps imitating Pitt, he prided himself on standing alone, on being
politically 'unconnected'; and, while swayed by his changing
moods, he boasted of being constant and consistent, which in a
sense he was. Of his gyrations and fluctuations I give one example.
During the anxious months, September–December 1762, while
the Peace Preliminaries were under discussion, he, then Secretary
at War, was courted by the Government and the Opposition,
and no one knew from day to day what line he would take. From
the mass of reported contradictions on this occasion I can here
pick out but a few: brief dicta which require no explaining.

'He laughs at the Ministry at night and assures them in the
morning that he is entirely theirs', wrote Rigby on 19 October.[3]
And Shelburne to Bute, on the same day: a friend of Townshend's
has reported that he was 'determined to support the King's
measures and your Lordship both statedly and steadily, and with

[1] 32881, f. 337.   [2] *Memoirs*, vol. iii, pp. 17–18.
[3] Bedford MS. 46, f. 56.

cordiality'.[1] But apparently the same day Townshend sent word
to Newcastle that the moment Newcastle and Devonshire called
upon him 'he was ready'[2]—what he was ready for is not specified.
On 28 October Fox reported to Bute that Townshend was freely
talking against the peace.[3] On 10 November Townshend con-
gratulated the King 'but coldly' on it, and criticized its terms.[4]
The next day Fox wrote to Bute: 'Charles Townshend is worse
than ever; upon my word, my Lord, we shall not be able to go on
with him in his employment and this fickle humour.'[5] Bute to
Shelburne on 12 November: '. . . as to Charles Townshend, I
beleive the best method will be to leave him to himself; . . . he
dare not oppose, and the day of retribution will come'.[6] Fox to
Bute on the 23rd: 'Mr. C.T. was [here], and any body who did
not know him, would have thought him not only a friend but the
most zealous one.'[7] And later on, the same day: 'Charles Townshend is intolerable. He will I beleive do all he can to ruin you;
but he has ruined himself.'[8] Rigby to Bedford on the 24th: 'There
is no guessing at Charles Townshend's intentions, but he continues yet to shuffle, and I dare say will resign or be turned out.'[9]
And the King to Bute about that time: Townshend may 'yet join
the Duke of Newcastle (which I can never think impossible)'.[10]

But here is the picture which, in the midst of these fluctuations,
Townshend drew of himself in a letter to an unknown corre-
spondent: 'It is my firm resolution to act the part of a man of
business and a man of honor; to be decided by things and not
men; to have no party; to *follow no* leader, and to be governed
absolutely by my own judgment, with respect to the Peace now
concluded, the approaching system of measures, and the future
Ministry.'[11] And he proceeds to retail his grievances: in the past
he was 'neglected and frequently injured' by Newcastle; 'dismissed from public office' by him and by Devonshire; left by
Pitt 'at the end of a successful Opposition, in an unpleasant office,
without communication or common respect'. Unconnected with
Newcastle, he would be inconstant if he adopted his resentments;
he must not act second to Devonshire's 'personal and private
disgusts'; he could never unite with Fox; and if he has declined

---

[1] Bute MSS.   [2] Newcastle to Devonshire, 21 October, 32943, ff. 32–40.
[3] Bute MSS.   [4] Sedgwick, No. 223.   [5] Bute MSS.
[6] Lansdowne MSS. at Bowood.   [7] Bute MSS.
[8] Ibid. The letter is wrongly docketed, obviously at a later date: 'December 1762'.
[9] Bedford MS. 46, f. 128.   [10] Sedgwick, no. 231.
[11] From an incomplete copy dated 10 November 1762, in the Charles Townshend
Papers of the Duke of Buccleuch.

Cabinet office (which he claimed had been offered to him) he
has done so 'not from want of ambition, but from a love of *consistency*'.

On 6 December he wrote to Bute that he wished 'to retire
from the office of Secretary at War'—the letter is noted in the
Register of Bute's Correspondence,[1] but I have failed to find it
among the Bute Papers; and Townshend's reasons for retiring are
nowhere stated. He actually resigned on the 8th, the day before
the Peace Preliminaries came before the House; was expected to
arraign them, but when the debate turned in favour of the
Government, spoke on their side ('C. Townshend . . . made the
finest speech I ever heard', wrote Rigby to the Duke of Bedford);[2]
and negotiations for his rejoining the Government followed soon.

These months of crisis are but one example of Townshend's
instability. Reacting negatively to group-ties, when in the Government he almost invariably cultivated the Opposition, and when
in Opposition made approaches to the Government. Much of his
time and energy was taken up by such shifts and manœuvres;
while his unbridled ridicule was practised on all alike, even on
Administrations which he tried to enter. The posts assigned to
him he usually felt to be beneath his rank and merit, which gave
a concrete form of grievance to his negative reactions. In fact, in
terms of office his career was disappointing: after five years as a
junior member of the Board of Trade, nearly two years at the
Admiralty, and one year in Opposition, from 1756 till 1761 he
was relegated to a Court sinecure; from February 1761 till December 1762 was Secretary at War, in the eighteenth century a
subordinate post not carrying Cabinet rank; for seven weeks,
23 February to 15 April 1763, he held the Board of Trade with
powers less extensive than he had contended for; from May 1765
till July 1766, the Pay Office, a lucrative but politically ineffective
post; and in July 1766 was made by Chatham to accept that of
Chancellor of the Exchequer, without a place in the Cabinet: the
Chancellor of the Exchequer as such, being merely an Under-
Secretary to the First Lord of the Treasury, had no claim to
membership of the Effective Cabinet, though Townshend in his
own right could have expected it. 'Cabinets meet, but Charles
never sent to', wrote Selwyn to Lord Holland on 5 August.[3] In
October 1766, after a good deal of sulking, Townshend managed to
wriggle himself into it, with the well-known disastrous results.

[1] 36796.   [2] Bedford MS. 46, f. 170.
[3] *Letters to H. Fox*, ed. Earl of Ilchester, p. 269.

Considered a dozen times for a Secretaryship of State, he was offered it at least three times, but declined. He showed poor judgment in joining or leaving Governments; resigned from Bute's on the eve of its greatest triumph, and rejoined it a few weeks before Bute's resignation; threw away his chances on the formation of the Grenville Government in April 1763, and joined it in May 1765 when it was doomed.

Poverty of heart warped even his judgment: too much preoccupied with his own person, he did not enter into the feelings of other men, lacked intuitive awareness, and so would misjudge situations. Instead of sensing reality, he would argue against it, as if able to impose on it his own conceptions. Here is an example. When in May 1765 George III was forced to reinstate the Grenville Government, the least obnoxious to the King of their conditions was the dismissal of Lord Holland from the Pay Office and his replacement by Townshend. Yet, that for the King this was part of the same humiliating transaction, Townshend refused to see or acknowledge; went about complaining of the treatment now meted out to him at Court;[1] and when told the obvious, that his acceptance 'had been unpleasing to the King, from the manner in which it had been *forced* upon him, at *such* a *time*, and with other similar *affronts* to him', Townshend denied the fact and recapitulated the circumstances: he had refused to accept without the King's approbation![2] A degree of obtuseness remarkable in one so clever and versatile.

The same lack of psychological understanding he showed in his dealings with America, the most important aspect of his career. These moreover reveal an unexpected, though hardly incongruous, facet of his character: his obstinate adherence to his own ideas unaffected by developments, and the persistence with which he tried to realise them. His fatal American measures of 1767, so far from being an improvisation, enacted at the end of his career a programme he had formulated at its start, in 1753–4; and there was a strong emotional colouring to that programme: a rebel towards his father and chiefs, he turned into a heavy father when acting for the Mother Country in relation to her offspring. To the subject of Townshend and America I shall devote the rest of this lecture.

[1] Newcastle to the Bishop of Oxford, 1 June 1765, 32967, ff. 1–7.
[2] See C. Townshend's two letters to his brother, Lord Townshend, 3 and 4 July 1765, *Grenville Papers*, vol. iii, pp. 65–9; and his letter to W. Dowdeswell, 25 June 1765, in the Buccleuch MSS.

In 1749 Charles Townshend started his official career, not at the Admiralty as he had wished but at the lowest Board, that of Trade and Plantations. His five years of apprenticeship there were of vital importance: he became acquainted with colonial problems and formed his ideas on America. In August 1753 instructions of a rather unusual character were issued to Sir Danvers Osborn, Governor of New York[1]—Horace Walpole, writing about 1755, described them as 'better calculated for the latitude of Mexico and for a Spanish tribunal, than for a free rich British settlement'.[2] These instructions Charles Townshend subsequently avowed in the House to have 'advised',[3] that is, to have drafted. They charged the New York Assembly with trampling upon the royal authority and prerogative by assuming 'to themselves the disposal of public money'; directed it to make permanent provision for the salaries of the Governor, judges, and other officials; and for the security of the province and any foreseeable charges. The money was to be applied by warrants from the Governor advised by the Council, the Assembly being merely 'permitted, from time to time, to view and examine . . . accounts'. In short, the royal executive was to be rendered financially independent of the colonial Assembly. A remodelling of colonial government was Townshend's aim, to which the raising of a revenue by act of the British Parliament became a necessary corollary.

In the summer of 1754, with war imminent, plans were discussed in America and London for a 'general concert' between the American Colonies for mutual defence. Townshend, promoted in April to the Board of Admiralty, was consulted by Newcastle on a scheme of union submitted by his recent chief, Lord Halifax, First Lord of Trade. This Townshend thought impracticable, and anyhow undesirable:[4] he did not expect the Colonies to reach agreement concerning their respective contributions; but if they did, they would continue their 'settled design' to draw to themselves by their annual Bills of Supply the prerogatives of the Crown, 'the only means of supporting . . . the superintendency of the Mother Country'. 'Whatever is done, can only be done by an Act of Parliament'; and the Provinces are more likely to accept 'a candid and just plan sent from hence' than form one

---

[1] For their text see *Gentleman's Magazine* (1754), pp. 65–6, and L. W. Labaree, *Royal Instructions to British Colonial Governors, 1670–1776*, vol. i, pp. 190–3.

[2] *Memoirs of the Reign of King George II*, vol. i, p. 397.

[3] Ibid., vol. ii, p. 173; debate of 20 February 1756.

[4] For Halifax's scheme see 32736, ff. 243–5 and 247–56, for Townshend's letter to Newcastle and his 'Remarks', ibid, ff. 508–13.

themselves. 'I shall endeavour to prepare such a plan for your Grace . . . with a fund which all the Provinces will, I am certain, approve and chearfully pay.' I have failed to trace that plan either among the Newcastle or the Townshend Papers. But Charles Townshend's unfounded belief that he could devise a plan for taxing the Colonies by act of the British Parliament which would prove acceptable to them, was to be repeated on later occasions — another example of his way of clinging to his own conceptions in disregard of reality.

In Parliament he continued to speak on colonial matters; and when in December 1759 peace negotiations were expected to start soon, he applied to Pitt to be made Plenipotentiary for America,[1] though this would have given him only the third place on the delegation.

When by the summer of 1762 Townshend talked of resigning the War Office, and the King and Bute too wished him out of it, a transfer to the Board of Trade was discussed. On 16 September Rigby wrote to the Duke of Bedford:[2] 'The world talks much of me as Secretary at War; . . . I believe Charles Townshend has a promise for his favourite American plan.' So far I have not found this plan which presumably reproduced the programme enunciated in 1753–4, and realized in 1767. And when after 8 December Townshend's return to office was discussed, the Board of Trade was again envisaged, but the powers to be conceded to him were once more the subject of weary negotiations. They do not seem to have been extensive when Townshend at last assumed office on 23 February; but anyhow his one remarkable performance concerning America during his seven weeks at the head of the Board of Trade was of a most irregular nature.

The account of it given by Bancroft[3] is inaccurate and confused. When on 4 March Welbore Ellis, Townshend's successor at the War Office, brought in the Army Estimates, it was he, and not Townshend, who stated 'that the American Force was intended to be paid for a future year by America'.[4] And when later on, about 20 March, Townshend proposed that a revenue be immediately raised in America by lowering the duties on French molasses and enforcing their payment, he acted entirely off his

[1] 32900, ff. 120–1.
[2] Bedford MS. 45, f. 220; the letter is printed in the *Bedford Corr.*, vol. iii, pp. 122–5, with the sentence about Townshend omitted.
[3] *History of the United States* (1856), vol. v, pp. 86–8.
[4] See Jenkinson's report of the debate, MS. North b. 5, ff. 87–8 and 94–9 at the Bodleian.

own bat, and not in a ministerial capacity as Bancroft supposed. The King, in an undated letter to Bute,[1] bitterly complains of other Ministers having remained silent on that occasion—'this subject was new to none, having been thought of this whole winter; all ought to have declar'd that next session some tax will be laid before the House but that it requires much information before a proper one can be stated, and thus have thrown out this insidious proposal; I think Mr. Townshends conduct deserves the dismissing him or the least the making him explain his intentions'. What action followed, if any, is uncertain; but on 30 March James Harris notes in his parliamentary reports[2] a dispute between Grenville and Townshend about American duties; after which the matter was 'adjourned to a long day'.

At this time the Grenville Administration was being formed. The intention was to remove Townshend to the Admiralty; against which he demurred. The danger of having him deal with America seems to have been appreciated. Thus Fox, in a letter of 17 March,[3] wished Townshend out of the Board of Trade, and to have 'that greatest and most necessary of all schemes, the settlement of America', effected by others. And James Oswald wrote to Bute on 13 April: '. . . nothing, surely, will embarrass the future administration more than Mr. Townshend's continuing in the resolution of remaining where he is. The settlement of America must be the first and principal object. . . . Can we imagine that either he [Mr. Grenville], Lord H[alifax], or Lord Eg[remont], or all these together, can manage C.T. in that department?'[4]

From April 1763 till May 1765 Townshend was out of office; and on 25 February 1764 Newcastle wrote to Townshend, as his expert on colonial affairs, about the forthcoming budget: 'The next point of consequence . . . is their disposition of North America . . . you must suggest to us what it may be proper to do there.'[5] And when on 7 March Grenville 'gave us', notes Harris, 'some general idea of his plan, particularly as to the taxing America', Townshend spoke strongly on the Government side: 'that our plan of expences being so great, America ought to share'. But when on 9 March Grenville fully developed his scheme, which included the American Stamp Bill, Townshend was absent, having gone to Cambridge to manage for Newcastle the contest be-

---

[1] Sedgwick, op. cit., No. 282.
[2] Malmesbury MSS.
[3] Fitzmaurice, *Shelburne*, vol. i, p. 148.
[4] *Memorials of James Oswald of Dunnikier* (1825), 413–19.
[5] 32956, f. 95.

tween Hardwicke and Sandwich for High Steward of the University.
The discussion of the stamp duties was deferred for a year. On
20 January 1765, in a debate on Naval Estimates, Townshend
went out of his way to assert 'the supremacy of this country over
the colonys—would not have them emancipated'.[1] And when on
6 February Grenville introduced his Stamp Bill, Townshend supported him in a speech which he concluded with a peroration in
the best paternal style: 'And now will these Americans, children
planted by our care, nourished up by our indulgence untill they
are grown to a degree of strength and opulence, and protected by
our arms, will they grudge to contribute their mite to releive us
from the heavy weight of that burden which we lie under?'[2] To
which Barré replied in a speech widely publicized in America:
'They planted by your care? No! your oppressions planted 'em
in America. . . . They nourished by your indulgence?' etc.

Townshend declined Cabinet office in the Rockingham
Administration, but remained in the wings as Paymaster General,
and had a share in shaping their American policy. After a good
deal of equivocation he, who in February 1765 had whole-
heartedly supported the Stamp Act, a year later voted for its
repeal while reasserting his own attitude towards America. In
the crucial debates on the subject he rarely intervened, which was
remarked upon at the time: only three speeches by him are
recorded, and reports of two have but recently come to light which
give a fully intelligible account of his argument.

On 17 December 1765 Townshend opposed Grenville's motion
declaring the Colonies in a state of rebellion. According to James
Harris, he owned his difficulties; would await further information
from America; spoke strongly for the supremacy of Parliament;
'yet . . . if you have done any thing to stop or injure their trade,
releive them and they will submit'. Here is in embryonic form the
policy of Repeal coupled with a Declaratory Act. When, contrary
to Newcastle's stated opinion, the resolutions asserting the right
of Parliament were made to precede the Repeal, the measures
were hammered out in two small informal meetings at Rockingham's, on 19 and 21 January, at which, of those present, Townshend was by far the ablest and best versed in American affairs.[3]

[1] Harris's parliamentary notes, Malmesbury MSS.
[2] The fullest report of the debate is given in a letter from Jared Ingersoll, agent for
Connecticut, to its Governor, Thomas Fitch, 11 February 1765; see *Collections of Conn.
Hist. Soc., Fitch Papers*, vol. ii, pp. 317–26. It was first published in 1766 in *Mr. Ingersoll's Letters relating to the Stamp-Act*.
[3] About the two meetings see 35430, f. 31 (misdated), and 32973, f. 224.

'I have had very little to do in the settlement of them,' wrote Newcastle to the Archbishop of Canterbury on 2 February; 'which, I understand, was done at a meeting with the three Ministers [Rockingham, Grafton, and Conway], Mr. Charles Yorke, Mr. Dowdeswell, and Mr. Charles Townshend'.[1]

None the less, when the resolutions came before the House, on 3–6 February, Townshend preserved silence, and only broke it on the 7th, when Grenville moved an address for enforcing the laws in America. The fullest account of Townshend's speech is preserved in the shorthand notes by Nathaniel Ryder (first Lord Harrowby) from which I quote: '*C. Townshend*. Does not rise to differ from the spirit and the temper expressed by the honourable gentleman who proposed this address. He feels for the situation of N. America as much as Grenville. He thinks if some proper plan is not formed for governing as well as quieting them at present and for the future, it will be extremely dangerous. The magistrates at present in many colonies elective, the judges dependent on the assemblies for their salaries.'[2] But Townshend opposed Grenville's motion as 'tending directly to the enforcing of the Stamp Act'. 'We are now without forts or troops. Our magistrates without inclinations and without power. Would you raise this temper while you are the most unable to resist it? If a delay is necessary, do not let us lose the fruits of this delay by this hasty, this preclusive measure. . . .' And Sir Roger Newdigate, when jotting down a few notes on Townshend's speech, singles out his remarks about the need to alter 'the plan of government in North America', about the position of governors, judges, and other officials, etc.[3] In short, Townshend was harping once more on his old theme, the remodelling and strengthening of the executive power in America.

The third speech by Townshend on the Repeal of the Stamp Act, on 11 February, again shows that over American taxation he was basically in agreement with Grenville. He declared, reported James West to Newcastle, 'he could not repeal the Act on account of the right whereby it was imposed, nor on account of the violence that had been used against it, but only if at all, on the impracticability, or inexpediency of it, or the inability of the Colonies to pay the tax'.[4] Surely very half-hearted support for what came afterwards to be considered the chief plank in the programme of the Rockinghams.

---

[1] 32973, ff. 342–4.   [2] Harrowby MSS., document 65.
[3] Newdigate MS. B. 2546/18, at the Warwicks R.O.   [4] 32973, f. 411.

Yet during the crisis caused by Grafton's resignation in the first fortnight of May 1766, Newcastle proposed making Townshend Secretary for America (a new office to be created for him), because of 'that attention to the settlement and government of our Colonies, which in their present situation they will require'; and 'Charles Townshend knows more of the matter than anybody'.[1] Conway agreed, and Rockingham was to speak to Townshend about it.[2] Of what passed between them we have only an obviously embroidered second-hand account, in a letter from Whately to Grenville.[3] All we know for certain is that the Rockinghams were about to entrust Townshend with the management of American affairs, and he apparently declined. True, at this juncture the colonial problems of immediate interest were the commercial regulations concerning North America and the West Indies and the free port in Dominica, on which Townshend was reputed an expert. But even so, in view of his attitude on American constitutional problems, it seems, to say the least, incongruous with the later claims of the Rockinghams that they of all people should have wished to put him in charge of American affairs.

In the Chatham Administration the Colonies were primarily Shelburne's concern, and when on 26 January 1767, over Grenville's motion that the expense of the Army in the Colonies be defrayed by them, Townshend pledged himself to raise a revenue there for the purpose, his action was unauthorized, an aggravated repetition of his intervention in March 1763; his methods and set purpose remained unchanged. Nor was his pledge a spontaneous reaction to a challenge. Shelburne, writing to Chatham on 1 February, correctly stated some parts of Townshend's plan which he had heard 'from general conversation'.[4] Townshend had obviously been preparing it, but had not submitted either its principle or its details to the Cabinet. With whom he prepared it is suggested by an undated draft of the Townshend duties among the Buccleuch MSS.: it is in the handwriting of Samuel Touchet, M.P., a bankrupt merchant of considerable ability but doubtful reputation, with whom Townshend associated a good deal, and for whom in June 1767 he tried to obtain financial provision from Grafton stating that 'he and he alone has the merit of whatever has been honorably done in this winter for the public and the

---

[1] 32975, ff. 89, 104. See also Fortescue, vol. i, p. 301.
[2] 32975, ff. 102 and 164 (misdated); and 33001, f. 225.
[3] *Grenville Papers*, vol. iii, pp. 235–6.   [4] *Chatham Corr.*, vol. iii, pp. 184–5.

Treasury in the choice of taxes'.[1] Townshend assured the House that the revenue would be drawn from America 'without offence',[2] presumably because of its external character, and then treated 'the distinction between external and internal taxes as ridiculous in every body's opinion except the Americans', which, as Shelburne remarked, was 'not the way to make any thing go down well in America'.[3]

A more exact indication of the duties was given by Townshend, incidentally, when on 13 May he introduced resolutions for punishing the delinquency of New York with regard to the Mutiny Act. Conway, disapproving of the measure, had refused to do so. Still, also in the case of Townshend there occurred a hitherto unexplained hitch. He was to have opened the plan on 5 May, but 'that very morning', writes Walpole, 'he pretended to have fallen down-stairs and cut his eye dangerously'.[4] Walpole's comment, however, that Townshend's 'strange irresolution and versatility could not conceal itself even on so public an occasion', is wide of the mark. It was his determination to free the royal officials of their dependence on the Colonial Assemblies which produced the delay. Townshend wrote to Grafton in an undated letter which must, I think, be placed on 5 May: 'Mr. Townshend ... sincerely laments that the opportunity has not been taken of soliciting his Majesty's assent to the proposition of independent salaries for the civil officers of North America: especially as he has pledged himself to the house for some measure of this sort; and had the assurances of Lord Shelburne in the last cabinet for the whole extent of the establishment and the D. of Grafton on Saturday adopted the idea at least as far as New York. In this distress, Mr. T. does not think he can with honor move the resolutions this day, and therefore hopes either to have the authority or that some means may be found of postponing the matter for a day or two till he can receive it. He feels his honor absolutely at stake.'[5]

By 13 May, when he moved the resolutions, he had obtained the desired authority, though in a restricted form. Horace Walpole's report of the speech,[6] which he described as 'consonant to the character of a man of business, and ... unlike the wanton sallies of the man of parts and pleasure', quotes him saying: 'The salaries of governors and judges in that part of the world must be

[1] Grafton MS. 454.
[2] Grafton, *Autobiography*, p. 126.
[3] Loc. cit.
[4] *Memoirs*, vol. iii, p. 15.
[5] Grafton MS. 445.
[6] Op. cit., vol. iii, pp. 21–4.

made independent of their Assemblies: but he advised the House to confine their resolutions to the offending provinces.' Charles Garth, M.P., agent for South Carolina, reported to its Committee of Correspondence Townshend's forecast of his 'plan for improving the system of government in the Colonies': he was going to propose 'that, out of the fund arising from the American duties . . . His Majesty should be enabled to establish salaries . . . better suited to support the dignity of the respective officers, and for which to be no longer dependent upon the pleasure of any Assembly'.[1] Confined 'to the offending provinces', these proposals were embodied in the sixteenth resolution of the Committee of Ways and Means which lays down that the duties to be raised in the Colonies be applied in making provision for the administration of justice and the support of civil government, in such Colonies 'where it shall be found necessary', and the residue be used for defence.[2] When on 2 July the American Bills received the Royal assent, Garth's comment was that this provision 'must operate to render the Assembly . . . rather insignificant'. 'Indeed', he added, 'the Bill did not pass the Commons without an intimation of this kind to the House, but the measure was taken, and the friends of America are too few to have any share in a struggle with a Chancellor of the Exchequer.'[3] Thus after fourteen years, towards the end of his career and life, Charles Townshend, the reputed weathercock, carried into effect the scheme which he had put forward as a very junior minister in 1753–4: a steadiness of purpose with which he has not been credited.

When Townshend died on 4 September 1767, Horace Walpole wrote: '. . . our comet is set! Charles Townshend is dead. All those parts and fire are extinguished; those volatile salts are evaporated; that first eloquence of the world is dumb! that duplicity is fixed, that cowardice terminated heroically. He joked on death, as naturally as he used to do on the living. . . . With a robust person he had always a menacing constitution. He had had a fever the whole summer, recovered as it was thought, relapsed, was neglected, and it turned to an incurable putrid fever.'[4]

I close with a reflection which often saddens a biographer; it is easier to analyse the shortcomings and mistakes of a man than to convey an idea of his genius, charm, or eloquence, unless they

---

[1] *So. Ca. Hist. and Geneal. Mag.*, vol. xxix (1928), pp. 227–30.
[2] *Parliamentary History*, vol. xvi, p. 376, and *Commons Journals*, vol. xxxi, pp. 394–5.
[3] Op. cit., pp. 298–300.   [4] To Horace Mann, 28 September 1767.

are transmitted in his writings, which is not the case with Charles Townshend. For us 'that first eloquence of the world' remains 'dumb'. The record we have is of a man of quite exceptional ability, unhappy and self-frustrated, and now best remembered for the disastrous part he played in the prelude to the American Revolution.

20

MONARCHY AND THE PARTY SYSTEM

I HAVE chosen for my subject a story with a happy ending, with a striking dénouement, unforeseen and unpredictable while it was shaping. Constitutional monarchy—the union of a hereditary Crown with parliamentary government—is, to quote Mr. Churchill, 'of all the institutions which have grown up among us over the centuries . . . the most deeply founded and dearly cherished'.[1] British monarchy detached from British politics has become the link of the Commonwealth of Nations, and the pivot of government in a number of co-ordinated countries; it is seen to secure basic continuity in government with a variability unequalled under any other system. But in the earlier stages the growth of constitutional monarchy was impeded rather than aided by conscious political thought—the 'odious title' of Prime Minister was decried, and the extinction of party prayed for. Even now constitutional monarchy, though anchored both in the thought and affection of the nation, depends for its smooth working on the continuance of concrete factors by which it was moulded. Hence the importance of discerning them.

What are the basic elements of constitutional monarchy? A Sovereign placed above parties and politics; a Prime Minister and Government taking rise from Parliament, and received rather than designated by the Sovereign, yet as 'H.M. confidential servants' deriving from the Royal Prerogative that essential executive character which an elected legislature could not impart to them; and an unpolitical Civil Service whose primary connexion is with the Crown, and which, while subordinated to party-governments, is unaffected by their changes: the two permanent elements, the Crown and the Civil Service, which not by chance together left the political arena, supply the framework for the free play of parliamentary politics and governments. Under royal government the sovereign was the undisputed,

[1] In the broadcast delivered on 7 February 1952, after the death of King George VI.

immediate head of the executive; under parliamentary government, it is the prime minister; but no clear-cut formula is possible for the intervening period of 'mixed government', during which the direction of government gradually passed from the sovereign to the prime minister by a process that can be logically defined but eludes precise dating. The prime minister replaced the sovereign as actual head of the executive when the choice of the prime minister no longer lay with the sovereign; the sovereign lost the choice when strongly organized, disciplined parliamentary parties came into existence; and party discipline depends primarily on the degree to which the member depends on the party for his seat. The sovereign can keep clear of party politics only so long as it is not incumbent on him or her to choose the prime minister. Thus constitutional monarchy as now understood hinges to a high degree on the working of the modern party system.

In 1761 not one parliamentary election was determined by party, and in 1951 not one constituency returned a non-party member. To trace how that change has come about will require a most thorough knowledge of constituencies and elections, of members and parliaments, and of constitutional ideas and realities throughout the formative period; to acquire that knowledge is one of the tasks of the History of Parliament on which we are now engaged, and can only be accomplished by a great collective effort. In this lecture I propose to set before you tentative outlines: suggestions rather than conclusions. I shall deal mainly with the earlier period covered by my own research; still, in a broad survey I am bound to travel beyond its limits, and I have drawn on the help and advice most generously accorded by fellow workers in our field.[1]

2

The king's business in parliament had at all times to be transacted through ministers; and as parliament grew in importance, so did the minister capable of managing it. Yet under 'mixed government' even for the securing of parliamentary support royal favour

[1] I name those who have either given me unprinted work to read or who have directly contributed suggestions bearing on my theme, or quotations illustrating my points. For such help I am indebted to Professor A. Aspinall, Mr. Asa Briggs, Mr. M. G. Brock, Mr. I. R. Christie, Mr. Kitson Clark, Professor Norman Gash, Mr. David Gray, Dr. R. W. Greaves, Mr. J. B. Owen, Dr. J. H. Plumb, Mr. R. R. Sedgwick, Miss L. S. Sutherland, Miss Joan Wake, and Professor Robert Walcott.

and confidence were needed, and as late as 1786, Robert Beatson, in his *Political Index* dedicated to Adam Smith, placed the names of the leading ministers under the heading 'A List of Prime Ministers and Favourites, from the accession of King Henry VIII to the present time'. The personal element inevitably determined the exact relation between the sovereign and his advisers, and at all times there were kings who yielded easy assent to ministers or deferred to the guidance of favourites; and few more so than George III, especially in the first decade of his reign. Horace Walpole, accurately informed by his friend H. S. Conway, wrote in 1769 that George III 'never interfered with his Ministers', but 'seemed to resign himself entirely to their conduct for the time' —a statement borne out by the king's voluminous correspondence wherein, as a rule, he repeats with approval advice tendered by his ministers. He would become active only when, in Walpole's words, 'he was to undo an administration'.[1] Still, 'the King's independency', that is, his right to choose and dismiss ministers, was a constitutional axiom; and however hard politicians strove for office, they would, each and all, declare their extreme reluctance to enter or retain it unless assured of the king's favour willingly accorded. Newcastle in 1759 voiced 'the most ardent wishes' for the Prince of Wales to succeed 'in such a situation as shall leave his hands free . . . to form his plan of government with advantage';[2] George Grenville claimed to have 'entered into the King's service . . . to hinder the law from being indecently and unconstitutionally given to him'—'to prevent any undue and unwarrantable force being put upon the Crown';[3] and Pitt repeatedly declared that he would not be forced upon the king by parliament, nor come into his service against his consent. When the Fox-North Coalition had succeeded in imposing themselves on the king driven to the brink of abdication, Fox, who treated Whig 'anti-monarchism as the main principle of the British Constitution',[4] addressed him, on 16 April 1783, in the following terms:[5]

> Mr. Fox hopes that Your Majesty will not think him presumptuous or improperly intruding upon Your Majesty with professions, if he begs leave most humbly to implore Your Majesty to believe that both the Duke of Portland and he have nothing so much at heart as to

[1] Horace Walpole, *Memoirs*, vol. iii, p. 66.
[2] 32889, ff. 136–7; quoted in my book, *England in the Age of the American Revolution*, p. 100.
[3] *Grenville Papers*, vol. ii, pp. 86 and 106.
[4] R. Pares, 'George III and the Politicians', *Transactions of the R. Hist. Soc.*, 5th series, vol. i (1951), p. 128.   [5] Fortescue, op. cit., vol. vi, p. 357, No. 4308.

conduct Your Majesty's affairs, both with respect to measures and to persons, in the manner that may give Your Majesty the most satisfaction, and that, whenever Your Majesty will be graciously pleased to condescend even to hint your inclinations upon any subject, that it will be the study of Your Majesty's Ministers to show how truly sensible they are of Your Majesty's goodness.

During the next forty years parties were gradually shaping in parliament, but they did not as yet dominate it, and in theory relations between king and ministers remained unchanged. 'If you do not like us why do you not turn us out?' asked the Duke of Wellington of George IV in July 1821.[1] And in March 1827 Stephen Lushington, M.P., Secretary of the Treasury, still attributed to the king the absolute and unqualified choice of his ministers;[2] while Canning, in language curiously reminiscent of that held by Bute sixty-five years earlier, inveighed against aristocratic 'confederacies', and discoursed on 'the real vigour of the Crown when it chooses to put forth its own strength'.[3]

When in 1834 William IV had dismissed the Melbourne Government, Peel claimed a 'fair trial' for the ministers of the king's choice; and its semblance was conceded by the Whigs who, having won the ensuing general election, refrained from a direct vote of censure on the Address.[4] As late as 1846, Wellington and Peel, at variance with a majority of their party, harped on their position and duties as Ministers of the Crown and declared that, were they to stand alone, they would still have 'to enable Her Majesty to meet her Parliament and to carry on the business of the country'.

> I was of the opinion [declared Wellington] that the formation of a Government in which Her Majesty would have confidence, was of much greater importance than the opinions of any individual on the Corn Laws, or any other law. . . .

And Peel, whose ideas of an independent executive similarly seemed to hark back to the earlier period, thus attempted to define his position:

[1] *The Diary of Henry Hobhouse (1820–7)*, ed. A. Aspinall, p. 67; see also *The Journal of Mrs. Arbuthnot*, 27 June 1821, ed. F. Bamford and the Duke of Wellington, vol. i, p. 103.

[2] S. R. Lushington to Sir Wm. Knighton, 26 March 1827: *Letters of King George IV*, ed. A. Aspinall, vol. iii, pp. 207–10.

[3] G. Canning to J. W. Croker, 3 April 1827: *The Croker Papers*, ed. L. J. Jennings, vol. i, p. 368.

[4] See G. Kitson Clark, *Peel and the Conservative Party. A Study in Politics, 1832–41*, pp. 211–12 and 237–8.

I see it over and over again repeated, that I am under a personal
obligation for holding the great office which I have the honour to
occupy . . . that I was placed in that position by a party. . . . I am
not under an obligation to any man, or to any body of men, for being
compelled . . . to undergo the official duties and labour which I
have undertaken. . . .

And next:

I have served four Sovereigns. . . . I served each of those Sovereigns at critical times and in critical circumstances . . . and . . .
there was but . . . one reward which I desired . . . namely, the
simple acknowledgment, on their part, that I had been to them a
loyal and faithful Minister. . . .

To this Disraeli retorted that the queen would never have called
on Peel in 1841 had he not 'placed himself, as he said, at the head
of the Gentlemen of England'.

I say [continued Disraeli] it is utterly impossible to carry on your
Parliamentary Constitution except by political parties. I say there
must be distinct principles as lines of conduct adopted by public
men. . . .
Above all, maintain the line of demarcation between parties; for
it is only by maintaining the independence of party that you can
maintain the integrity of public men, and the power and influence
of Parliament itself.[1]

Here then were two conceptions of the ministers' relations to
Crown and Party: one reflecting the past but still adducible
without patent absurdity; the other, much more in harmony
with the realities which then were shaping, and which, once
shaped, were soon to be mistaken for primordial elements of the
British Constitution. The past and the future, capable of neat
definition, impinged on a period of mixed character, first, by a
theoretical carry over, and next, by historical antedating. As a
result, 'by a double distortion', to quote Mr. Sedgwick's summing
up, George III 'has been represented as having endeavoured to
imitate the Stuarts when he ought to have anticipated Queen
Victoria'.[2]

3

According to contemporaries the complex system of the 'mixed
form of government' combined 'by skilful division of power' the

[1] Hansard, vol. lxxxiii, 3rd series, 22 January 1846, cols. 92–3, 120, and 123.
[2] Sedgwick, op. cit., Introduction, p. viii.

best of the monarchy, aristocracy, and democracy; and it was
viewed by them with pride and satisfaction. Mechanically
minded and with a bent towards the ingenious, they relished its
'checks and controls', and the 'mutual watchfulness and jealousy'
which its delicate balance demanded from all concerned; and
they cherished a constitution which safeguarded their rights and
freedoms when 'in almost every other nation of Europe' public
liberty was 'extremely upon the decline'.[1] George III, that much
maligned monarch, was truly representative when, abhorring
both 'despotism' and 'anarchy', he extolled 'the beauty, excellence, and perfection of the British constitution as by law established'.[2] What was bound to escape contemporaries was the
insoluble contradictions of a political system which, incongruously,
associated a royal executive with parliamentary struggles for office.
Yet the two had to coexist in an organic transition from royal to
parliamentary government.

A parliamentary régime is based on the unhindered alternating
of party-governments. But while contending party leaders can
in turn fill the office of prime minister, how could the king freely
pass from the one side to the other, and in turn captain opposite
teams? It was far more consonant with his position to try to heal
'the unhappy divisions that subsist between men' and form an
administration from 'the best of all parties' than to quit 'one set
of men for another'. Could he give up with unconcern the
ministers whom he had chosen and upheld, and in whose actions
and policy he had participated? In 1779 it was but natural for
him to stipulate that on a change of government past measures
should 'be treated with proper respect' and that 'no blame be
laid' on them. And here is a naive but sincere statement of his
position: 'I have no wish but for the prosperity of my Dominions
therefore must look on all who will not heartily assist me as bad
men as well as ungrateful subjects.' And on another occasion:
'. . . whilst I have no wish but for the good and prosperity of my
country, it is impossible that the nation shall not stand by me; if
they will not, they shall have another King.'[3] He did not think in
terms of parties; but their existence prevented the king, while he

---

[1] David Hume, *Essays Moral, Political, and Literary* (1742).

[2] *Correspondence of King George III*, vol. iv, pp. 220–1, no. 2451; the King to Lord
North, 14 November 1778.

[3] Fortescue, op. cit., vol. i, p. 375, No. 353, the King to Pitt, 15 July 1766; vol. iv,
p. 517, No. 3875, the King to the Lord Chancellor, 11 December 1779; vol. iv, p. 507,
No. 2865, same to same, 3 December 1779; vol. vi, p. 151, No. 3973, the King to Lord
North, 4 November 1782; vol. iv, p. 65, No. 2230, same to same, 17 March 1778.

remained the actual head of the executive, from leading an undivided nation.

Yet it was impossible to eliminate party from parliament: an assembly whose leaders contend for office and power was bound to split into factions divided by personal animosities and trying to preserve their identity and coherence in and out of office. Consequently when in office they laid themselves open to the accusation of monopolizing power and of 'keeping the King in fetters'; in opposition, of distressing the government with intention to 'storm the Closet' and force themselves, unconstitutionally, on the king. No consistent defence of parties was possible under the 'mixed form of government', and this undoubtedly retarded their development and consolidation. To Bolingbroke parties when based on a 'difference of principles and designs' were 'misfortune enough', but if continued without it an even greater misfortune, for then they were mere 'instruments of private ambition'.[1] David Hume denounced them as subversive of government and begetting 'the fiercest animosities' among fellow citizens; but he next conceded that to 'abolish all distinctions of party may not be practicable, perhaps, not desirable, in a free government'.[2] Burke squarely contended that party-divisions were, for good or evil, 'things inseparable from free government'; and in his well-known euology of party as a union of men endeavouring to promote the national interest on a common principle, gave a forecast of parliamentary government. Men so connected, he wrote, must strive 'to carry their common plan into execution with all the power and authority of the State'; in forming an administration give 'their party preference in all things'; and not 'accept any offers of power in which the whole body is not included'.[3] While professing adherence to the Revolution Settlement, by implication he eliminated the rights of the Crown, and obliquely argued that in fact the royal executive had ceased to exist, replaced by the monstrous contraption of a cabal set on separating 'the Court from Administration'. The 'double Cabinet', a product of Burke's fertile, disordered, and malignant imagination, long bedevilled his own party and their spiritual descendants.

That the House of Commons might ultimately 'engross the whole power of the constitution', wresting the executive from the

---

[1] *A Dissertation upon Parties* (1734).

[2] Op. cit., part I, essay VII, 'Of Parties in General', and part II, essay XIV, 'Of the Coalition of Parties'.

[3] *Observations on a late State of the Nation* (1769); and *Thoughts on the Cause of the Present Discontents* (1770).

Crown, was apprehended by Hume. How then could they be
'confined within the proper limits?'

> I answer [wrote Hume] that the interest of the body is here re-
> strained by that of the individuals. . . . The Crown has so many
> offices at its disposal, that, when assisted by the honest and disin-
> terested part of the House, it will always command the resolutions
> of the whole so far, at least, as to preserve the antient constitution
> from danger.

He thus discerned within the House itself the main obstacle
to parliamentary government: a majority of its members were as
yet by their ideas, interest, and pursuits unfitted for a system of
party politics.

4

Parliamentary struggles for office necessarily produce a dichotomy
of 'ins' and 'outs'; and two party names were current since the
last quarter of the seventeenth century: hence in retrospect the
appearances of a two-party system. In reality three broad divisions,
based on type and not on party, can be distinguished in the
eighteenth-century House of Commons: on the one side were the
followers of Court and Administration, the 'placemen', *par
excellence* a group of permanent 'ins'; on the opposite side, the
independent country gentlemen, of their own choice permanent
'outs'; and in between, occupying as it were the centre of the
arena, and focusing upon themselves the attention of the public
and of history, stood the political factions contending for power,
the forerunners of parliamentary government based on a party
system. Though distinct, these groups were not sharply separated;
wide borderlands intervened between them, in which heterogeneous types moved to and fro.

The Court and Administration party was a composite, differen-
tiated body; but common to them all was a basic readiness to
support any minister of the king's choice: even in their parliamentary capacity they professed direct political allegiance to the
Crown, either on a traditional semi-feudal, or on a timeless civil-
service basis, or merely as recipients, in one form or another, of
the king's bounty; and adherence to the king's government, so
long as compatible with conscience, was far more consonant with
the avowed decencies of eighteenth-century politics than 'formed
opposition'. A second, concomitant, characteristic of the group

was that whether they were great noblemen, or minor ministers of an administrative type, or hard-working officials, or political parasites, they tried through a direct nexus with the Crown to secure permanency of employment: wherein they were, by and large, successful. A third common feature, induced by natural selection and inherent in the character of the group, was that its members did not play for the highest political prizes: peers of the first rank and great wealth and desirous of making a figure in the country, or great orators or statesmen in either House, would wellnigh automatically move into the centre of the arena and take their place among the leaders of political factions.

Here are examples of non-political groups in Court and Administration. The Brudenells were in the second half of the eighteenth century prominent at Court, and although they invariably had two, and mostly three, peerages, and at least four seats in the Commons—'I do not think', says their historian, Miss Joan Wake, 'that they were ever much interested in politics.'[1] The Secretaries of the Admiralty were civil servants with expert technical knowledge, and though from Pepys to Croker they sat in parliament, in the eighteenth century not one went out on a change of government. Croker resigned with Wellington in 1830; 'till our own day', he wrote in 1857, 'the Secretary was not looked upon as a political officer, did not change with ministries, and took no part in political debate'.[2] The Secretaries of the Treasury, forerunners *inter alia* of the modern Parliamentary Whips, were civil servants concerned in the management of the House of Commons. In 1742, the Duke of Bedford took it for granted that Walpole's Secretary of the Treasury, John Scrope, would be dismissed, 'through whose hands such sums of money have passed, and who refused to give any answer to the Secret Committee about those dark transactions. . . .'

. . . what your Grace mentions is absolutely impracticable [replied Pulteney]. Mr. Scrope is the only man I know, that thoroughly understands the business of the Treasury, and is versed in drawing money bills. On this foundation he stands secure, and is as immovable as a rock. . . .[3]

[1] Miss Wake, when sending me the eighteenth-century chapters of her forthcoming book, used the sentence quoted above in a covering letter.

[2] *The Croker Papers*, vol. i, p. 81.

[3] The letters are printed in the *Bedford Correspondence*, ed. Lord John Russell, vol. i, pp. 4–8. Their text reproduced above is corrected from the originals at Woburn Abbey. In the letter from Bedford to Pulteney the editor through a slip omitted 'about those dark transactions' followed by fifteen more words.

When in May 1765 the king was obliged to take back the Grenvilles, they meant to exact explanations from some Members of
Parliament who held quasi-civil service posts and of whose attachment they felt uncertain; but they dropped this design when told
by one of them that

> he would faithfully support the administration of which he was a
> part but that he would on no consideration combine with any body
> of subjects against the undoubted right of the Crown to name its
> own officers. . . .[1]

And in 1827 J. C. Herries, M.P., Secretary of the Treasury, thus
defined his position:[2]

> I am pursuing my own laborious vocation. . . . I am not in the
> following of any party. My business is with the public interests and
> my duty to promote the King's service wherever I am employed.

Horace Walpole admitted that among the 'Treasury Jesuits', as
he called them, were 'some of the ablest men in the House of
Commons, as Elliot, Dyson, Martin, and Jenkinson'; yet he
ascribed to 'secret influence' their continuance in office 'through
every Administration', and echoed Burke in calling them 'the
Cabinet that governed the Cabinet'.[3]

Whether a post was held by quasi-civil service tenure often
depended on its holder. Lord Barrington, M.P., never out of
employment between 1746 and 1778, was nineteen years at the
War Office under Newcastle, Devonshire, Rockingham, Chatham, Grafton, and North; but Henry Fox as Secretary at War
was a front-rank politician. Soame Jenyns, a littérateur of distinction and with good connexions, held the post of a Lord of
Trade from 1755 till he left parliament in 1780; for Charles
Townshend it was the first step in his political career. The character of Court offices was even more uncertain: Lord Hertford,
the head of an eminently political family, who between 1751 and
1766 had been Lord of the Bedchamber, Ambassador to Paris,
Lord Lieutenant of Ireland, Lord Steward, and then from 1766
onwards, Lord Chamberlain, wrote to the king on the fall of the
North Administration: 'Let me . . . as a personal servant to your

---

[1] From Gilbert Elliot's 'Account of the crisis of May–June 1765', Elliot MSS. at
Minto House, vol. vii, No. 3; reproduced from a copy in the Liverpool Papers, 38335,
ff. 120–33, in N. S. Jucker, *The Jenkinson Papers*, p. 367.

[2] J. C. Herries to Sir Wm. Knighton, 27 February 1827, *Letters of King George IV*,
vol. iii, p. 200.

[3] Horace Walpole, *Memoirs*, vol. ii, p. 221; vol. iv, pp. 75–6.

Majesty, not be involved with Ministers to whom I have never belonged. . . .'

Not 'to belong to Ministers' was sometimes raised to the level of a principle. Harry, sixth Duke of Bolton, early in the reign of George III sided with the Opposition and rejoined them in 1770; but on succeeding to the dukedom in July 1765, declared that in future

> his attachment shall be to the Crown only—that he sees how contemptible, and weak it is for a peer of England independent as he is, and with a great estate, to be dragged along in the suite of any private man or set of men whatever; and to become the mean instrument of their views, their faction, or ambition.

And Lord Egmont declared in the Cabinet on 1 May 1766: '. . . that I had no predilection for this or that set of men—that my first duty was to Your Majesty.' Or again, in January 1783, Lord Hood, when put up in his absence as candidate for Westminster, wrote that though he had no ambition for a seat in the House of Commons, he would accept, but would then 'studiously steer clear . . . of all suspicion of being a *party man* . . . for or against the Minister', as he thought this 'unbecoming a military servant of the King'.[1]

To sum up: so long as government was truly the king's own business, and the king's permanent servants could sit in parliament, there was nothing reprehensible or illogical in members refusing, from legitimate interest or on grounds of conscience, to commit themselves to parties and leaders.

5

The country gentlemen (and certain urban counterparts of theirs)[2] were the very antithesis of the Court party. Their watchword was independence: attachment to the Crown but no obligations to ministers. They entered the House with a sense of duty to the public; their ambition was primacy in their own 'country' attested by being chosen parliamentary representatives for their

---

[1] Fortescue, op. cit., vol. i, p. 27, No. 21, Lord Hertford to the King, 3 April 1782 (misdated by the editor as 1762); vol. i, p. 158, No. 134, Egmont to the King, 12 July 1765; vol. i, p. 300, No. 304, same to same, 2 May 1766; vol. vi, p. 209, No. 4062, Lord Hood, 16 January 1783.

[2] Men like John Barnard or William Beckford—rich business men not seeking government contracts but representative of the independent business community.

county or some respectable boroughs (or else they sat for complete pocket boroughs of their own, preferably without voters for whom favours might have to be obtained from Administration). Office, honours, or profits might have impaired rather than raised their standing;[1] the sovereign had therefore little occasion to disappoint them, or the minister to reward them; and they were treated with the respect due to the independent part they played. They were critical of financial extravagance on Court, sinecures, or on costly (and unnecessary) wars; and they were suspicious, or even contemptuous, of the ways of courtiers and politicians; they loathed government contractors and pensioners in the House—the locusts that devoured the land tax—and were easily roused against them. But not playing for office, they were not bound to factions: when on 12 February 1741 the Opposition Whigs moved for Walpole's dismissal, 25 country gentlemen normally in opposition to him voted against the motion, while 44 left the House.[2]

Governor Pitt wrote to his son on 16 January 1705:[3]

> If you are in Parliament, show yourself on all occasions a good Englishman, and a faithful servant to your country. . . . Avoid faction, and never enter the House pre-possessed; but attend diligently to the debate, and vote according to your conscience and not for any sinister end whatever. I had rather see any child of mine want than have him get his bread by voting in the House of Commons.

About 1745 the story was told[4] that a peerage had been offered to Sir Watkin Williams Wynn (M.P. for County Denbigh from 1722 till his death in 1749):

> . . . his answer was that as long as His Majesty's Ministers acted for the good of their country, he was willing to consent to anything; he

---

[1] With regard to honours the position had changed by the beginning of the nineteenth century: numerous peerages had been conferred by Pitt on leading county families, and seem to have stimulated further applications. On 5 November 1814, Lord Liverpool, having repeatedly discussed the creation of peerages with the Prince Regent, wrote to E. Wilbraham Bootle, M.P., that in order to keep the number within reasonable bounds, it was found necessary 'explicitly to refuse the application of every country gentleman, whatever his fortune or pretensions', and confine new peerages 'either to persons who had claims on the ground of some public service, official or in the field', or 'who were already Scotch or Irish peers' (38260, f. 96).

[2] Rev. H. Etough to Rev. Dr. Burch, n.d., Coxe, *Memoirs of Sir Robert Walpole*, vol. iii, pp. 562–3.

[3] H.M.C., *Fortescue MSS.*, vol. i, p. 18.

[4] H.M.C., *Hastings MSS.*, vol. iii, p. 49; Lord Hastings to his father, Lord Huntingdon, n.d.: 'This I had from Sir Walter Bagott's son, who had it from his father.'

thanked His Majesty for the Earldom he had sent him, but that he was very well content with the honours he had and was resolved to live and die Sir Watkin.

And the boast of the typical country gentleman was that he was neither the minion of Administration nor the tool of faction.

Originally the country gentlemen tried to exclude all office-holders from the House; their failure left the door open for parliamentary government. But as a rule they practised what they had preached—it would have been a handicap for a knight of the shire, relying on the support of the country gentlemen, to hold office or to have received personal favours from government: in 1830 Sir Thomas Gooch, M.P. for Suffolk 1806–30, had to make excuses on the hustings for having solicited a Crown living for his son.[1] Before about 1830 even 'too marked a party line' was apt to be considered incompatible with true independence; in 1806, W. R. Cartwright (M.P. for Northamptonshire 1797–1830) was criticized for having consistently supported Pitt when 'a Knight of the Shire should vote as an individual and not as a party man'.[2] In a speech in parliament, on 21 January 1819, Sir George Sinclair, M.P. for Caithness, thus defined the attitude of the country gentlemen:[3]

> . . . neither to withhold entirely their confidence from Government, nor implicitly to sanction their proceedings; sometimes to oppose their measures, but never to impeach their motives—to combine political candour with constitutional vigilance—rather predisposed to approve than predetermined to condemn; resolved to favour but not to flatter; to controul, but not to embarrass.

And he rightly added:

> I am well aware that no individual is more obnoxious to both parties than one who will not absolutely bind himself to either.

Thus the country gentlemen had this in common with the Court group that they too, though for widely different reasons, refused to be tied to parliamentary parties and leaders; further, that they also were neither orators nor leaders; for again, any one of them who rose to such pre-eminence, automatically joined the politicians in the central arena.

[1] *Suffolk Chronicle*, 14 August 1830.
[2] See E. G. Forrester, *Northamptonshire County Elections and Electioneering, 1695–1832*, p. 92.   [3] *Parliamentary Debates*, vol. xxxix, cols. 55–9.

I

6

Little needs to be said about the outstanding, historical figures among the politicians: these were the men who played for the highest prizes, for Cabinet posts and the conduct of the king's business in administration and parliament. It was in their power to procure ease to the king's affairs in parliament, or to obstruct them; they could therefore claim the king's favour, and in a crisis compel it. But who were the rank and file of the political factions? In the first place the relatives, friends, and dependants of great peers usually returned for seats at their disposal; and next, the political following of commoners who could aspire to the highest offices and hunt as equals with the oligarchical groups. But these followers, in search of places or profits, did not differ essentially from the minor ministers or political parasites of the Court party. In fact, the same men are found at various times on either side of the fence, and happiest when there was no fence: when their group was so firmly established in office that it could hardly be distinguished from the Court party.

Though these were three main groups in the eighteenth-century House of Commons, in action there could be but two: the ayes and the noes, the Government party and the Opposition—which fact has reinforced the delusion of a two-party system. The Government side was invariably a junction of the Court party with a group of politicians; to the attractive force of Crown patronage was added the political ability of parliamentary leaders. When the dissolution of the first Rockingham Administration seemed imminent in January 1766, members forming the core of the official group, in a survey of the political scene, thus described their own position:[1]

> Those who have always hitherto acted upon the sole principle of attachment to the Crown. This is probably the most numerous body and would on trial be found sufficient to carry on the publick business themselves if there was any person to accept of a Ministerial office at the head of them, and this is all they want.

In other words, the Court could supply numbers and workers but not political leaders and a parliamentary façade—for this in 1766 it had to turn to the Rockinghams, or the Grenvilles and Bedfords, or to Chatham. Even when the leading minister was

---

[1] N. S. Jucker, *The Jenkinson Papers*, pp. 405–6.

the king's choice—Bute in 1762, Chatham in 1766, North in 1770, or Pitt in December 1783—the king had often to accept some ministers displeasing to himself. But when his relations with the dominant political group were distant or uncertain, he would try to introduce into the Cabinet some ministers of his own: thus Northington and Egmont entered the Grenville and the first Rockingham Administration, and Thurlow those of Rockingham and Shelburne in 1782–3; and it gave rise to comment in March 1783 when the king was not allowed a single member of his own choice in the Coalition Government.[1] The theory of the Cabinet as a joint board of king's men and politicians was, unconsciously, formulated by Horace Walpole when the Duke of Richmond, in discussing Cabinet reconstruction in 1767, objected to Camden because he 'would be the King's'—'I asked', writes Walpole, 'if they expected that every man should depend on King Rockingham, and nobody on King George.'[2]

When a First Minister was known to enjoy the favour of the king, the Court party would naturally adhere to him; and every group of politicians in power tried to fill places at Court, administrative posts, and seats in government boroughs with their own men; these, if their group long continued in office, would permeate the Court party and coalesce with it. But if then a separation supervened, it remained to be seen how much government property the politicians would get away with—places for life, reversions, parliamentary seats, etc.—and how many friends, glued to the flesh-pots, they would have to part with. Moreover, men who had long 'upheld the rights of the Crown', condemning 'formed opposition' as factious and disrespectful to the king, found it difficult to enter it themselves: as was seen in the case of Newcastle in 1762, and of Wellington in 1830.[3]

In normal circumstances the king's authority and support were sufficient to keep the average group of politicians in office, but no government could survive for long if either the king or public opinion turned definitely against them. Between 1742 and 1832 the country gentlemen and their city counterparts increasingly became the spokesmen and indicator of public opinion; and that group, about a hundred strong, when solid would carry with it a good many men of its own type and class but of less

---

[1] Horace Walpole, *Last Journals*, vol. ii, p. 500.

[2] Horace Walpole, *Memoirs*, vol. iii, p. 47.

[3] See *Three Early Nineteenth Century Diaries*, ed. by A. Aspinall, Introduction, p. xxxv: 'Wellington said that he could not bear the idea of being in opposition: he did not know how to set about it.'

pronounced independence and normally voting with the Court or with political groups. When in 1764, over General Warrants, a great many of the country gentlemen voted with the Opposition, the Government was in serious danger.[1] When in February 1781, 59 out of 80 English knights of the shire were listed by John Robinson, Secretary of the Treasury, as opposition,[2] the end was near; and when on 18 March 1782, Thomas Grosvenor informed North 'in his own name, and in those of some other country gentlemen' that they would withdraw their support from his Government, its fate was sealed. Even members of the Court party were now breaking away, or at least absenting themselves from the House: some from conviction, others from caution. When Wellington was defeated on 15 November 1830, only 15 out of 82 English county members voted for him and 49 against; and in 1831 'only six . . . English county-members in the new House were anti-Reformers'.[3]

Unengaged in struggles for office, the independent country gentlemen were a retarding element in the growth of parliamentary government, but the charge of favouring 'prerogative', sometimes levelled against them, was as uncorrelated to political realities as were their own attempts at constructive action—for instance in the confusion after the fall of North, when the weight of the independent members was felt more than under stable conditions. Thus early in 1784, 78 members—the St. Albans Tavern group—endeavoured to contrive a reconciliation between Pitt and Fox and a coalition which was probably desired by neither, and least of all by the king: for these country gentlemen party wrangles were meaningless, and a nuisance if likely to bring on the dissolution of a parliament which had run only half its course. Another, even more naive, move in 1788 is set forth in a circular[4] endorsed by 30 Lords and Commoners. In this 'such Members of the two Houses as hold themselves independent of, and unconnected with, the parties that now exist, and are desirous of contributing their best endeavours to promote the general interests of the Country', were invited, while not considering themselves 'under any restraint, or tied down to follow the sentiments of the majority', to 'act in unison with each other'. And here is the 'analysis of the House of Commons' given in the circular:

[1] See my book, *England in the Age of the American Revolution*, p. 202.
[2] Abergavenny Papers.
[3] See *Three Early Nineteenth Century Diaries*, Introduction, pp. xxii–xxiii and xxxvi.
[4] The circular headed 'Proposals' is in the Braybrooke Papers, in the Essex Record Office, Chelmsford (D/DBy C9/44).

1. Party of the Crown 185
   This party includes all those who would probably
   support his Majesty's Government under any
   Minister, not peculiarly unpopular.
2. The Party attached to Mr. Pitt . . . 52
   Of this party were there a new Parliament, and
   Mr. P. no longer Minister, not above twenty
   would be returned.
3. Detached Parties supporting the present Administration viz:
   1. Mr. Dundas 10
   2. Marquis of Lansdowne . . . 9
   3. Earl of Lonsdale 9
   4. East Indians 15
4. The independent or unconnected Members of the
   House . . . . [108][1]
   Of this body of men about forty have united together, in conjunction with some members of the
   House of Peers in order to form a third party
   for the purpose of preventing the Crown from
   being too much in the power of either of the two
   other parties who are contending for the government of the country, and who (were it really
   necessary) might with the assistance of the
   Crown, undertake to make up an administration
   to the exclusion both of Mr. Pitt and Mr. Fox,
   and of their adherents.
5. The Opposition to the present Administration
   1. The Party attached to Mr. Fox . . 138
   2. Remnants of Lord North's Party . 17
6. Absentees and Neutrals 14

The names of Whig and Tory do not appear in this list, nor in
any other compiled in those years; nor have I used them so far
in this lecture, for they explain little, but require a good deal of
explaining.

7

Whig and Tory were 'denominations'—names and creeds—
which covered enduring types moulded by deeply ingrained
differences in temperament and outlook. But when was a clear
party division covered by them? Even before 1714 some scholars

[1] The number is not given here, but lower down in a summary list of the parties.

now discern merely a number of groups and connexions of a Tory or a Whig hue, or of uncertain colouring; for hardly ever was there anything like straight party voting. About the middle of the century the names were deprecated, described as out-worn and meaningless, and yet they were used; for names there must be in a political dichotomy, even if their meaning is uncertain and their use misleading. In parliament even under the first two Georges disaffected Whigs supplied the most inveterate leaders of the Opposition and most of its voting strength. But in a good many constituencies the names of Whig and Tory still corresponded to real divisions: partly perhaps because local factions could hardly have been denoted as 'Government' and 'Opposition', and partly because the most enduring distinction between Tory and Whig—High Church versus Low Church and Dissent—retained more vitality and significance in local struggles than at Westminster.

A ruling group will always try to place its opponents under a ban, and the natural consequence of the practice of Walpole and the Pelhams was that anyone who wished to play at politics and for office, adopted the name of Whig: the Finches, Seymours, Legges, Leveson-Gowers, Wyndhams, Foxes, etc. In fact by 1750 everyone at Court, in office, and in the centre arena was a Whig, while the name of Tories, by a process of natural selection, was left to the residuum who did not enter politics in pursuit of office, honours, or profits, that is, to the country gentlemen and to the forerunners of urban radicals.

The nomenclature, as further developed in the first decade of George III's reign, is correctly stated by Horace Walpole in a passage of his *Memoirs*, penned late in 1768, or more probably in 1769:[1] 'The body of the Opposition', he says, 'still called itself Whig, an appellation rather dropped than disclaimed by the Court'; 'the real Tories still adhered to their old distinctions . . . and fluctuated according as they esteemed particular chiefs not of their connexion . . . '; but 'their whole conduct was comprised in silent votes . . . '. Thus Walpole knew the difference between 'real Tories' and the Court Whigs who had become the 'Tories' of Opposition Whig pamphleteers; but as he habitually flavours accurate perceptions with current cant, a footnote, added in the 1780's, emphatically asserts that Lord North 'was a Tory'. About the same time Burke, in a letter of 24 December 1782, describes the phalanx of 130–50 placemen and place-hunters

[1] Horace Walpole, *Memoirs*, vol. ii, p. 67.

ranged behind North to secure the survival of places, refers
to them as 'the body, which for want of another name, I call
Lord North's'; and then adds: 'I ought to have excepted out
of the profligates of Lord North's corps five or six Tories who act
on principle, such as it is.'[1] Less than two months later, the
Rockinghams formed a coalition with the 'profligates' by con-
ceding to them that nothing more should be done 'about the
reduction of the influence of the Crown' by economical reform.

Who were now the 'Tories'? The younger Pitt never used the
name and after his death his successors went merely by that of
'Mr. Pitt's friends' (apparently George Canning was the only one
who occasionally called himself a 'Tory'). On 5 October 1809,
Perceval wrote to Lord Melville:[2]

> Our Party's strength, dismembered as we are by Canning's and
> Castlereagh's separation from us . . . has lost its principle of cohesion.
> We are no longer the sole representatives of Mr. Pitt. The magic
> of that name is in a great degree dissolved, and the principle on
> which we must most rely to keep us together, and give us the assis-
> tance of floating strength, is the public sentiment of loyalty and
> attachment to the King. Among the independent part of the House,
> the country gentlemen, the representatives of popular boroughs, we
> shall find our saving strength or our destruction.

In short: here is once more the basic structure of eighteenth-
century parliamentary politics, with increased regard for the
country gentlemen but no trace of a two-party system, or at all of
party in the modern sense; and the group which in 1760 went by
the name of Tories, a generation later is referred to simply as
'independent country gentlemen', the name of Tory being
practically in abeyance. It is the history of those party names,
and how they were applied, which calls for careful study free of
confusion between names and realities, or rather between the
differing realities which the same names were made to cover;
and next the history must be traced of party realities as shaped
by interaction between the constituencies and the House of
Commons. Nineteenth-century parliamentary historians now
seem agreed in deferring the full emergence of the modern party
till after the Second Reform Bill: what preceded it were intermediary forms which should not be treated anachronistically in
terms of a later age.

[1] See E. B. de Fonblanque, *Political and Military Episodes . . . from the Life and Correspondence of . . . John Burgoyne* (1876), pp. 418–21.   [2] Perceval MSS.

With regard to the second half of the eighteenth century, the idea of party conducive to parliamentary government is usually linked up with the Whigs; which, for what it is worth, is a matter of nomenclature rather than of ideology: the politicians, and not the Court group or the independent country gentlemen, were the party-forming element, and the politicians called themselves Whigs. But among the politicians the attitude to sovereign and party did not depend on the degree of their Whiggery: those who enjoyed the favour of the Crown, and coalesced with the Court party, were naturally less of a party-forming element than those in disfavour, or uncertain of royal support, who had therefore to rely primarily on parliament and seek to form their following into a coherent party. This was specially true of political groups which had forced themselves on the king: the Grenvilles after September 1763, the Rockinghams in 1782, and the Coalition in 1783.

The fourth Duke of Devonshire, the 'prince of the Whigs', was in every way an outstanding personality among them: disinterested and generous, he acted from a sense of duty but according to the canons of the time. As Lord Chamberlain he had to deal in August 1761 with a crisis in the King's Bedchamber.

> Lord Huntingdon Groom of the Stole [he writes] came to Lord Ashburnham who was in waiting and told him that he would put on the King's shirt. His Lordship reply'd to be sure if he pleased but then he must take the whole waiting. The other said no, I will only put on the shirt, Lord Ash[burnham] said I give you notice if you do it I shall quit the room. . . .

And so he did. Lord Rockingham and other Lords of the Bedchamber agreed with Ashburnham, 'were much dissatisfy'd, thought it lowering their employments, and that they could not stay'; but when Bute became 'very warm' over the matter Devonshire warned him that if five or six of the most considerable lords threw up their employment as beneath them, others too would quit, and Bute 'would get nobody to take it that was worth having it'. The late king, said Devonshire,

> had piqued himself on raising the Bedchamber by getting men of the first rank for them to take it, and that [if] it was lower'd they certainly would not remain in, that it was a very cheap way of keeping them steady to support Government.[1]

---

[1] Devonshire MSS. 260. 339.

Indeed, in 1761 the Lords of the Bedchamber included seven-teen peers controlling at least double the number of seats in the House of Commons, and three courtesy lords, all in the House; and Devonshire was giving the right advice on how to put Court offices to the best use in managing parliament. But in that advice, given by a leading Whig at the end of the so-called Whig era, there is nothing which would even distantly foreshadow parlia-mentary government based on party.

For that, owing to circumstances, we have to turn much rather to the Grenvilles. Two months after the king had, in August 1763, unsuccessfully tried to get rid of them, a by-election occurred in Essex, and on 28 October, John Luther, one of the candi-dates, called on Lord Sandwich and expressed his concern at hearing that Sandwich was taking a part against him.

> I told him [wrote Sandwich to Rigby] that I considered myself meerly with regard to Essex as a party man, that my interest and that of my best friends was at stake, as far as related to the support or downfall of the present Administration . . . that I had seen Mr. Conyers, who had told me that he embarked himself in my system, and that he meant if he succeeded, to be a true and steady friend to *this* Administration. Mr. Luther answered me that he had given the same assurances to Mr. Grenville . . . that he was a friend to *Government*, . . . I said that *Government* was a loose word . . . was he a friend to *this* Administration, and more so to *this* than he should be to any Administration of which Mr. Pitt was a member, at that he smiled and hesitated a little, but soon answered that he was a friend to this Administration and would shew himself as such while they acted *consistently*. . . . I answered . . . that his own words obliged me situated as I am to act against him; that this country must be governed by combinations of people, and that those who would act in the combination that I belonged to would have a right to my support. . . .

But Luther, according to Sandwich, kept a back door open by constituting himself 'the judge of what was *consistency* in the Administration'.[1]

Or again, in 1764 the Grenvilles intervened in East India Company elections (the first government to do so), with the purpose of helping Clive to get back his *jagir*, he having pledged himself to support them in or out of office—to which promise he adhered. And when they and the Bedfords were turned out by the king, they withdrew their men from Administration and the

[1] Sandwich MSS.

Court; whereas a year later, the Rockinghams showed so little understanding of party management that they left Chatham whomever he chose to retain. Ideas and a political practice are things of slow growth; parliamentary government, wise as it is as a system, was not born like Pallas Athene.

*

To sum up: Parliamentary government based on the party system is not an ingenious device, the product of creative thought, for which credit is due to one set of men, while another is to be blamed for lack of foresight or virtue in not anticipating it. Its bases are deep down in the political structure of the nation, which was being gradually transformed during the period of so-called mixed government. An electorate thinking in terms of nation-wide parties is its indispensable basis; and it is therefore at least as much in the constituencies as in parliament that the growth of these parties will have to be traced. In the eighteenth century parliament was without that background of enfranchised masses thinking in terms of party; it was to a high degree a closed arena, with its own life and divisions, still dominated by Court and Country on the periphery, but containing the forerunners of political parties in the centre. To clear up these antecedents must be the contribution of us, eighteenth-century historians, to the essential work on the least explored period of British constitutional history, the nineteenth century, now started by a group of keen, able, and what is important, mostly young, historians.